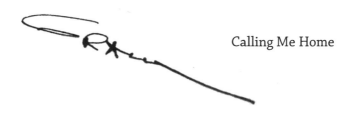

Calling Me Home

UNIVERSITY PRESS OF FLORIDA

Florida A&M University, Tallahassee
Florida Atlantic University, Boca Raton
Florida Gulf Coast University, Ft. Myers
Florida International University, Miami
Florida State University, Tallahassee
New College of Florida, Sarasota
University of Central Florida, Orlando
University of Florida, Gainesville
University of North Florida, Jacksonville
University of South Florida, Tampa
University of West Florida, Pensacola

University Press of Florida

*Gainesville · Tallahassee · Tampa · Boca Raton*

*Pensacola · Orlando · Miami · Jacksonville · Ft. Myers · Sarasota*

BOB KEALING

# ❧ Calling Me Home ❧

Gram Parsons and
the Roots of Country Rock

This book may be available in an electronic edition.

17  16  15  14  13  12   6  5  4  3  2  1

LIBRARY OF CONGRESS CATALOGING-IN-PUBLICATION DATA
Kealing, Bob.
Calling me home : Gram Parsons and the roots of country rock / Bob Kealing.
p. cm.
Includes bibliographical references and index.
ISBN 978-0-8130-4204-6 (alk. paper)—ISBN 0-8130-4204-6 (alk. paper)
1. Parsons, Gram, d. 1973. 2. Rock musicians—United States—Biography.
3. Country musicians—United States—Biography. 4. Country rock music—
History and criticism. I. Title.
ML420.P275K43  2012
782.42166092—dc23
[B]
2012009908

University Press of Florida
15 Northwest 15th Street
Gainesville, FL 32611-2079
http://www.upf.com

In Memory of Charlie Louvin,
1927–2011

Charlie Louvin with the author, City Auditorium, Waycross, Ga. (Michael Robinson)

Up close, Parsons looked—to my own sophomore eyes—remarkably self-possessed and confident. He was lean, with longish dark hair. He was good-looking and cool. Holding my books, I felt a certain amount of awe and more envy that a contemporary could be so far along that road to the American Dream we grew up on: the path to being Elvis.

DAVID W. JOHNSON

Gram Parsons at Harvard, 1965. (The Newseum, Ted Polumbaum Collection)

# Contents

Calling Me Home

**1**

## Cosmic Roots

In Gulf Shores, Alabama, on a sun-drenched sliver of white sand, sea oats, and rolling dunes, Avis Johnson Bartkus opened up about being part of her Uncle Gram Parsons's complicated legacy.

After he died, Bartkus's mother, Gram's baby sister, would never play his records, or the Rolling Stones. Bartkus was thirty-four years old the first time she heard her uncle's pioneering music.

"She never talked about any of it," Bartkus reflected while gazing at the restless Gulf of Mexico. "It was painful for her to listen to."

Pain and tragedy run like perilous fault lines through three families that make up Gram Parsons's family tree: the Connors of Tennessee, the Parsons of Louisiana, and a wealthy central Florida citrus family, the Snivelys. Within all of them, addiction has taken a toll like canker to an orange crop.

Bartkus's mother and grandmother were also named Avis. "Avie" as friends call her, does not suffer from addiction as her mother and grandmother did. Avie has her own family and can file away her late mother's bad memories and poignant writings about family struggles. Occasionally, Avie questions where her uncle would be now if he'd made it out of the desert of addiction alive.

"His heart was back home in the South," she said. "I think there was definitely some draw in Tennessee and Nashville and that area." In 1973, at just twenty-six, Gram Parsons came back south in a box. The circumstances surrounding his death explain why some blood relatives like Avie, aren't fully aware of his importance to the world of contemporary music.

It's far too simplistic to say Gram Parsons is the father of country rock; many artists share that distinction. Beginning in the late 1960s, Parsons spearheaded the cultural desegregation of both idioms. At the height of America's generational firestorm over Vietnam and civil rights, his vision helped heal the bitter divide between peacenik, hippie rockers, and the conservative America-love-it-or-leave-it crowd. Given his musical, freewheeling young adulthood and upper-middle-class southern upbringing, Parsons was an amalgam of both.

Parsons never wanted to be anointed the avatar of country rock, a label he didn't care for. In the early 1970s, he thought music from groups like the Eagles to be "plastic" and not true to the soulful, bluesy side of country music. That's what people didn't understand; Parsons was actually playing pure country with contemporary lyrics and attitude. He retained a deep admiration for the purveyors of so-called "white man's blues," authentic American artists like George Jones and Merle Haggard.

Gram Parsons referred to what he was doing as "Cosmic American Music." Many of those close to him, including former collaborator Chris Hillman, have been at a loss to define what he meant.

What Parsons called Cosmic American Music was born in the mid-1950s; its own roots can be traced to hymns and sacred spirituals sung for generations in southern churches. In the middle of the twentieth century, artists like Ray Charles and Elvis Presley brought a blending of seemingly disparate musical styles that accelerated purely through the magic of invisible radio waves.

"Radio did not obey the law," wrote journalist and scholar William McKeen. "Radio travelled through the air and the air did not recognize arbitrary lines drawn by men. Radio did not respect Jim Crow laws so it became the great unsung subversive force that brought about social change in America."

The force filtered its way to teenagers through another crucial innovation. "The transistor radio was a big breakthrough," declared Rock and Roll Hall of Fame inductee Roger McGuinn. "It gave kids the ability to listen to what they wanted to when they wanted to as opposed to what their parents wanted them to listen to."

The music they heard on the radio brought young people together and provided hope for a way out of the hardscrabble towns where so much of it was born. Children of the South like Parsons didn't need to choose between the music of Ray Charles, Little Richard, Elvis Presley, Patsy Cline, or Bob Dylan. To them, it was all good.

Despite violence and intimidation, in the segregation era courageous folk musicians performed alongside black artists. During the Vietnam War, Cosmic American Music for the first time brought California folk rockers to the ultraconservative Grand Ole Opry; hippies and cowboys found common ground in Austin, Texas; and outsider country artists no longer had to adhere to the slick Nashville way.

The South, where Gram Parsons grew up, is Cosmic America—a region rife with musicians and storytellers spinning tales of sin and redemption, love and heartache, troubadours and reprobates. This definitive region produced a gumbo of musical styles rooted in places like Memphis, Muscle Shoals, Nashville, New Orleans, Austin, Waycross, Macon, and Winter Haven. There's Mississippi Delta blues, the Chitlin' Circuit, New Orleans jazz, traditional country, rockabilly, and now something we'll call the youth center circuit.

In the 1960s, Florida youth centers incubated what came to be known as southern rock from the Allman Brothers, Lynyrd Skynyrd, and the Outlaws. Hybrid artists Gram Parsons, Jim Stafford, and Bernie Leadon played this circuit. Mainstream rockers like Tom Petty, Don Felder, Stephen Stills, and Les Dudek honed their chops in Florida youth centers as did traditional country musicians and writers like Bobby Braddock and John Anderson. No matter how big or small, towns and cities all over Florida had their own teen centers where underage kids had a chance to get paid to play, and where nationally known artists came to perform. This youth center circuit is the Sunshine State's great unsung musical tradition.

What lies ahead is an examination of Gram Parsons's own Cosmic American roots, planted deeply within the Georgia red clay and Florida myakka. This is literary journalism: a serendipitous adventure through Parsons's myriad southern musical stopping-off points and beyond. Even at a young age, Parsons had an uncanny ability to surround himself with musicians far better than he, immersing himself in important music scenes in a Forrest Gump-like way.

Once Parsons moved away from Florida to pursue musical fortunes in Cambridge, New York, and eventually Los Angeles, he came back south to perform, gain inspiration, collect trust fund payments, and recruit musician friends to play on his recordings. His landmark solo records included an all-star cast of southern studio players. Jim Stafford, one of his most important influences, was like an older brother. Bluesy baritone and south Florida folk legend Fred Neil was another key influence.

In early 1968, Parsons brought his bold creative vision to the most influential rock-and-roll band in America, the Byrds. When that confederation split apart, Parsons co-founded the archetypal "country rock" band with a more hip, California attitude, the Flying Burrito Brothers. Years later, Parsons hit his stride with a southern musical soul mate, Emmylou Harris, and seized on the opportunity to express his pioneering vision as a solo artist.

"I don't know if I'm playing with fire or if I'm doing the right thing even," Parsons once told an interviewer. "I think I am. When I say that longhairs, shorthairs, people with overalls, people with their velvet gear on can all be at the same place at the same time for the same reason, that turns me on."

Parsons committed to country music while few thought of it as a cool thing to do. During the peace and love era, he became the movement's standard bearer along with other highly influential hybrids like Linda Ronstadt, Bob Dylan, Richie Furay, Gene Clark, Doug Dillard, Roger McGuinn, Chris Hillman, the Nitty Gritty Dirt Band, Mike Nesmith, Bernie Leadon, Creedence Clearwater Revival, Dickie Betts, and the Band.

In the late 1960s and early 1970s, the idea of Led Zeppelin front man Robert Plant recording alongside a country singer like Dolly Parton would have been about as likely as the Eagles playing country rock in matching business suits.

Forty years later, the mainstream music establishment lavished upon Plant and bluegrass belle Allison Krause a bushel basket of

Grammys for their collaboration. Is it any wonder Plant had taken to wearing a Gram Parsons T-shirt?

When Tom Petty re-formed his own central Florida youth center circuit-era band Mudcrutch, he invoked the name of Gram Parsons as an inspiration. Musicians as diverse as Elvis Costello, Dwight Yoakum, Ryan Adams, Patty Griffin, and Steve Earle have also paid homage to alt-country's patron saint, the Cosmic American hipster.

Emmylou Harris's Country Music Hall of Fame catalog is rich with Gram Parsons songs and his seminal influence. That alone is validation of his legacy.

It's impossible to tell a Gram Parsons story without taking a serious and sober look at the devastating effects of drugs and alcohol. Within the context of Parsons's contemporaries who survived, we'll consider the notion of surrendering to addiction and finding redemption. Descendants like Avis Johnson Bartkus know all too well how Gram Parsons's extended family has been ravaged.

So now we travel the road a little deeper, to many southern people and places that shaped the life of a Florida boy with deep Georgia roots. Through a newly discovered group of historic images of Parsons, dozens more rare photographs provided by Parsons's family, letters, and many new primary source interviews, you'll meet the remarkable array of musicians and regular folk with whom Parsons collaborated and from whom he gained inspiration. You'll travel to the most important stages in Gram Parsons's fleeting career: some hidden, others only a memory.

Most chapters begin with what we'll call a "revisit" to persons or places important to this story. Together we'll feel the vibrations of history as we go back to where Parsons and his friends wrote, played, and performed.

Find out why Gram Parsons, like so many other southern kids who came of age in the 1950s and 1960s, had a singular focus and burning ambition to be like Elvis. Relive the remarkable opportunity Parsons had to see the King of Rock and Roll and a stellar roster of greats who appeared with Presley. In the place it happened, we'll speak with a legendary performer who was there.

Take a trip to rock and roll's most important region, the Cosmic American South. Wait and listen for all those forgotten, far-off voices crackling in via AM radio. Remember the sweet smell of citrus, hickory, and evergreen wafting through the air, slight and vague, but cherished like a distant memory. Run the dusty back roads and orange groves with barefoot children, climb on top of the boathouse, and gaze at the stars framed through strands of Spanish moss.

Come along now, to a long-gone era in the low country, with a few detours to points northeast and west. That's where we're headed.

## 2

# Legacy versus Legend

On a bluff overlooking a bend in the St. Johns River, boys in short-sleeved shirts and ties mingle with attractive girls in summer outfits, pausing from intellectual pursuits to watch planes landing in the distance at the Naval Air Station Jacksonville, Florida. In this serene setting, spectral strands of Spanish moss dangle in the cooling breezes. For decades, young people on the precipice of adult lives, beginning to shape dreams and opinions, have taken time out here.

On the back reaches of the Bolles School, Gram Parsons used to come to a stone gazebo to fight off depression the way he always did: with his poetry and guitar. At other times this place was simply a hangout: somewhere to grab a smoke, pass the time with classmates, and enjoy a view of the St. Johns River winding its way north.

"Oh, he was a beautiful boy back then," recalls his friend and confidante from those days, Margaret Fisher. Girls swooned when Parsons performed solo at the Bolles School's gymnasium or nearby at Bartram School for Girls, where Fisher was enrolled. His hair was longer than that of the other boys, and his perpetually tanned skin, talent, and southern gentlemanly way gave Parsons the kind of social status usually reserved for the school's royalty—the jocks.

On this day decades after Parsons left Bolles, the vibrations of his time here are palpable. Many of the classmates, friends, and teachers who mentored him have remained in the area. Fisher was among them, living in a beach town forty-five minutes or so from the prestigious school's campus. Arriving at the guard house in a dark, past-its-prime Jaguar, Fisher too had an air of withered, world-weary grandeur. She had come back to Bolles to relive the bittersweet memories of meeting Gram Parsons for the first time, in the gazebo.

"I tried to be as far from him as I could get," remembers the formerly blond and bookish ingénue from a moneyed Jacksonville family—a doctor's daughter. "He was playing his guitar and performing, and I was so socially awkward I buried my face in a Truman Capote book and tried not to notice him."

As the bookish, fair-haired girl clutched her copy of Capote's *Other Voices, Other Rooms*, Parsons, always able to be the person he thought he *needed* to be, struck up a literary conversation. At that moment Parsons found a friend who would come in and out of his life for the next decade. When they met here in Florida, Parsons was beginning a quick upward trajectory, his confidence at an all-time high: his ambition and possibilities boundless; his ultimate success all but a certainty.

Fisher has come to be known as the woman who was with Gram Parsons a decade later when he died. Since then, Fisher has lived with the regret of not being able to stop him or somehow find a way to keep his death from happening.

"Imagine," she said flatly, "being defined by the worst day of your life."

As Fisher strolled past her first meeting place with Parsons, she was three thousand miles from that dark day, remembering the awkward but bright and beautiful waif she used to be, meeting the magnetic, handsome young musician. No tragedy, no drugs, no booze, no guilt, no questions why. They were just a couple of "inconvenient kids" sent to a boarding school by parents who had other things to deal with.

It was too much for Fisher to actually sit down in that gazebo and let memories of that first meeting with Parsons overtake her. That would have to come another time. "Not now," Fisher said with certainty. "I've had enough for one day." As quickly as Fisher led us back to that special stopping-off place where she and Parsons met, we were walking back to the Bolles School's front gate, to our cars, to the safe tedium of today.

Gram Parsons has also been defined by the worst days of his life—pigeonholed by the bizarre and tragic events surrounding his death—as if time froze in September 1973 when he died at twenty-six. Critics minimize Parsons as a selfish, trust-fund dilettante, who didn't have to work, suffer, and sell records for the fame all musicians crave. All he had to do was die young.

Had Gram Parsons found redemption, he'd have been inducted into the Country Music Hall of Fame with the angel-voiced singer he introduced to the world, Emmylou Harris. For his fans, the vision of Parsons as an older, successful, and esteemed founder of the alt-country genre torments them. *Why couldn't he just have lived?*

Gram Parsons's lack of chart success and longevity make it impossible for him to ever achieve mainstream success or recognition. Unlike so many of his contemporaries who got caught up in the rock-and-roll life's excesses, Gram Parsons got no second or third act. Thus, *Rolling Stone*'s description of him as "rock's greatest cult figure" is particularly apt. Because of his early exit from this earth absent any meaningful stay on the Billboard charts, many stalwart music fans will forever say, "Gram who?"

Keith Richards of the Rolling Stones said the two most "pure musicians" he knew were John Lennon and Gram Parsons. "Gram wrote great songs," Richards wrote. Entertainer Jim Stafford—Parsons's childhood friend, bandmate, and mentor—said of those songs, "They're underground classics." One-time friend and bandmate Chris Hillman said Parsons "could've been quite a driving force in country music. Everything he wanted and dreamed he could've been." By contrast, one country music legend confided he found Parsons's playing "loose" and of his enduring appeal said, "I don't get it."

Scholar Clay Motley offers this explanation of Parsons's influence: "A close examination of Parsons's lyrics reveals a fascinating tension between raucous hedonism and religious redemption—'Sin City' and the 'City of God.' This unresolved tension running through Parsons's musical career reflects his luminal position as a path-breaking figure between traditional country music and '60s rock and roll."

The key to Parsons's appeal lies in the fact that he put so much of himself into the music. It may not have been technically correct by Nashville standards, but no one can deny Parsons radiated vulnerability, soul, and effortless cool. When he warbles, "I'm your toy, I'm your old boy," in the poorly titled "Hot Burrito #1," it's as if all the need and longing in Parsons's real life is right there at the surface. When he sings "her comb still lies beside my bed" in "Brass Buttons," how can those who know his life story not be reminded of Parsons's mother, Avis, who also died young?

Some believe one of Parsons's best songs, the evocative "Hickory Wind," is an ode to the good times he spent hunting and fishing with his war-hero father. The lyrics reflect an intimacy with a place and time in the South he would never again recapture, much like the sudden realization that the man he looked up to and depended on was gone.

In addition to enormous wealth provided by Gram's grandfather, Florida citrus baron John Snively, Parsons's other inheritance was the family addiction and melancholy. The extensive citrus holdings, family fortune, the white-columned mansion situated in the middle of Cypress Gardens in Winter Haven, Florida—none of it could buy Parsons or his sister a sense of home or family warmth.

In 1973, the news of his death and the bizarre chain of events that followed brought him a macabre kind of legend he likely would have relished. But it's a kind of notoriety we might associate today with reality-show stardom: being famous for nothing particularly important.

It has taken decades, but finally his pioneering legacy is catching up. Gram Parsons has become an underground icon for the right reasons: creating a genuine country crossover blend of music that brought together disparate groups of fans and to this day provides the roadmap for legions of other hybrid artists to follow.

The next stop in this journey is an outpost in southeast Georgia, a railroad town named Waycross.

# 3

## Pilgrimage to Waycross

In the far reaches of southeast Georgia lies 685 square miles of black-water swamp called "Okefenokee," meaning "trembling earth." Underfoot, you feel and hear the squish squish of the spongy ground. In winter, the mosquitoes are sparse and venomous snakes lie low. Put in a flatwater boat along any of the swamp's 120 miles of canoe trails and there's a pretty good chance the only human form you'll see is your own, reflected in the mocha-colored water.

Two rivers are born from this swamp: the St. Mary's and the Suwannee. At sundown, frogs sing in a communal chorus until all at once, they stop. In the spellbinding din of silence at twilight, constellations come into view. Generations of southern grandmas have told their babies all those twinkling stars are just holes in the bottom of heaven.

At Grand Prairie the tangle of downed trees, deep wooded thickets, and dense swamp gives way to a vast, miles-wide horizon. There seems to be little separation between earth, water, and sky. At sundown, wispy clouds travel along the fading hues of orange, red, and indigo. From this intimate vantage point you are one with this silent, intense place in nature—the head waters of Cosmic America.

On the Okefenokee's northeastern edge in a railroad town called Waycross, local radio stations in the late 1950s reflected American music's evolving sounds. WACL for "Atlantic Coast Line" and WAYX, short for "Waycross," played infectious dance numbers by Macon native "Little" Richard Penniman, soul-stirring Ray Charles from Florida's panhandle, and emerging rockabilly sensations like Louisiana-born Jerry Lee Lewis and Carl Perkins hailing from Tiptonville, Tennessee.

Most locals loved the tried-and-true country and gospel favorites. Hank Williams had the uncanny ability to translate the feelings of hard living in the South; the Louvin Brothers' "high-lonesome" harmonies crossed over to gospel and secular audiences; trailblazers like Kitty Wells and Mother Maybelle Carter charted a course for women.

At night, radio waves traveled far and wide like invisible shooting stars. Kids tuned their transistor radios to the 50,000-watt blowtorch that was Nashville's WSM-AM, home of the most important country music show in America: the Grand Ole Opry.

Then along came the distillation of it all, wrapped into one young Cosmic American king, from Tupelo, Mississippi, by way of Memphis, Elvis Aaron Presley. It's impossible to overestimate Presley's impact on the evolving youth culture of the 1950s. Before he became the biggest star in the world, Presley, like rock and roll's Johnny Appleseed, performed live and captivated young audiences in myriad out-of-the-way southern towns.

Ingram Cecil Connor III was a pudgy, dark-skinned nine-year-old who liked to play practical jokes on his little sister Avis. On Saturday mornings he threw dance parties for neighborhood kids in the Florida room of his parents' upper-middle-class ranch house at the corner of Suwannee Drive and Seminole Trail in Waycross. Even at that young age, the child his friends called "Gram" had already tuned in to the changing styles of contemporary music, and he liked what he heard. "I would get country music mixed with some rockabilly and I would listen for the rockabilly and I liked some of the country music," he reflected many years later. "Some of the early Ira Louvin and Charlie Louvin and Louvin Brothers stuff, early Everly Brothers, the stuff which was considered country at first, turned me on, and so I listened to this combination of rockabilly."

Like many of his peers in Waycross who came from money, Gram took regular piano lessons from a teacher named Miss Bessie Maynard. "You just knew music was going to be part of his life," said Gram's childhood friend Henry Clarke. "Everything he did had something to do with music." On weekends, Gram and two friends who were as close to him as brothers, Clarke and Dickey Smith, rode bikes downtown to the Ware Tire Company on State Street. Along with Goodyear tires, the store had a housewares section with records for sale. Sometimes the boys would spend half a day there listening to albums. The store even had a little booth you could sit in for a free preview. Gram's mother, "Big Avis" Connor, kept an open account for her son; he could always come home with the new single he'd heard on the radio.

During those Saturday morning parties, Gram's friends brought over their own records. "They'd say 'Gram, I want you to listen to this record' and he'd sit down at the piano and pick it out," said Clarke.

"I knew how to play the Boogie Woogie and he did too," remembered Nancy Gill, a schoolmate of Gram's younger sister "Little Avis." In his room Gram had "these giant waist-high bongos," Gill recalled.

Gram had a prankster streak and liked to tell jokes. One day he convinced Little Avis and Nancy he was carrying a long, dark snake over his shoulder. Turns out it was nothing more than your garden-variety, nonvenomous, black-leather belt. When he wasn't torturing his sister with practical jokes, Gram was also her protector.

Smith remembered Gram's ability to take the latest Little Richard song, listen to it four times, then go straight to the piano and play it. "Couldn't read a lick of music," Smith recalled. "He was uncanny." One afternoon Gram marched into the Smiths' kitchen, where Dickey's hard-working, no-nonsense mom spent a lot of time.

"Mrs. Smith, I just wrote a song and I want you to listen to it," Gram announced.

Dickey was amazed Gram had the gumption to interrupt his mother's Saturday routine. She dropped what she was doing and followed him into the living room to the Smiths' piano. Gram sat down and started working away on a number he'd put together himself. When it was over, Dickey's mom asked him to play it again. "He called it 'The Gram Boogie,'" Smith recalled. "He impressed my mother and that was hard to do."

When Gram wasn't preoccupied with music, the Connor kids could play on their "shoot to shoot" in the backyard. It consisted of a line running from tree to tree that they could ride along by means of a handle for hours of carefree enjoyment. In their beautiful Cherokee Heights neighborhood, prosperous couples raised loads of children in suitably comfortable brick homes. Towering pine trees bordered unpaved roads. Springtime was awash with pastel-colored azaleas and dogwood in bloom. It was nothing unusual to ride on horseback through the neighborhood. The kids knew Friday and Saturday as "play-out nights." They built bonfires and played football, kick the can, and hide-and-go-seek. The parents socialized at someone's home or at the country club.

In this small southeastern Georgia town, families like the Connors were royalty. Gram's mother hailed from a Florida citrus family of vast wealth and real estate holdings, the Snivelys. Her father "Poppa" John started out as a fertilizer salesman. During the depression, he bought up vast tracts of land homesteaders put up for auction. Snively built a citrus empire and became a millionaire many times over. He owned and sold the land upon which Cypress Gardens was built. The Snivelys' white-columned mansion to this day sits rather incongruously in the middle of the old-time Florida fun park. Poppa John set aside large trust funds for all his grandchildren, including Gram and Little Avis. Big Avis and her husband, World War II fighter pilot Ingram Cecil Connor II, nicknamed "Coon Dog" for his sad eyes, were married at the mansion.

Though intelligent, Coon Dog was quiet and gentle, not known for business acumen. Poppa John set him up in a supervisory position at his box-making operation in Waycross, guaranteeing his son-in-law the kind of salary and status befitting a man married to his daughter. There wasn't a whole lot for Coon Dog to do, and Poppa John made it plain his input on big-picture decisions was neither welcomed nor needed.

"There were some weeks," remembered Coon Dog's employee of more than a decade, Claud Goble, "where he might not come down here but once or twice a week." As long as the boys at the box plant were producing, Coon Dog could turn his attentions elsewhere. A gregarious man who liked to fish and hunt, in his spare time Coon Dog took on the role of scoutmaster to the neighborhood boys. It was clearly something he relished, even taking the boys on out-of-state camping trips.

"He would take us out there with BB guns or 22s and he would show us the safety, how to handle guns," recalled Henry Clarke. Even though Dickey Smith wasn't a Scout, he remembered fondly the times Coon Dog showed him the old jalopy he kept in the garage. Once in a while he drove them around Cherokee Heights in the old relic. "Boy, we thought that was unbelievable," recalled Smith. In addition to his love of vintage cars, Coon Dog collected authentic Native American headdresses, pulling them out on special occasions.

Coon Dog regaled the boys with riveting stories from his days as a fighter pilot. He didn't hesitate to discipline them, but Coon Dog was better known for his warm and jovial side. Those who grew up around him find it hard to forget Coon Dog's smile. Gram's dad was their hero too.

"I was much more comfortable with him than my mother, who was nervous and had all sorts of rules to keep," remembered Little Avis. "I remember baseball games and hardware stores, harvest moons, sourgrass and pumpkins when I think of him, but the thing I remember most about Coon Dog is his sad eyes."

His descendants say Coon Dog likely suffered from post-traumatic stress disorder stemming from the dozens of bombing runs he flew in the war. And he had a wandering eye for the ladies surpassed only by an appetite for booze. "I'm sure there was a lot of stress he didn't deal with," said his granddaughter Avis Johnson Bartkus, "Mom said he always seemed sad." By his granddaughter's estimation, Coon Dog was a "functioning alcoholic," who from time to time needed to "go and dry out when he was a mess."

Big Avis had prom-queen looks and long, curly brunette hair. Her striking appearance wasn't lost on Gram's friends even at nine or ten years old. Said Henry Clarke, "She was one of the prettiest women I'd ever seen."

Big Avis made sure her children were not left wanting—to the point of spoiling her son and daughter. There wasn't any real work for them to do besides homework. "It would have been embarrassing for Gram to have to mow the yard or do the dishes," said Smith, who cut his own grass with a push mower.

As she'd been accustomed to growing up in a wealthy central Florida family of the segregated South, Big Avis hired a black couple, Carrie and Johnny Barnes, to help cook and clean. If there were school clothes to buy, Avis had them delivered from the store. For better or worse, the Connor children had no worries about anything even resembling chores. Johnny drove Gram and his buddies to the record store, and every Christmas Carrie rode the train with them to Winter Haven to visit relatives.

The kids from Waycross never believed crazy stories Gram told them about his rich Florida grandparents. "Then I got down to Florida," Smith chuckled, "and said, 'Lord, he's been tellin' us the truth.'" For a couple of weeks during summer vacation with Gram, Dickey and Henry were transported to what must have seemed like a kid's paradise: having the run of a gigantic mansion situated in the middle of Florida's premier (pre-Disney) theme park, Cypress Gardens. Servants at the mansion never let the kids do anything for themselves. They could watch water-ski shows, then go backstage and hang out with the performers. To this day, Smith recalls in amazement, "The guy who taught me how to ski, his picture was on the skis!"

During a hunting trip, the boys ran out of shotgun shells; a new batch was brought in via helicopter. Henry Clarke marveled at how nonplussed Gram was by it all. "He was not that arrogant person, I'm rich or I come from a rich family," Clarke said. "I think Coon Dog had a lot to do with that."

Imagine the letdown when Gram's friends had to go back home to reality. "I got chastised a great deal," said Clarke. His parents reminded him they didn't have servants to wake him up, lay out his clothes, or take him anywhere he wanted to go. If that didn't do the trick, a crabapple switch would.

Nancy Gill remembered Big Avis lying in her king-sized bed flipping the channels back and forth with something wondrous she'd never seen: a remote control device. Lunch time at the Connors' house, Carrie Barnes or one of the other maids cooked up exotic things like Cuban sandwiches, the kind you didn't get at any other kids' homes.

There was a little table for four in the kitchen where the kids ate. "The adults would eat later," Gill recalled. "A lot of times they were sitting around the living room having cocktails. Then they might go out."

At the Okefenokee Golf Club, Gill's father joined in on late-night partying with the Connors. "There was a lot of wild stories of Big Avis at the golf club, and my Dad was there so he saw all that," recalled Gill. In one instance, Avis commandeered a fire truck and rode it around the country club grounds. And who would dare do anything about it? With their social status, the Connors and the Gills were practically a law unto themselves. But there was a price: in a small town like Waycross, that kind of juicy gossip was going to get around and probably be exaggerated.

To his childhood friend Dickey Smith, all the talk had at least one very real trickle-down effect for Gram. Parents outside of the cocktail set didn't want their children going over to the Connors and being exposed to his parents' vices. "Besides me and Henry," Smith said, "he didn't have a whole lot of friends, personal friends."

Playing and listening to music was like a refuge for a bright kid like Gram Connor. "If we ever had a concert come through town, I don't think he missed it," recalled Henry Clarke.

Then came the show that proved to be Gram's musical epiphany. On Wednesday, February 22, 1956, nine-year-old Gram begged his buddies to go with him to an evening concert at the Waycross City Auditorium. A twenty-one-year-old rockabilly star-in-the-making named Elvis Presley, would be headlining two shows.

"C'mon," Gram begged.

"Nah," said his skeptical pal Dickey, "never heard of him."

"This guy's gonna be real famous!" Gram urged.

"I'll wait until he becomes famous," Dickey retorted with finality.

Undeterred, the budding ladies' man Gram convinced a pair of older twin girls from another moneyed Waycross family, Diane and Daphne Delano, to go with him to the first of two shows that night.

Only at a fleeting crossroads in the Deep South could a small-town kid see live in one night such an assemblage of iconic musicians: Charlie and Ira Louvin, Mother Maybelle and the Carter Sisters, and the young star-on-the-rise Gram and the rest really wanted to see. Billed as "Mr. Dynamite, the nation's only atomic-powered singer," Elvis

Presley was on the brink of breaking out big nationwide. In a 500-seat hall, the blueprint for Gram's musical future converged: high-lonesome harmonies infused with Gospel, archetypal country from its first family, and a raucous, sexualized form of rhythm and blues sung by a white man, heretofore unseen in the segregated Bible Belt. On Sundays in Waycross, by local ordinance, the town's radio stations carried nothing but church programs until two in the afternoon.

Presley would never again be so accessible—and young Gram Connor never more impressionable. With all the night's excitement, Dickey Smith at the last minute went by the packed auditorium, "Just to try to get a peek."

Mother Maybelle and the Carters started off the evening. Young June Carter "talked corn but wore a big diamond." Her junior Minnie Pearl shtick belied the fact that June was a big-time talent, touring with her family and taking acting lessons from Elia Kazan in New York. It was twelve years before her marriage to Johnny Cash.

Enjoying the beginning of what would be their most successful year ever, Ira and Charlie Louvin belted out "God Bless Her Because She Is My Mother," and their most popular song of the night, "There's a Hole in the Bottom of the Sea."

With all the evening's warm-up acts finished, the lights went down. Here's how the *Waycross Journal-Herald*'s correspondent, using the nom de plume "A. Musik Lover," described Elvis's entrance: "The rather tall, dark complexioned youth came on stage wearing a lime green shirt with rhinestone cuff links and dark hair slicked back. Pandemonium."

Presley had just recorded what would become his first number-one hit, its title reported in the local paper as "Heartburn Motel." The only syllable Claud Goble heard from that song was its very first:

"Weeeellll—"

"That's all I'd hear with the women screamin' and hollerin'," laughed Goble. "But he put on a show!"

Many enthralled fans filtered out of the early show and lined right back up for the late concert. A hard-driving executive from the Waycross paper confronted Elvis backstage. "Someone's gonna pay for this ad ya'll run in our paper!"

"Uh, yessir," replied the humble young rock and roller.

Gram was deeply moved by what he saw happening on stage and all around him. He told an interviewer he actually managed to commandeer a seat in the front row. From that point, he said, no one tried to make him move. "He came on, and the whole place went bonkers," he recalled. "It all penetrated my mind."

On this tour, Ira Louvin had had what turned out to be a very expensive run-in with the future King of Rock and Roll.

Elvis sat at a piano backstage and played "Amazing Grace." "Now, this is the kind of music I like," Presley commented.

Probably feeling some pangs of jealousy that he and his brother were being upstaged by Presley, the notoriously hot-tempered, hard-drinking, old-school Ira Louvin challenged Presley:

"If that's what you like, then why do you play that crap out on stage?"

"When I'm out there, I do what they want to hear," Presley shot back. "When I'm back here, I do what I like."

Had Presley been a little older, Ira's brother Charlie believed the two men would have come to blows. As it was, Presley never recorded a Louvin Brothers record. The battle of words between Ira and Elvis likely resulted in the Louvins missing out on a small fortune in royalties.

Presley's effect on young Gram was immediate and long-lasting. For a boy already so interested in music, the die was cast, and nothing else mattered.

## Like Elvis

At Billy Ray Herrin's Waycross music store, it's not uncommon to find four generations of pickers playing and forever swapping stories. Herrin is also a clearinghouse for all things having to do with the boy who spent his first twelve years of life in this town as Gram Connor. It's no coincidence the name of Herrin's business, Hickory Wind, is also one of Gram's trademark songs. And he'll swear to you the oak tree Gram refers to in the song sits right next to the Waycross City Auditorium where Elvis played—not in South Carolina as the song goes.

With just a few phone calls, Herrin brought together a small group of Gram's friends from those days. I spent hours talking to childhood friends including Dickey Smith and Henry Clarke and waiting for a seventy-year-old retired CPA to show up and take me for a ride. Henry's cousin Haywood "Boo" Clarke played a part in another of young Gram's musical milestones. He obliged to take me where it happened.

The home at 1520 St. Mary's Drive sits just a block down the pine-tree-lined street from where Gram used to live. It was here, Gram told friends, that he picked up a guitar for the first time. And it was his buddy's cousin Boo Clarke who showed him how to play. Decades later, as Clarke sat on the porch of the home his parents built, you could hear a hint of amazement in his voice. "I often wondered how that got out that I taught him some chords," Boo reflected. He didn't find out that Gram gave him the credit until many years later.

To a legion of kids like Gram, Elvis Presley seemed impossibly cool, driving the girls wild with sexy gyrations, strumming his guitar with complete abandon, wearing what no one else wore. Writer Stanley Booth, also a Waycross native, described the natural rebellion Presley represented:

> They were not named Tab or Rock, not even Jim, Bill, Bob. They all had names like Leroy, Floyd, Elvis. All outcasts, with their contemporary costumes of duck ass haircuts, greasy Levis, motorcycle boots, T-shirts for day and black leather jackets for evening wear. Even their unfashionably long sideburns (Elvis's were furry) expressed contempt for the American dream they were too poor to be part of.

Booth, who also lived many years in Memphis, observed that it took real "daring" for Elvis to be from that crowd and promote himself as a singer.

Bob Dylan told historian Doug Brinkley, the first time he encountered Elvis's voice it was like "busting out of jail." Dylan was referring to the Elvis of his youth, Cosmic Presley: "I wanted to see the powerful, mystical Elvis that had crash-landed from a burning star onto American soil. The Elvis that was bursting with life. That's the Elvis that inspired us to all the possibilities of life."

To a Georgia boy in the fourth grade, the appeal was less about rebellion and more about the overflowing star power this young rockabilly God exuded. Gram started putting Brylcreem in his hair and slicking it back. "If he saw something he liked that made him look like Elvis," Dickey Smith said, "he'd wear it, and he didn't care what anybody would think."

One day Gram showed up at the Clarke house, where he'd heard some of the older boys, home on school break, were playing guitars. In those days, Boo Clarke and his cousins preferred country with some folk music thrown in: Hank Williams, the Kingston Trio, and the Carter Family were favorites. "I remember he just came in and liked what we were doing," Boo Clarke reflected. Using his Gibson acoustic guitar, Clarke showed Gram some basic chords—building blocks of the songs he was hearing on the radio. Not only did Gram look like Elvis, now he could begin to play the instrument that so many young boys his age thought transported them to instant cool and helped get them more attention from girls.

Once Gram got a guitar, friends say he carried it "everywhere he went." The Saturday morning parties usually included Gram performing something from Little Richard on the piano. After the Elvis concert, Gram moved his shows outside to the Connors' front porch.

It was Little Avis's job to emcee the show and introduce her brother. Even at that young age, friends like Henry Clarke say Gram knew how to make an entrance. "He was a very stunning and dashing figure," recalled Clarke, one of the regulars in Gram's audience. "He would sing and strum, even shake a little bit." Dickey Smith laughed, "If I'd had any sense, I'd have been Colonel Parker and charged people for it."

To Gram's boyhood friends, there was no question that seeing Elvis Presley solidified his ambitions. In grade school he'd shown an interest in things like football and basketball; most of that ended after seeing Elvis perform.

Gram started to develop a kind of star power in his hometown. When Dickey had to go into the hospital to have his appendix removed, it was Gram's idea to get a group of buddies together to dedicate their get-well sentiments via WACL radio. The disc jockey introduced "Gram Connor and his friends," who all relayed their good wishes over the airwaves. Only in those days could a group of kids walk in off the street and literally step right up to the microphone of a local radio station.

But beneath the attention Gram received was an undercurrent of resentment and disdain. Some peers felt Gram was, "conceited and lying all the time." For Dickey, Gram's unpopularity in the face of his growing star power was palpable. "At one point," Smith confided, "I didn't particularly tell people that I went over to his house."

The resentment from small-town friends would soon be the least of Gram's problems. When Big Avis had been drinking and Gram did something she didn't like, she would often chastise him in front of friends. "My God, Gram," she exclaimed, "why can't you be more like Dickey and Henry?"

But at the same time, his mother had come to the conclusion that Waycross public schools weren't providing the kind of education she thought Gram needed. Said Henry Clarke, "Gram was intelligent and I don't think he was being challenged in our grammar schools. And I think he realized even at that stage he needed a challenge intellectually and musically." Gram was no longer a little kid, and his parents chose to pull him out of local, public school and the comfortable routine to which he was accustomed.

Their solution was an Old South military school: the Bolles Academy in Jacksonville, Florida. Snap inspections, shined shoes, salutes, and drills replaced the carefree life Gram had come to know of domestics, music, play-out nights, and Saturday morning parties. His mother's decision to send him to boarding school would drive a rift between them.

Due to serious alcohol abuse and mutual infidelity, those who knew Gram's parents felt they were experiencing serious marital problems. Fights between Big Avis and Coon Dog were becoming common. Before 1958 ended, the fun-loving, high-living country-club Connors of Waycross would reach a breaking point.

# 5

# Coon Dog's Secret

In Waycross, the brick house on Dixon Trail looks out of place. It sits in the middle of what used to be a pea field on the Dixon property but is now an area of commercial buildings and retail stores. This is what has become of the Connor family's upper-middle-class house from Cherokee Heights. Long after the Connors moved out, a local sheriff named Robert E. Lee took up residence. One election night in the early 1970s, part of the home literally exploded and burned. Talk of the town has always been that the sheriff was the target of some sort of political vendetta. There were plans to tear the place down.

"My husband Wendall was a house mover and knew the man who was going to remove the remains of the house," said Arlene Dixon. She can still remember picking peas in the field where Wendall decided he wanted to relocate the home in which Gram grew up. As she recalled the strange turn of events that ended with the home being moved, Dixon stood on the porch where Gram gave his first performances as a little boy. These days the weeds have started to take over the first couple of steps, and there's a sizable spider web to avoid. The front entrance doesn't get much use.

"They cut the home into four pieces to move," she remembered. Coincidentally, Wendall had been a steel guitar player in a group called the Waycross Express. He also attended Presley's 1956 performance at Waycross City Auditorium.

"Wendall had a lot of high praise for Elvis," Dixon's widow remembered. Wendall was also "right proud" of his association with the home's history. In much of the music Gram made during his career, he hired some of the great pedal steel guitarists of the day and loved the sound.

To live in Gram's former home meant the Dixons had to put out of their minds the explosion, the fire, and the tragedy that caused the Connors to move out. Said Arlene Dixon: "It doesn't bother me my bedroom is the one where Coon Dog died."

\*   \*   \*

At Bolles School in 1958, the atmosphere was much like boarding school life depicted in the film *Dead Poets Society*: regimented and traditional, not a place for free-spirited, independent, artistic types. The boys had four hours of academics in the morning. Time after lunch was reserved for the rigors of military training and athletics. In the 1950s, many in the Old South still saw military school as the ideal rite of passage to honorable manhood. Many of the young cadets went on to West Point. For a sensitive twelve-year-old who enjoyed music and the arts, it had to be pure hell.

Former Dean of Academics Rufus McClure said, "I knew Gram well enough to know he would not have cared for the military. But he would have gone along with it because he had no choice." Some boarding students had parents who sacrificed a great deal to send them to Bolles; they stayed in close touch and monitored their children's progress closely. "Then there were others who dropped their kids off and said 'see you at Christmas,'" McClure said. "Gram was more of the latter."

When Gram was twelve, reel-to-reel recorders were all the rage for kids interested in music. Since smaller, more compact machines weren't widely available in 1958, an average Phillips or Webcor reel-to-reel came in a big, heavy box. It could cost as much as $29.95, making it as important a Christmas present as a new bicycle or guitar.

Perhaps feeling some guilt about all the time he missed with his son while he was away, Coon Dog planned to give Gram a fancy reel-to-reel recorder for Christmas. After buying the machine, Coon Dog embarked on making a special recording for his son. "Gram's daddy was like the emcee," recalled Dickey Smith.

"Here's Dickey and he wants to tell you merry Christmas," Coon Dog announced. He did the same with a number of Gram's other close friends. It would be a particularly warm way for Coon Dog to welcome his son back home for the holidays. The Connors always bought a pile of presents for Gram and Little Avis. Christmas was a lavish affair usually spent at the Snively mansion in Winter Haven.

"It was a prism of images: silver trays, ginger ale, ice tinkling in crystal glasses, puppies and ponies and perfume and the whole of Winter Haven in every room," Little Avis remembered. "All these images dissolve into the dark by one overshadowing moment."

On Sunday December 21, 1958, Coon Dog dropped off his wife, son, daughter, driver Johnny Barnes, and maid Louise Cone at the Waycross train station. As usual, the group was heading down to celebrate Christmas with Poppa John and Grandma Hainie.

"Take care of my Avie," he called after them. His family expected Coon Dog to drive down to Winter Haven the next day.

On Monday December 22, Coon Dog's employee Claud Goble saw him in his office over at the box factory looking "just like he always did." Alone in his house on December 23, no one knows exactly when, Coon Dog Connor put a loaded revolver to his head and pulled the trigger. As a clue to what was coming, Coon Dog had sent a recent photo of himself back to his mother in Tennessee. Co-workers recalled a sense of calm that had come over him in recent days; clearly he'd been studying on a way out of the box factory job he never really liked. But how could he abandon the children he adored?

"My mother was one of the first people to see Coon Dog," Henry Clarke remembered. "It was a tragic thing." Goble was thunderstruck; no one had seen this coming. In a hushed tone he said: "It's amazing a man with such a high rank in the service that had a family and all, would kill hisself that way." Boo Clarke and all the boys who saw Coon Dog Connor as a war hero, scoutmaster, and father figure were inconsolable. "Oh man, it devastated us," Clarke said. "We couldn't get over it."

In deference to Coon Dog Connor's social standing in Waycross, the coroner ruled his death an accident. Editors at the newspaper dutifully reported the ruse, but everyone in town knew different. The police brought Dickey Smith and other kids down to the station to listen to the tape Coon Dog had made for Gram. Coon Dog had apparently recorded some sort of farewell message on the tape recorder. But all that remained were the words, "I love you Gram."

Much of the talk centered on Coon Dog's relationship with Avis. Was someone having an affair? Was the marriage about to end? Coon Dog's struggles with alcohol are well-documented. In truth, there's much more to it than that. For years Coon Dog had been living with a painful secret: he'd fathered a child out of wedlock.

Around the time Little Avis was born, a divorcee in town gave birth to a son—Coon Dog Connor's second son. "She was recently divorced," said Coon Dog's granddaughter Avis Johnson Bartkus. "Her family would not let her keep the baby so she put the baby up for adoption." Bartkus feels Gram and Little Avis never knew they had a long-lost half-brother. But what did Big Avis know? And when did she find out? The child grew up in an orphanage and didn't seek out his father's identity until well in to adulthood. Bartkus said the family resemblance is there.

"I suspect it may have added to his demise," Bartkus said of her grandfather. "There might have been some guilt about that." To find out about Coon Dog's second son after so many years was a jolt to his descendants. "It blew my mind a lot," said Bartkus.

In 1958, Big Avis was also deeply involved with someone else; without doubt, the family had fallen apart. Nancy Gill's parents told her later about Big Avis's affair with another man. "I hate to mention names," said Gill discreetly, "I know 'em." Gill spent many nights at the Connor house and witnessed "lots of drama" between her friend's parents.

Despite his serious wanderings, to Coon Dog, the end of his marriage had to be akin to the end of his life. "He was a victim of a broken heart," Gill said. "He was a man totally dependent on Avis's income with the box factory in Waycross." With his wife's considerable financial means, she could practically erase him from the children's lives.

A small contingent from Waycross made the trip down to Winter Haven, where the Snivelys held Coon Dog's funeral a few days after Christmas. For Claud Goble, the experience was surreal. "Right after the funeral the family was back at it," said Goble, "serving drinks, business as usual." To make matters worse for the Connors who'd travelled from Tennessee, Gram and Avis weren't there.

"The Snivelys took Gram and my Mother to a state fair," remembered Bartkus. "The Connor side was furious about it."

Christmas of 1958 had to be torturous. When Gram and Avis were finally made aware, the effect of suddenly losing their father with little explanation must have been shattering.

Little Avis remembered: "I was left to find comfort from somewhere inside myself: 'Dear God please make Daddy come back.' But mother said he'd never come back, so I revised my prayer: 'Dear God, please bless Daddy and tell him to wait for me.'"

For Gram, a period of confusion and anguish began. Henry Clarke urged Gram to come back up for a visit sometime soon. "I'll never come back to Waycross," Gram told him. That didn't end up being true, but at the time, Gram's carefree boyhood he'd had before being sent to Bolles ended in a sudden, shattering instant.

One day several years after his father's death, Gram was driving with a schoolmate to Winter Haven. Even on the narrow, winding roads, Gram was driving at an alarmingly high speed. When his friend Paul Broder asked him why, Gram hinted at a death wish: "If I ever get in a wreck I don't want to be maimed." Broder argued there had to be a better way, but Gram told him: "Everyone I've ever loved ends up dying."

Big Avis never expressed a sense of responsibility or even much remorse for her husband's suicide; that chapter in her life seemed to close quickly.

After Coon Dog's suicide, in Waycross it was as if the entire Connor family was dead and gone. "They disintegrated," said Dickey Smith. For years, the Clarkes had been close friends and neighbors of the Connors. "That's the last I saw of them," remembered Boo Clarke. After the loss of her husband, Avis relocated her family to the mansion in Winter Haven.

Back at boarding school, Gram was miserable and urged his mother to let him return home. There was no one there to help him through the grief and suffering. "The school made no effort on his behalf beyond 'I'm sorry to hear about that,'" said Rufus McClure. "We had no such person as a chaplain in those days." Avis resisted her son's pleas. "I think Gram's mother went to more drinking," said Dickey Smith. "I think Gram and his mother split a little bit. I think he wanted to come home and she didn't want to deal with that." Gram became such a disciplinary problem, he was asked not to return to Bolles the following school year.

That summer, Avis took the children on a grand train trip across America. For his little sister, Gram tried to step into his father's shoes. Little Avis called her brother, "a male comforter who put things in their proper perspective. We grew very close to one another." Big Avis seemed to come out of her shell too, though her quirks puzzled the children. "She held our hands and closed her eyes when we went over bridges," Little Avis recalled. "She had a hand-carved wooden dog which she carried with her everywhere and could not sleep unless it was by her side."

* * *

In 1959, the music that occupied much of Gram's time became his lifeline. "It's what saved him," said Waycross musician and Gram devotee Billy Ray Herrin. Fortunately for Gram, his new home in Florida would nurture his ravenous appetite for music and provide the rudder he needed. If all else was grief, anger, and despair, there was always the music.

Gram's new central Florida home was becoming a music hotbed in the South. In a tiny five-mile stretch between the towns of Winter Haven and Auburndale, Gram befriended and benefitted from a constellation of singers, songwriters, and entertainers on the rise.

The dawning of Florida's great garage band era was drawing near.

## Gram's Domain

Avis and the children lived at the Snively mansion only until she could find a home of her own. In late 1959, she relocated to an upscale middle-class ranch home in a new Winter Haven subdivision. Decades later, I was there with a childhood friend of Gram's who witnessed the next phase in his life.

Sunlight broke through the window on an otherwise dreary central Florida afternoon. In a bedroom of a well-kept but otherwise unremarkable suburban tract home, one of Gram Parsons's best childhood friends in Winter Haven, Jim Carlton, stood bathed in the sunlight. Looking a little out of sorts, he stood hands-on-hips as if to brace himself against a tidal wave of fuzzy images coming back in to view.

"It's just a flood of memories, a torrent," Carlton offered. "It's really a letter from home here, I tell you."

The letter came with a 1960 postmark; for the first time in more than forty-five years, Carlton was standing in the room he practically called home back then. Referring to this little area as "Gram's domain," just like that—Carlton was thirteen again.

He recounted all the little things about Gram's domain that most other boys their age didn't have: a private bathroom and shower, walk-in closet, television, piano, swimming pool in the backyard, and an enviable record collection that included Peter Nero, James Moody, the Ventures, and comedy albums by the Smothers Brothers, Jonathan Winters, and a new sensation, Bob Newhart. "This was a pretty cool pad to have when you were thirteen years old," said Carlton.

From the minute he got up, Gram was at the piano tinkering—making up songs "about whatever girl he was going with at the time," Carlton recalled, "Pam or Carol or Karen, the girl du jour." When he was ready to leave the house, Gram took a guitar with him almost everywhere he went. "It was like his wallet," Carlton deadpanned.

Carlton is one of the most important friends Gram made upon his arrival in Winter Haven. The two shared a similar sarcastic wit, natural talent, and a love of girls, cars, and music. They were bandmates and even did a knockoff of the Smothers Brothers comedy routine. In later years, Carlton became an authority on this pivotal point in Gram's life. He also produced an album of his friend's urban folk recordings.

Carlton tried to conjure memories and find his way around the neighborhood along Piedmont Drive where he once felt at home. He stopped by to visit with a woman who'd lived there since the early days.

"I still remember hearing Gram singing and playing guitar on the back porch," she said with a hint of a smile. Then the wistful tone fell away. "It's a sad thing that happened to their family. It's as if they all just came apart."

Only half a year after losing her first husband, Big Avis embarked on a whirlwind romance with a bon vivant New Orleans businessman named Bob Parsons. Immediately, the Snively clan believed Parsons had designs to marry Avis and gain entrée to her money. Gram didn't like Parsons either at first, suspecting he was some kind of "carpetbagger."

"I met him in the deep end of a swimming pool," recalled Little Avis. "He had a big black birth mark on his back so I decided I didn't like him. On the other hand, he wore a gold St. Christopher medal around his neck. Now that was something."

Parsons had a kind of Hugh Hefner persona. Always a snappy, if sometimes garish dresser, he tooled around in a Jaguar and brought a dose of faster living to the former Connor clan. Parsons had a serious disease to please, loved to socialize, and sat next to Avis matching her drink for drink. Barely a year after Coon Dog's death, Bob Parsons was ready to become the man of the house.

To say Parsons was only in it for the money, though, is neither fair nor accurate. If anyone could understand what Gram was going through, it was the new man in his mother's life. When Bob Parsons was a child in New Orleans, his own father deserted the family. To help his mother make ends meet, young Parsons delivered papers in the French Quarter. When he got older, Parsons rode the bus to his job at a men's clothing store and developed a keen sense of style. Even if he had little money, Bob Parsons knew how to dress as if he did. By marrying Avis at the end of 1959, Bob Parsons was providing a loving father figure for Gram and Little Avis, the way no one ever did for him.

Up at the top of the driveway next to the home at 941 Piedmont Drive, Gram and Avis wrote their names in the wet concrete, just their first names: "Gram, Avis." In this period of transition and uncertainty, it's as if that's all the two could still claim of the life they'd known and the father they'd lost.

In the fall of 1959, his mother shipped Gram off to another boarding school, Graham-Eckes Academy in Palm Beach. "I'm not crazy about it," Gram wrote to a girl named Connie O'Connell in Waycross. "All the girls here are stuck up." It's clear the bitterness toward his old hometown had worn off: "I love Waycross so and all of the wonderful people that lived there." Gram told Connie he'd started playing electric guitar in what may have been his very first band, Red Coats Now. That band and Gram's stay in Palm Beach were short-lived. By Christmas he'd convinced his mother to let him come back to their new home in Winter Haven.

Next, his mother enrolled Gram in Saint Joseph's parochial school, even though she didn't raise her children Catholic. One day at lunchtime, Gram met a new classmate, Jim Carlton. "Everyone was calling each other by their last names," Carlton remembered, "except one, they were just calling him Gram." The two boys went outside and ate their brown-bag lunches at a picnic table. After, they started walking around the ball fields, cracking jokes. "He was funny and I was funny," Carlton said. "And there's nothing better than that. That's a real bond."

Gram often had to spell his name. When asked to do so, one of his favorite retorts was: "Gram, like the measure, not the cracker."

Carlton accepted Gram's invitation to come over to his house, but then hesitated when a black man arrived at school to pick them up. It was still 1960 in the segregated Deep South, the days of separate white and colored waiting rooms, drinking fountains, motels, and hospitals. Kids had once derided Carlton for taking a sip from the colored fountain at the Kwik Check store. Now he was getting a different perspective on things; his new buddy Gram made a crack about the situation and was not at all threatened by persons of color. "It's all right. C'mon," Gram reassured him. Johnny Barnes had stayed with the family after Coon Dog's suicide. To Gram, he was far more than the family's handyman, gardener, and driver. Barnes, his wife, and their son were trusted friends.

Carlton had a near-religious experience that first time Gram invited him to his home on Piedmont Drive. He saw a piano, guitar, and rows of records. When he spent the night, maids brought Canadian bacon, peanut butter, and Pepsi for breakfast. "I thought that was the coolest thing in the world!" Carlton exclaimed. "I had the sense he had a lot more freedom than I had." When Gram arrived after school, Carlton watched him blast an air horn and exclaim, "Gram's home." But often, no one was there to hear it.

Gram was to thereafter find out about Carlton's affinity for music, too. Gram learned that Carlton's father was a professional jazz musician from Chicago and ran the music store in downtown Winter Haven. Piano jazz legend Marian McPartland was a close family friend and Jim's godmother. For aspiring young musicians, a place that sold rows of gleaming new guitars and drew others who could dispense advice on becoming a better player—it might as well have been a house of teen worship.

Parsons and Carlton screamed down Piedmont Drive in Gram's go-cart and later skulked around at night with a BB gun looking for streetlights to fire upon. Somehow they got hold of teachers' phone numbers, ringing them up at impossibly late hours. Carlton had come up with a pretty fair JFK imitation; in the mirror Gram did a spot-on goof of crooner Neil Sedaka complete with a preening pinkie wet-down of both eyebrows.

At night the boys wolfed down popcorn and stayed up watching old movies like Jimmy Cagney's *Fighting 69th*, run so often on Tampa's WTVT channel 13, it became a joke between them. In those days kids their age had to be satisfied with watching whatever came on the two or three main stations, making unmerciful sport of what they saw. Of the seniors dancing to Guy Lombardo's orchestra Gram exclaimed, "My God, it's a sea of bald heads!"

When it came to girls, Gram's good looks, social standing, stylish clothes, and good manners gave him a leg up on his gangly, less mature peers. He went further sooner than his admiring and sometimes envious friends. However, Gram could also be quiet and withdrawn. And because his family had money, some immediately assumed Gram was a snob.

"I knew that wasn't true," said one of Gram's former girlfriends, Donna Class. "Gram wasn't the slap-you-on-the-back, rough-and-tough boy. He was just a musician. He was gentle and communicative and a good friend."

Class came from another upper-middle-class Winter Haven family. Her father trusted Gram so much that he would drop his daughter by Gram's house early in the morning. Other times, Donna and a friend would show up at Gram's side door when he and Jim were having a sleepover. "I still remember the color of his bedspread," Class recalled.

Gram would get up in the morning and go straight to the piano. "Every song I sing is for you," he told Class. Even at that young age she knew "he told that to a lot of girls." As she spoke about her early friendship and eventual romance with Gram, Class could still sing part of the lyric he wrote for another girlfriend, Pam Cairns.

It must really seem absurd,
How one small three-letter word
Could so change and disarrange me,
I hear your name, and I'm aflame—Pam.

According to Carlton, cleaning the swimming pool was the single chore Gram had to complete to earn his hefty five-dollar-a-week allowance. By comparison Carlton remembered, "I had to work really hard for my two dollars." The boys always had money to go see big-name acts like Roy Orbison and Jerry Lee Lewis stopping in Lakeland for a gas-money gig between Miami and Atlanta. They also went to Lakeland to visit one of their favorite stores, Casswin Music.

In 1960, Gram Connor was about to take another musical step up and out. It was the dawning of a new decade filled with good times, music, and tragedy. He would play all over the South, write some of his best songs, and ride the wave of surfer-boy music, hootenanny folk, rock, and cosmic country.

# ❧ 7 ❧

## Red Coats, Pacers,
## and Legends

U.S. Route 27 runs like a spine right up the agrarian center of the state of Florida. Through old citrus, lumber, and railroad towns like Frostproof and Haines City, the divided highway once provided an important link for northern travelers to reach pre-Disney tourist attractions like the Bok Tower, Cypress Gardens, and spring-training baseball. Just off U.S. 27 sits Dundee, one of those blink-and-you-miss-it towns near Winter Haven.

Situated along the old Atlantic Coast Line railroad tracks, the roughly three thousand residents of this hamlet take a lot of pride in the century-old train depot made out of native pine and cypress. Legend has it the town's first baby was born in a tent beneath an old camphor tree that still stands next to the community center. In this small and beautifully restored depot, another birth of sorts happened in 1960; Gram Connor performed his first of many public concerts throughout the state of Florida.

The depot is a good example of how musicians growing up in the South made history in unexpected places: garages, farms, Florida rooms, gymnasiums, dry-cleaning stores, rural juke joints, churches, country clubs, cinder-block strip clubs, and recreation centers. Early recordings were made in private homes, back rooms, even at social clubs for women. These places nurtured the talents of some of America's most important singer-songwriters and performers of this era.

If bands were cars, the first group Gram Connor joined in Winter Haven, the Pacers, was aptly named. An older kid from nearby Auburndale named Jimmy Allen had become friendly with Gram and even gave him some guitar lessons. Gram's potential was obvious to Allen, who invited him to join his group, consisting of Marvin Clevenger on bass and Skip "Flat Top" Rosser, a big but generally gentle kid, on drums.

From the spring of 1958 through March of 1960, Elvis's white-hot career had been interrupted by a stint in the army. One of the great soul balladeers, Sam Cooke, emerged during this era. Elsewhere, vanilla crooners like Paul Anka, Frankie Avalon, and Pat Boone filled the talent vacuum, with varying degrees of success. Gram looked for alternatives to their loathsome ballads through jazz, rhythm and blues, country, and comedy records.

When Allen invited Gram to join the Pacers, the few Elvis moves he remembered from his Waycross days as the front-porch, half-pint Presley got him immediate notice from the girls. He took over as the band's lead singer and focal point. Not all of this sat well with Allen, who wanted to keep things clean-cut.

Not much is known of the Dundee depot gig except that the band wasn't much good. But to the young teen crowd watching it didn't matter. Gram, with his gleaming new Fender Stratocaster, looked the part. The fifty or so kids in attendance gave their loud approval. For a kid bent on stardom, it was further validation of his aspirations. The quartet played some Elvis, Buddy Holly, even a couple of country tunes. The event set the tone for life as Gram would know it all through his formative years in Winter Haven.

Donna Class saw Gram perform at the country club's "teen room" while playing with this same group of boys. To Class, Gram's first foray into the world of garage bands was further indication of what she already knew. "He was a musician," Class reflected. "He didn't have to become one; he just was, naturally. His music just took precedence over everything else."

Gram's family life was also at a turning point.

*   *   *

On a night the two siblings Gram and Little Avis "buddied up" in the same bedroom, their mother came in unexpectedly. "She made a big speech there in the dark between us about how Bob had asked her to marry him," wrote Little Avis. She said she wouldn't give him an answer until she knew the children wanted him for a father.

After giving the children time to discuss it in private, Big Avis came back for an answer. "We told her about how much we liked Bob and she cried and kept asking us if we were sure," Little Avis remembered. "Until Gram told her to be quiet and let us get some sleep."

After their marriage, Mr. and Mrs. Robert Ellis Parsons, pursued their own romantic agenda and partied with a revolving circle of friends. Little Avis had a donkey named Old Tuck and a riding teacher she was close to named Sabra Schiller. Avis immersed herself in riding and horse shows. She confided to Schiller her father had killed himself and grew close to her teacher. "I liked to pretend she was my mother," said Little Avis.

Gram found music a new way to get some positive reinforcement at home. Avis and Bob often called Gram to play piano and perform for their friends. For Bob Parsons, encouraging Gram's music was a way to ingratiate himself to Avis's standoffish son. However, Class witnessed a troubling part of Avis and Bob's routine: "I was over there a lot of mornings, and to remember they were *drinking* a lot of mornings is kind of shocking when you think about it."

Jim Carlton has pleasant memories of Big Avis, often referring to her as his "other mother." To many, the extent of her drinking problem was not obvious. When Big Avis was sober, she was very much a part of the Winter Haven upper crust—tooling around in her Cadillac, traveling with Little Avis to her riding competitions, and supporting Gram in his music.

When she was older, one of the few stories Little Avis ever told about her mom involved photographers who clamored to get shots at those riding competitions. "The photographers knew Big Avis would be drunk at the shows and would buy all the pictures of my Mom," recalled Avis Johnson Bartkus. "So they would take tons of them."

Despite Avis's hard-drinking ways, she became pregnant and gave birth in the fall of 1960 to a healthy baby girl named Diane. Little Avis was thrilled and insisted Diane sleep in her room just as soon as the family's crusty nursemaid would allow it. With all the ups and downs at home, the one constant in Gram's life was his love of music.

*　*　*

Having had his first taste of stardom, Gram wanted to branch out and start a band of his own. He met a young guitar prodigy from nearby Eloise named Jim Stafford, who was two years older. One afternoon Gram told his new buddy he planned to tell the Pacers he was done. "I remembered how big Flat Top was, and I warned him not to go out there," Stafford recalled. But Gram wasn't afraid.

Sure enough, when Gram made his intentions known, Flat Top Rosser got mad and slapped him around. Gram might have been a sensitive kid, but over the years he had learned to take a punch. Since his departure was abrupt, perhaps Gram figured Rosser had the right to be a little steamed. He held no ill will. "I remember when Gram came back he had red marks under his eye," said Stafford, who admired Gram for having the guts to tell the older guys he was out. Upon seeing his old bandmates at a later gig, Gram actually told Jim Carlton not to make fun of them. To Carlton it was clear the Pacers still weren't having much luck getting their sound in gear.

In the five-mile corridor between the towns of Winter Haven and Auburndale, scores of kids in the rock-and-roll era saw music as a way out of the dull, workaday, churchgoing lives their parents pursued. One of those with whom Gram would come into contact again and again was future Country Music Hall of Fame songwriter and Auburndale resident Bobby Braddock. In his memoir, *Down in Orburndale* (a reference to how locals pronounced the name of the town), Braddock reflected on how uncommonly musical Polk County was in the early 1960s:

> In my memory, the music was everywhere, as if it were being piped in through the trees and coming up from the cracks in

the sidewalks. Rock and Roll was the music of the young and we couldn't imagine ourselves or the music ever growing old. When Elvis's "Jailhouse Rock" arrived at our local radio station, the teenage deejay Ronnie Brown played it continuously for one hour, with no interruptions or commercials. Because I had fallen in love with country music, my favorite rock n' roll was by the artists who had country roots, such as the Everly Brothers and Jerry Lee Lewis. I think I loved music so much that one kind of music just wasn't enough for me.

Braddock's lyrical memory of old Florida could have reflected Parsons's sentiments; both had a keen awareness of the musical melting pot in which they were raised. Elvis carried with him the notion that it was cool for a working-class kid to sing and perform. Dylan and the Beatles later personified the idea of writing their own, more introspective material. The combination was akin to splitting the atom, given the ensuing explosion of garage bands that populated the Florida peninsula throughout the 1960s.

Gram's early self-confidence was reflected in the name of his new band, the Legends. It bears pointing out, kids his age changed bands like school clothes; members came and went quickly. The 1961 through early 1962 Legends line-up included Gram on guitar and piano, his buddy Jim Carlton on upright bass, a school chum Lamar Braxton on drums, and Jim Stafford on lead guitar.

Stafford possessed an unflinching desire to be an entertainer and pursued it with a raw ambition and strong work ethic. Where his younger friend Gram wanted to be a rock star in the tradition of Elvis, Stafford wanted to entertain people any way he could. The first time one of his jokes made someone laugh, Stafford remembered, "It was absolutely like a religious experience for me. I mean it was really thrilling."

Stafford's father Woody toiled at the International Fruit Corporation in a mill-town enclave between Winter Haven and Auburndale known as Eloise. Compared to the Snivelys, the Staffords were far down the social ladder. One look at the humble surroundings where Stafford lived as a child illustrates that point. Down the dusty road in front of his small, wood-frame home, Stafford often walked barefoot.

His was the family's first generation to have indoor plumbing; Stafford had to wait years to witness the wonders of television in his own home. But music, which helped erase Jim Crow racial boundaries in the South, also became a sort of equalizer among social classes. None of that stuff mattered to his musician peers because teenaged Jim Stafford was already a guitar god.

"FABULOUS guitarist, great potential musician," Bobby Braddock wrote of Stafford in a diary from 1962, concluding "far better than me." This was serious praise from a guy who was older, already playing professional gigs, his own skills on keyboards held in high esteem.

At the Carlton music store in downtown Winter Haven, Stafford took lessons from Carlton's father, Ben. An intelligent pragmatist who played a variety of instruments like upright bass and banjo, Ben Carlton moved his family from Chicago to Winter Haven to write promotional jingles for the citrus industry. He sat the boys down and tried as strongly as he could to discourage them from life as professional musicians. He pronounced Gram's name "Gray-um."

"If you don't get an education," Ben Carlton warned, "You'll be out pickin' shit with the chickens."

Gram was getting the opposite message at home from Bob Parsons, who encouraged him to play. As for Jim Stafford—a dire warning like that would have only made him practice more. Stafford played all the time anyway. He brought his guitar to the dry-cleaning store run by his family, practicing in-between helping customers.

When Gram invited Stafford to jam, the country boy from Eloise got a taste of how the other half lived. "Jesus, a swimming pool!" Stafford exclaimed. Today backyard pools in central Florida are almost as common as mailboxes out front, but that was not the case in the early sixties. "That was a very exotic and wondrous thing," Stafford remarked. "I couldn't get over it."

For some reason, Stafford's work ethic didn't translate to the ragtag collection of friends called the Legends. Stafford recalled, "The thing we didn't do, I don't know why, but I don't remember us setting up in somebody's garage and really working on things." When their earliest gigs rolled around, the guys decided there on the spot what songs they'd sing and who would do what part. "Our set list had to be just abysmal," Jim Carlton said. "Did we know twelve songs?"

Given Gram's affinity for writing songs after girls like "Pam"—"Sherry" by the Four Seasons made the Legends' set list. The repertoire included other contemporary hits like Ray Charles's "What'd I Say" and the Ventures' "Walk Don't Run."

Carlton remembered Gram performing Johnny Ray's "Little White Cloud That Cried" at an early gig. "He just steals the show with this little song," marveled Carlton. The song was so syrupy by Carlton's estimation that the crowd could have gone into "insulin shock." Gram seemed to have an instinct for what slow songs the ladies in the audience would like.

Their first show, each guy was supposed to get ten dollars. After all the money was counted, the promoter couldn't pay in full. "Tell you what," offered Gram, "we'll take eight bucks apiece and you can keep the rest." Gram made the promoter happy and solved the problem diplomatically.

Abruptly, his friends became aware of another big change in Gram's life.

"When I met him, he was Gram Connor," Stafford said. "A few weeks later, he was Gram Parsons." Although Jim Carlton was a lot closer to Gram, he, too, became aware of the change suddenly. One day after school Gram told him, "My name is now Ingram Cecil Parsons." Bob Parsons had adopted Gram and Avis and gave them his last name. "I could tell he was happy about that," Carlton remarked.

The last vestiges of the Connors of Waycross were gone. Gram barely, if ever, spoke of his natural father or what had happened. "He had some distress about that obviously," Carlton said. But Gram carried it with him in silence. There was now an obvious divide between his new life in Winter Haven as faster-living Bob Parsons's son, and his first twelve years in Waycross as war hero Coon Dog's boy. To the Parsons of Winter Haven, on the day of Gram and Avis's adoption, Coon Dog Connor "ceased to exist."

Bob Parsons had an ex-wife of his own who had borne him two daughters, Jan and Becky. For a month every summer, the girls would come visit their father and new half-siblings. Big Avis went along with having the girls visit. Her routine wouldn't change all that much anyway. "I remember Gram being this kind of cool, hip guy who was six years older," recalled Becky Parsons. "I remember being so fascinated by the fact that there was this music room on the house that was soundproofed and he could play his music."

The neighborhood children welcomed Bob's daughters to town by throwing a party. Each received a little combination diary and autograph book. Gram added the first autograph to Becky's book: "My signature will be worth something one day."

For teens like Parsons, Bobby Braddock, Jim Stafford, and Jim Carlton—kids burning with a desire to write, sing, play, and entertain—there was a way out of Polk County. Even though many of them weren't old enough to drive, shave, or play with any real professionalism, aspiring teen musicians across Florida could ply their trade in the most important music incubator of the 1960s: youth centers.

# The Youth Center Circuit

Before Twitter, Facebook, MySpace, and cyberspace this building was the teen place. Most people who stop in or happen by this drab, 1950s-era structure on Orlando's Lake Formosa have no idea how it used to rock. In recent years it's been called the Loch Haven Neighborhood Center, inhabited mostly by seniors or grade-school kids pursuing quiet social activities. The front, obscured to passing motorists by a hedgerow, looks dated and dowdy.

This forgettable-looking place used to be the Orlando Youth Center, the crown jewel venue for teenaged musicians and their stalwart fans. From Auburndale to Zephyrhills and many towns between, youth centers gave young musicians a paying place to play. Barely in high school, they could tour the region, develop a following, and gain confidence as performers.

The minute you step inside, the old youth center's ugly duckling veneer falls away. On the bottom level, there's still a wide, terrazzo dance floor and an elevated stage in the corner. Most striking is the sweeping glass wall overlooking the sprawling back porch. Large shade trees frame the lake view, making it easy to see why this area was teen make-out heaven.

It's impossible not to feel the vibrations of all the raucous live music that came from within these walls, played by groups like the Legends, the Outlaws, We the People, Tin House, the Tropics, the Purple Underground, even big-name acts like the Turtles. In its day, this youth center developed such a cool reputation that older kids actually had fake IDs to prove they were *young* enough to get in.

Across the lake, a young Rollins College student named Eric Schabacker started his own talent and booking agency for these young acts. He shot some of the earliest promotional videos of the bands with the lake as a backdrop. Lugging around a portable two-inch tape machine, he could showcase his talent to prospective clients. Later, Schabacker opened Bee Jay Recording Studio, giving these young acts a chance to immortalize their sound on vinyl. In later years, Schabacker recorded the likes of Michael Jackson in his out-of-the-way Orlando studio.

This is just one snapshot of the budding Florida youth center circuit that awaited Gram Parsons and his garage band mates.

For his son's first serious venture into the world of garage bands, Bob Parsons bought a Volkswagen bus and had "The Legends" emblazoned on the side. Big Avis bought a dozen matching red sport coats and creased black pants of varying sizes for any number of young guys who might be in the band for a gig or two. Thanks to his parents, Gram had a pretty cool set-up for a kid who was neither sixteen nor old enough to drive his own tour bus, so Jim Stafford often took the wheel. "You'd mash down on the accelerator and five seconds later the thing would start moving," Jim Carlton cracked.

The Legends played up and down what became the I-4 corridor, mostly in the youth centers. "There were juke joints like Club 27 and Club 92," said Stafford. "The Hobnob and Spider's Web, those were *joints*, you know?" But most nightclubs and bars weren't about to let fifteen-year-old kids play there; that's why youth centers were so important. And nothing else could provide the kind of money young people made playing these youth-oriented venues.

In 1962, the Legends opened at the Orlando Youth Center for eighteen-year-old Bruce Channel, whose monster number-one hit, "Hey Baby," featured Delbert McClinton on harmonica. From Winter Haven, the drive to the Orlando was more than an hour, so the boys got to stay overnight in a hotel, another exotic perk of playing the circuit.

"We took pride in leaving behind a pyramid of beer cans," Carlton remembered. That summer a regionally popular British group named the Beatles opened for Channel in London.

As part of a book she's working on, "Playin' the Peninsula: Garage and Teen Center Bands of the Florida I-4 Corridor," a youth center stalwart Susan Martin catalogued the staggering number of area garage bands of the 1960s and 1970s.

"Garage bands were everywhere," she recalled of that era. "Their big time was the high school dance, a radio station 'remote,' a flatbed truck used as a stage in a parking lot, a youth center or a teen club." Most never saw the inside of a recording studio, but those bands lucky enough to make a record could wind up having it hit Orlando radio station WLOF's "Funderful Forty." Before radio became the bastion of a handful of conglomerates and homogenized playlists, stations like WLOF were local yet nationally influential.

If deejays like Bill "Weird Beard" Vermillion or Dick Shane took a shine to a local youth-club band like Nation Rocking Shadows, or a strong regional act like Detroit's Bob Seger System, they could end up on the local charts right alongside big names like the Beatles:

If I don't make it to Orlando,
You know my runnin' days are done

**"Song to Rufus," Bob Seger System**

"As a kid of about 14, I used to hang out at WLOF on Saturday afternoons learning everything I could about broadcasting," Martin wrote. "I was also on the 'advisory board.' Vermillion would pull something out of his stack of stuff to preview and we'd start playing 'em. If I said something really reeked, he'd Frisbee it across the room, slamming it into a wall or trash can broken to bits."

Like a scene from the film *American Graffiti*, Orlando disc jockeys would broadcast from the glass booth of a two-story tower in front of Chastain's Restaurant on the Orange Blossom Trail.

The WLOF guys had a hearse they'd take around to remotes. When the old rig died, the station decided to hold a contest: The listener who could guess where the old hearse was hidden would win a new Mustang.

Since the youth center was the mainstay location for WLOF remotes, one smart guy decided the old rig must be hidden under the main stage. Sure enough, those zany deejays had compacted and stashed it under there in a big metal cube. The guy who won the Mustang still has it and proudly drove it to a recent reunion of youth-center bands.

The Legends had a small Premier sound system with two speakers. You plugged the lone microphone into the main unit and shared lead and backup vocal duties on it with everyone else. The boys had Fender amps into which Gram plugged his Stratocaster and Stafford his Jazzmaster. Dressed in matching red jackets, black pants, and black ties, even if the boys didn't play so hot—they cleaned up well. For a prestige gig at the Admiral Farragut Academy in St. Petersburg, band members substituted white dinner jackets.

According to Carlton, the amount of attention you received at a youth-center gig sent a clear message: "You felt you were really legit when the kids stopped dancing and stared at you."

The Legends were part of a broad mosaic of well-known musicians who started out in this era, up and down the Florida peninsula. As a young teen, the Eagles' future lead guitarist Don Felder joined up with a military brat named Stephen Stills in the Continentals. After a gig at a Palatka prom, Felder recalled the liberating qualities of staying in a hotel room and swigging Jack Daniels. "We were laughing and bouncing around, breaking bedsprings, and having a gas. It was probably one of my fondest memories of that whole time," wrote Felder.

During his early years in Gainesville, Felder forged a close friendship with Gram's future bandmate in the Flying Burrito Brothers, one of the unsung mainstays of the alt-country genre, Bernie Leadon. After Leadon co-founded the Eagles, he recruited his old Florida garage-band buddy Felder to play lead guitar. The two played a teen club in Daytona Beach called the Wedge, becoming friendly with future southern-rock legends Duane and Gregg Allman. At one time, the Allmans were a clean-cut Beatles cover band called the Escorts. Then they played all over Florida as the "Allman Joys."

After Duane's death in a motorcycle accident in 1971, the Allman Brothers Band hired Auburndale guitar wizard Les Dudek from a youth center band called Power. The Allmans' first song on which

Dudek played alongside Dickie Betts was their breakthrough hit "Ramblin' Man."

Tom Petty played in the Epics and Sundowners. His next garage band, Mudcrutch, played the Orlando Youth Center, a cinder-block strip club in Gainesville called Dub's, and an annual outdoor show called the Mudcrutch Farm Festival that attracted hundreds of fans.

Country singer John Anderson from Apopka played some of his early gigs in a local youth center. It's not hyperbole to say central and north-central Florida, Winter Haven to Orlando to Jacksonville, turned out more important rock and country rock guitarists of the 1960s and 1970s than anywhere else.

The roots of the youth center circuit can be traced to the seminal influence of Elvis. From 1955 through his early mammoth success in 1956 and 1957, Presley performed sold-out shows in Florida cities big and small: Miami, Tampa, Orlando, Daytona Beach, Jacksonville, St. Petersburg, West Palm Beach, Ocala, Sarasota, Fort Myers, and Pensacola.

On August 8, 1956, Elvis played three shows at Lakeland's magnificent Polk Theater. The *Lakeland Ledger* assigned four reporters to cover the mayhem Presley's appearance brought to Polk County. To this day, the spot where Presley signed the wall in his third-floor dressing room has been preserved under plastic.

In 1961, Tom Petty decided he wanted to become a music star after seeing Elvis shoot a movie on location in Ocala. It's impossible to quantify the width, depth, and breadth of Presley's effect on the culture of the South and kids like Gram Parsons. Guitar sales boomed, and young kids strummed, strutted, and plugged in. Like never before, teens and rock and roll became synonymous.

Sometimes bona-fide rock stars would appear live at Florida teen hangouts: "I remember seeing Jerry Lee Lewis at the Kissimmee Youth Center," Jim Stafford marveled. In the early 1960s, after Lewis revealed he'd married his teenaged cousin, he'd become a pariah in the music business. He had to accept whatever paying shows he could, no matter how small.

Thanks to Gram Parsons's ability to ply his connections for better-paying gigs, he was able to start recruiting talent from and occasionally sit in with rival garage bands like the Dynamics, headed up by

Kent Lavoie. Under the name Lobo, Lavoie would enjoy chart success in the 1970s with the songs "Me and You and a Dog Named Boo" and "I'd Love You to Want Me."

"I always thought Lavoie had a real commercial voice when I didn't know what a commercial voice was," Jim Stafford said. Lavoie is a no-nonsense guy who, at a 2001 reunion of Polk County musicians nicknamed the Polkats by Bobby Braddock, notoriously remarked that Gram Parsons couldn't sing, play, or write. Not all the musicians in attendance disagreed.

On his way to a guest appearance with the Dynamics at the Tiger's Den Youth Center in Cocoa, Gram's bus ran over a cow. Despite having a cracked rib, bloodied face, and being generally freaked out by it all, Gram fulfilled his promise to play. Parsons had other reasons for working with Lavoie's band.

One Saturday afternoon at the Auburndale municipal building, Gram sat in with the Dynamics' rhythm section, consisting of Jon Corneal on drums and Gerald "Jesse" Chambers on bass and harmony vocals. "Gram was showing an interest in two-part harmony," Chambers remembered. He also recalled the key to Gram's dexterity on piano: "God, he had such long fingers." A couple of days later, the phone rang at the homes of Corneal and Chambers. It was Gram asking them to join the Legends. "I got this real good guitar player named Jim Stafford," Gram told them. He also offered the promise of more money. "That's what appealed to us," Corneal remarked.

Upon visiting Gram's house for the first time, Chambers had a reaction similar to Stafford's. Chambers's family had moved to Auburndale from northern Alabama in 1952. His father could barely read or write, and they had very little money. "I remember standing and crying trying to get my Dad to sign to get a Montgomery Ward Airline guitar," Chambers remembered. "He did. In retrospect it was an enormous thing to do. He didn't do credit—you paid for it. We didn't have anything but we didn't owe anything."

Chambers, along with his brother Billy and cousin Carl, had started on the youth center circuit right out of church, where they learned to sing and harmonize gospel standards and contemporary numbers by the Louvins and Everlys. Jesse Chambers was among the first to sing duets with Gram. Chambers "wasn't terribly impressed" with Gram's early singing, but slowly the two worked up songs like "Let It Be Me" and "Love Hurts." For a fast number they picked Little Richard's "Rip It Up."

Jon Corneal's father owned a lumber yard and had a home bigger than Gram's. Still, he was impressed by his gleaming white Fender guitar with "gold-plated everything." It was a look to which Gram had grown accustomed, given that even the bathroom fixtures in his home were gold-plated.

*　　*　　*

Meanwhile, a new family drama was developing. Avis and Bob planned to build a big new lakeside home in Winter Haven. The couple enlisted the help of their neighbor, renowned architect Gene Leedy. To their embarrassment, according to Bob's daughter Becky, "they found out they didn't have the money to pay him."

Avis sued her brother, John Snively Jr., whom she felt had looted her portion of the family fortune. Papa John Snively had died in 1958, and John Jr. had been in control of the money. The Snivelys suspected Bob Parsons of encouraging the lawsuit as a way to further alienate Avis from her family. It was eventually settled, and Avis's portion of the estate was restored, meaning the trust funds for Gram and Little Avis also remained intact. However, the new lakeside home never got built.

For the most part, Gram didn't let the family drama get him down. Stafford described him as a "freewheeling kid, he didn't ever tell you that something was really rough for him." To the contrary, Gram would call him up and say, "Let's play guitars, let's play guitars!" There was an enthusiasm and passion for the music. And there was always Gram's considerable gift for gab; like many southern boys, he was a natural storyteller. The Legends' new lineup consisted of Gram on keyboards, guitar, and vocals, Jim Stafford on lead guitar, Jesse Chambers on bass and vocals, and Jon Corneal on drums. As the band got better, they generated a regional buzz that brought new and exciting opportunities. They were about to graduate from youth centers to the world of live, local television in the tradition of Dick Clark's *American Bandstand*.

Gram Parsons and then-unknown Emmylou Harris on stage at Liberty Hall, Houston, Tex., 1973. (Larry Sepulvado)

Avis Johnson Bartkus in Gulf Shores, Ala. (Michael Robinson)

The view of the St. Johns River from the gazebo at the Bolles School in Jacksonville, Fla. (Michael Robinson)

The Snively Mansion, Winter Haven, Fla. (Bob Kealing)

Deep within the Okeefenokee Swamp. (Michael Robinson)

*Above:* Gram Connor grade school photo, undated. (The Estate of Robert Parsons)

*Right:* Gram and Avis around the time of their father's death. (Avis Johnson Bartkus)

Avis Snively and Ingram "Coon Dog" Connor's wedding at the Snively Mansion, Winter Haven, Fla., March 1945. (Avis Johnson Bartkus)

*Left:* Ad for Elvis Presley concert in Waycross, Ga., February 1956. (The estate of Robert Parsons)

*Above:* Haywood "Boo" Clarke, the man Gram Parsons credited with teaching him his first guitar chords. (Michael Robinson)

City Auditorium in Waycross, Ga. (Michael Robinson)

Ingram Cecil "Coon Dog" Connor on his wedding day. (Avis Johnson Bartkus)

Rufus McClure, Gram Parsons's academic advisor at the Bolles School, Jacksonville, Fla. (Michael Robinson)

The front porch of Gram Parsons's boyhood home in Waycross, Ga. His first stage. (Michael Robinson)

The Waycross train station. (Michael Robinson)

Jim Carlton, inside Gram Parsons's "domain" for the first time in forty-five years.
(Bob Kealing)

The Dundee train depot, believed to be the site of Gram Parsons's first public performance with his band the Pacers. (Michael Robinson)

*Above:* Where Avis and Gram wrote their names in the driveway of their Winter Haven home. (Michael Robinson)

*Right:* Avis with her beloved donkey Old Tuck. (Avis Johnson Bartkus)

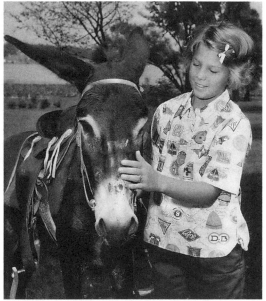

*Right:* Gram Parsons as a young teen. (The Estate of Robert Parsons)

*Below:* Big Avis and Little Avis at Ponte Vedra Beach, Fla., circa 1962. (The Estate of Robert Parsons)

Advertisement for Legends concert. (Avis Johnson Bartkus)

The Legends. (Carl Chambers, http://www.dizzyrambler.com)

The former Orlando Youth Center, a premier venue on the youth center circuit where the Legends opened for Bruce Channel. (Michael Robinson)

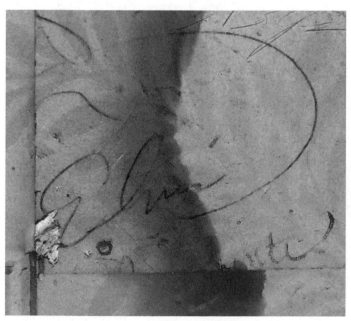

Elvis Presley's signature on the water-damaged wall of his dressing room at the Polk Theater in Lakeland, Fla. (Michael Robinson)

Les Dudek at the Winter Park Youth Center, circa 1967. (Les Dudek)

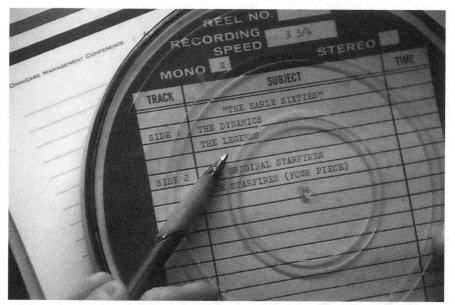

The reel-to-reel of what is believed to be Gram Parsons's earliest surviving live recording from the Hi-Time television show, WFLA-TV Tampa, Fla., circa 1962. (Michael Robinson)

Soundproofing tiles still on the wall of Ernie Garrison's home recording studio, Lakeland, Fla. More recently being used as a master bedroom storage area. (Michael Robinson)

What is believed to be Gram Parsons's earliest surviving acetate. (Michael Robinson)

Ticket to WFLA-TV's Hi-Time television show. (Carl Chambers, http://www.dizzyrambler.com)

Gram Parsons during his urban folkie period, circa 1964. (From the personal collection of Marilyn Platt)

Advertisement for the Other Room coffee house, Lakeland, Fla.
(Rick Norcross)

# 9

## High Times and
## Earliest Recordings

"I've been accused of living in the past," confessed self-proclaimed pack-rat Carl Chambers. Because of his compulsion to "hang on to stuff," the world has a much better idea of what Florida's historic garage band era was like. In his backyard recording studio in Auburndale, Chambers can play you one of his own compositions or take you on a time travel to hear what some of the most popular youth-center bands of the era sounded like when they were starting out. He and his brother Jimmy and cousin Jesse were in any number of them: the Legends, We the People, the Dynamics, the Starfires. One of Eric Schabacker's earliest videos shot in Orlando includes Carl on guitar and Jesse on bass doing justice to Neil Diamond's "Solitary Man."

Fans owe Carl Chambers a debt of gratitude for making and preserving Gram Parsons's earliest-known live recording. A musician's musician, since the late 1950s Chambers has lived for the music. He's traveled the world and played on four number-one hits for the Bellamy Brothers. In 1982 Chambers wrote Alabama's number-one single, "Close Enough to Perfect." He's chased fame and seen fortune elude him like a desert mirage. Chambers is living proof that road musicians don't have 401(k)s, pensions, or health plans. When they come off the road having entertained tens of thousands of fans, they often have little money to show for it, and worse, they see what weeks and months of absence have done to their family lives—if their loved ones have chosen to stay around.

Chambers is webmaster of "DRO," short for Dizzy Rambler Online (http://www.dizzyrambler.com). Named after one of his later bands, Chambers's website is the definitive primer on northern Polk County's considerable music history. For years, Chambers has dutifully catalogued the lives and careers of many local pickers who went on to fame and fortune. His writings give us a distinct flavor of what it was like growing up there in the 1960s, and many of his photographs and recordings are one of a kind.

Part of his inspiration to do Dizzy Rambler came from the realization that many of the old reel-to-reel recordings he made in those early days were in danger of being lost. The oxide that holds the sound to the tape had started to flake off. He transferred as much as he could to digital files and posted them on the web. As a result, you can hear Parsons's first forays into high-lonesome harmonies with Jesse Chambers, Bobby Braddock's early keyboard work, and young Jim Stafford's blazing guitar.

Every Saturday afternoon at 4:30 came Tampa's answer to *American Bandstand*: the *Hi-Time* teen dance show on WFLA channel 8. Each weekend, kids lucky enough to have a ticket traveled from all over the region, crowding into the station's studios on Jackson Street.

Teens today would be amused at the formality of the studio audience members looking as if they were all dressed up for church: boys in coats, ties, and dress shoes; girls made up as if going to a debutante ball. Like locally owned radio stations, shows like *Hi-Time* nurtured the teen music scene and took the popularity of garage bands to a regional level.

All musicians had to do was write the show's producers to let them know about their band. "Hi-Time was something all the bands wanted to play," Carl Chambers remembered.

By the time Jesse Chambers and Jon Corneal became regular members of the Legends, they were *Hi-Time* veterans. Jesse rode the school bus over to Tampa to be an audience member. Later, he and Corneal appeared on the show as the Dynamics, with cousin Carl Chambers on lead vocals.

Gram was worried about Jesse's old-school greaser look. "You need to wash that stuff out of your hair and comb it this way," Gram instructed. "And by the way, here's a bottle of Canoe." For boys that age, English Leather was the working man's aftershave. Canoe was the white-collar scent.

Gram passed along more than fashion tips. When it became apparent that Jesse Chambers's old Airline guitar would not pass for a bass, he and Gram headed over to Cannon Music in Lakeland. There on the wall was "the most wonderful Gibson guitar in the world." The salesman offered Chambers $60 for his old guitar and amp, leaving him exactly $100 short to buy the Gibson. "Gram put up the $100," Chambers remembered. "I owe Gram for that and I've thought of that several times in my life." It was Chambers's first bass guitar of many he played during his decades-long career as a successful sideman and road manager for Ricky Skaggs.

Gram received regular trust fund payouts and would share some of the cash with friends. One classmate hit up Gram for twenty bucks. Gram obliged, but the look on his face was indication he knew the money would never be paid back. When it came to helping Chambers buy his first bass, for Gram it was a means to an end: helping his band sound and look more professional. For Chambers, "that was like manna from heaven."

When the Legends appeared on *Hi-Time*, back at home Carl Chambers alligator-clipped a microphone on the front of his family's console television. "I was recording Jesse," he said. The host, WFLA's weatherman Jack Stir, did the introduction: "And now some young and upcoming musicians who are doing a fine job, local fellas from Winter Haven and Auburndale, the Legends and a good tune called 'Rip It Up!'" Backed by Corneal's steady drumbeat, Gram sang lead and Jesse harmony. Stafford supplies the screaming guitar solo.

At the beginning of the second song, Ray Charles's "What'd I Say," it sounds as if Gram's voice is still getting comfortable with puberty. After some more jaunty licks by Stafford on lead, at the song's end Stir makes a memorable blooper. He's commenting to one of the girls exhausted from dancing: "Oh that's tiring, isn't it? While you're catching your breast, uh breath. . . ."

The standout song from Chambers's recording of the Legends on *Hi-Time* is undoubtedly the Everly Brothers' standard, "Let It Be Me." From a historical perspective, it's the earliest example of Parsons's high-lonesome sound that would become a trademark of his later recordings and the alt-country genre. Had it not been for Carl Chambers's dogged commitment to documenting these performances, they would have been lost to history.

*Hi-Time*'s producer, Jean Morris, invited the Legends back for several more appearances. The band enlisted the help of a friend, Sam Killebrew, to act as its manager. During another *Hi-Time* performance, Corneal recalled Dick Clark actually being at WFLA. "Clark was there plugging his cavalcade of stars," Corneal remembered. "We performed that day and the stars didn't." This must have seemed like the next best thing to being introduced by Ed Sullivan himself. After a string of successful appearances, *Hi-Time* awarded the Legends, "Band of the Year." Still, Corneal remembered more mundane aspects of being on television, like the producers wanting the boys to wear blue shirts instead of white. Back behind the station, the cramped alley made the load-in and load-out a pain.

With regional success came arguments over the band's direction. "There were some strong personalities—Jim, Jon, and Gram. And they all had strong ideas and dreams," said Jesse Chambers. He continued, "I'm just wantin' to play bass—not everybody can be the star." Because of the bickering, Sam Killebrew's stint as manager was fleeting. According to Sam, "The band argued so much I handed them the booking schedule and said 'ya'll do it.'"

A special-projects producer for WFLA-TV said none of these *Hi-Time* shows was saved. As is the case with many television stations across the country, old shows are treated like old news. One year a new general manager came in and gave the order to pitch many of the films and tapes in the station's archive. The producer literally had to pull from the dumpster the station's film footage of JFK's historic Tampa visit one week before his assassination in Dallas.

Carl Chambers's *Hi-Time* recordings are believed to be Gram Parsons's earliest surviving live performances.

To make early acetate records, garage bands often had to travel to makeshift home recording studios. The Allman Brothers made their first such recording in a backyard cottage in Ormond Beach. Gram Parsons made his earliest surviving acetate in a small home in suburban Lakeland. A local recording engineer named Ernie Garrison had a recording studio that he ran out of his home.

The 1964 Lakeland phone directory indicated Garrison's modest house was located on the east side of town. Luckily, when pulling up unannounced at the home on Granby Street, a friendly man named Pete Davis happened to be letting his two dogs get a little exercise in the front yard. And even luckier, Davis was agreeable to letting my photographer Mike and I take a quick look for the history we hoped to find.

This 1950s single-story, cinder-block home, in a working-class neighborhood, had a large room that had been added on to the back side of the carport. "My wife and I have been using it as our master bedroom," Davis told us. When he let us in and flipped on the light, the room's configuration was the first clue we were in the right place.

The entryway had a small bookshelf with yet another doorway into the much larger sleeping area. It was obvious the bookshelf had been a window between the two rooms. The clincher was the large, white tiles lining the walls—soundproofing tiles, still there after so many years. Pete Davis's bedroom had been Garrison's home recording studio. The entryway would have been where the balding, middle-aged engineer sat with his equipment. Many important early recordings of central Florida's garage band era were made here.

For fifteen bucks, Garrison would cut the performers an acetate on the spot. One day a package arrived in the mail at Jim Carlton's house; he pulled from the envelope a Garrison 45 rpm acetate. The song titles were typed on a plain record label in block lettering: "Big Country" and "Racing Myself with the Wind." The artist's name: "G. Parsons."

Carlton still has the scratchy old single—believed to be Parsons's earliest surviving studio recording. It's unclear how many copies

Garrison made or Parsons sent out. The lyrics to "Big Country" ring true for young Gram. A better version of the song is included in the album *Gram Parsons: The Early Years, 1963–65*:

> So give me the road
> And a strong heart to travel with
> A mind that's always free
> I don't even know if I'll be back again
> I've got a lot of things to see
> It's a mighty big country

The songs on that early acetate are plaintive acoustic numbers. The mix of Parsons's vocals is so muddy it's hard to distinguish anything about them beyond their earnestness. "Big Country" was written and financed by Jay Erwin, part owner of Casswin Music in Lakeland. It didn't matter that Ernie Garrison's operation was nothing more than a little studio back behind his carport. For kids just starting, the idea of making any sort of record was a rush. "I thought I was at Columbia in Nashville," Jim Carlton quipped.

Gram did any number of early recording sessions, the results of which are long gone or have not yet been dug out of the right box in someone's attic. Bobby Braddock unearthed the fact that Gram Parsons hired him for a session at the Auburndale municipal building in January 1963; Parsons would have just turned sixteen. "I remember him as a rich kid who wore glasses and owned the first Wurlitzer electric piano I ever saw," Braddock wrote. "If I had known he was going to be a legend, I would have paid more attention."

As a teenager in a little central Florida town, Gram already knew to hire the best sideman around. It's amazing to think Braddock would go on to write one of the most celebrated country songs of all time, "He Stopped Lovin' Her Today," for George Jones, one of the artists Gram Parsons credited with bringing him to the realization that country was white man's blues and the genre he wanted to pursue.

"Bobby was really an incredible keyboard player," remembered Jon Corneal. "It raised all our proficiency just by virtue of the quality of his playing." Over at a tiny studio inside Casswin Music in Lakeland, Corneal played on another of Parsons's early sessions: "I remember us recording two Gram songs, one was 'Pam' and one was 'Joan.'"

\*    \*    \*

Kids in Florida and across the country started to focus on a genre that had been gaining momentum: folk music. The music of Woody Guthrie, Pete Seeger, and the Weavers gave a voice to the working class and their increasing calls for social change. From that simple and unadorned acoustic template came more commercially viable and less socially conscious acts like the Kingston Trio and the New Christy Minstrels. Singer-songwriters like Fred Neil, Bob Gibson, Ramblin' Jack Elliott, Bob Dylan, and Joan Baez carried the torch of introspective blues, social justice, and workers' rights to a new generation. The magical sounds emanating from their twelve-string guitars resembled church bells. Their harmonies spoke to the soul, providing more meaningful music in the mostly sterile void between Elvis's early years and the Beatles' conquest of America.

In 1963, Gram Parsons was ready to incorporate folk music into his growing stable of sounds. It became another musical distraction from the growing turmoil in his personal life; Gram was raising himself.

# ❧ 10 ❧

## Folk in the Other Room

In Lakeland's Dixieland district, a forgettable-looking single-story strip mall sits along busy South Florida Avenue. The façade has been updated, giving the complex a new look, but not in a convincing way. One of the businesses is a medical office and the other two spaces are empty. All around, there are signs of economic distress that forced most businesspeople to relocate to more prosperous parts of town. Yet in its day this complex was home to an important part of central Florida's music history.

One end of this strip used to house Fat Jack's Deli, the kind of down-home diner cherished by locals and undiscovered by most tourists content to stop at close-to-the-highway burger joints. In the middle was Casswin Music, where Gram Parsons took his first serious interest in folk music and liked to mingle with the like-minded musicians who hung out there. On the other end was Lakeland's first coffeehouse during the folk era, the Other Room. Looking at the "for rent" sign now, you'd never guess this was once an important cultural corridor. Everything here is a distant memory.

In the early and mid-1960s, small coffeehouses and clubs like the Other Room opened and catered to folkies all over Florida. Just like the youth center circuit, Florida's burgeoning folk scene was home to an impressive roster of future stars. Some are national names, while others became regionally respected.

In Miami, in 1962, a still-unknown folkie named David Crosby and local singer-songwriter Bobby Ingram opened what's believed to be South Florida's first coffeehouse. The most universally revered Florida folk singer, Fred Neil, whom Bob Dylan credited with giving him his first Greenwich Village gig, found a home in Coconut Grove. Vince Martin, who had a 1957 hit with the Terriers, "Cindy, Oh Cindy," teamed up with Neil to become kings of the South Florida folk scene. Their 1964 album on Elektra, *Tear Down the Walls*, still holds up.

Some of the best-known coffeehouses in South Florida were the Flick, Gaslight South, the Coffee House, the Catacombs, and Pegasus. In time, Parsons would find his way to Neil, Martin, and the Grove.

Orlando and Winter Park had the Carrera Room; in Tampa Bay the 18th String and Beaux Arts coffeehouses opened. A series of classic black-and-white pictures of Parsons were taken at a beachside Jacksonville coffeehouse, Café Espresso. Who took them remains a mystery.

Even after the popularity of folk had run its course commercially, these Florida coffeehouses nurtured the careers of Gamble Rogers, Paul Champion, Jimmy Buffett, David Crosby, John Sebastian, Odetta, Joni Mitchell, Will McLean, Van Dyke Parks, Jim Lauderdale, Cass Elliott, comedian/banjoist Steve Martin. . . . The list is endless.

Folk music brought Parsons his first professional gigs outside of Florida and opened up a whole new world: Greenwich Village. He developed a friendship with Neil, one of his most important influences. The trip brought Parsons and his high-school buddies close enough to touch the kind of success of which kids dream, and which adults find cruelly elusive.

Gram's friendship with Donna Class developed into romance. "It always just seemed really natural that we'd be together," she remembered. "The thing I recall about Gram," Class reflected, "He was particularly kind and easy to be with." At sixteen, his parents gave Gram an Austin Healey Sprite sports car. He buzzed around town with Class to places like Jack's drive-through restaurant. They spent a lot of time boating with Gram's first cousin Rob Hoskins and another close friend, Dick McNeer.

Class rode with the same horse trainer as Little Avis. "Avis and her first cousin Susan Snively were always competitive in their classes and always took turns winning," Class remembered. "It must have been hard for both girls with the families so competitive. They were both wonderful riders." Class said that Gram usually went to the horse shows and cheered for his sister: "I can remember Gram skiing behind a horse once for some sort of silly class."

At a horse-show banquet Gram played piano and impressed a young horseman, Buddy Freeman, who had become friendly with the Parsons family. Freeman recalled Gram "sitting at the piano playing like he was performing on stage." From that point, Freeman seemed smitten with the young man's talent. Gram was only too happy to take full advantage and leveraged Freeman's interest in helping his career.

Gram's stepfather, Bob Parsons, did a lot of business out of the country selling heavy equipment. He even brought back an exotic pet ocelot that quickly claimed territorial rights to all of the Parsons's backyard and swimming pool. With his stepfather's long absences and mother's drinking, Gram was often left to his own devices. "Gram was kind of isolated in his part of the house," remembered Class. Along with that isolation came the temptation to sample his parents' liquor supply and his mother's prescription pills. Gram had also begun smoking pot and developed a rather sophisticated way of getting it.

"Gram had received some in the mail, literally, it came inside a book," said Class. "We were at a park in Lake Alfred with a girlfriend of mine from North Carolina, and I remember laughing and having so much fun together." It was her introduction to pot, and Class insisted that's as far as drugs went for her. The same could not be said for Gram. With all the music, freedom, and partying, one important aspect of his life was severely neglected: school.

At Winter Haven High, Gram joined the tennis team long enough to have his picture taken for the school yearbook. By his junior year, education was no longer a priority. No one seemed to notice his academic slide. Class put it bluntly: "Gram was around for tenth grade; eleventh he skipped most of school. He never showed up." Once Gram's parents were made aware of the severity of the situation, they put him on "restriction."

"I got custody of the Sprite because he couldn't drive it," Jim Carlton remembered. That meant Carlton also got to serve as Gram's chauffeur the mornings he attended school and commented "He was late, so I was late."

For Gram there were too many distractions. He'd developed a new love interest, a striking blonde named Patti Johnson. Gram bought a twelve-string guitar and formed a folk trio that included Johnson and Gram's buddy McNeer. Named after an influential New York City nightclub, the Village Vanguards would entertain during intermission on Gram's regular gigs with the Legends.

Gram convinced Jim Stafford to take some publicity pictures with him. "It was all his idea, and as a matter of fact I'm pretty sure he brought the shirts," Stafford remarked. At a photo studio down the road from Stafford's house, the two teens dressed sharp, held guitars, and looked like brothers. "I never would have thought to take a publicity picture, but it certainly occurred to him," said Stafford. *Rolling Stone* magazine published one of the photos as part of a 1974 interview with Stafford, who was riding the success of hit singles "Swamp Witch" and "Spiders and Snakes."

Jon Corneal remembered, "He had a line into those social things." At a horse show banquet at the Haven Hotel, each member of the Legends was paid a hundred dollars. Then Gram turned around and got his folk trio booked into the women's club across the street. They played Nora Mayo Hall, a long-time site for graduations, art shows, and social events. "He was into playing music and doing what he was doing, and I just don't think he was going to school," said Corneal.

For kids who weren't so well connected, it was difficult if not impossible to find any local clubs where they could play folk music. Many adults saw folk as the music of the communist left or overly idealistic college students. Pete Seeger stood up to the House Un-American Activities Committee and found himself effectively blackballed as a communist sympathizer. Nonetheless, his songs were cherished by Parsons and young people all over the country.

Folk concerts, known as "hootenannies," became popular showcases for local talent. In 1963, a young musician named Rick Norcross won a hootenanny contest at the Polk Theater in Lakeland. That inspired Norcross, a Florida Southern College student, to explore opening up a coffeehouse in town.

Norcross approached Jay Erwin, the man who wrote and backed Gram's early single. Erwin was an affable musician and teacher who ran Casswin Music and supported local bands. "I pushed the Casswin guys into opening a club in Lakeland," said Norcross, "and the Other Room held forth as the folkie center of that part of Florida." Norcross and a couple of other local musicians, Kayle Payne and Sammy Schneider, became regular entertainment at the Other Room. Located in that strip of three shops with cars buzzing by a few steps out the front door, Casswin Music and the Other Room are where Jim Carlton believes Gram Parsons finally went "full bore" into folk music.

"Gram used to come over to Casswin's for strings and picks and stuff," Norcross said. "On one of his trips he brought a very fancy Ode banjo." When the Other Room opened, it gave Parsons a new place to showcase his growing interest in folk and performing solo.

The club was a hole in the wall with fifteen tables, modern paintings, and ropes and fish nets hanging from the ceiling. Candlelight created a dark and dramatic atmosphere. Patrons were asked to drop a one-dollar cover in "the kitty." "This provides the salary for performers which I might add, is very little," said a local newspaper writer. "But I believe they derive as much pleasure from performing as the people in the audience do from listening to them."

When the boys wanted to do Peter, Paul and Mary songs, sixteen-year-old Emma Smith provided the female voice. She recalled Parsons coming in late, sometimes with Stafford or other musicians. "I thought Gram was adorable," Smith remembered. "He wasn't a brash guitar kind of guy. What he sang was thoughtful."

Another musician who asked that his name not be used resented Parsons for immediately letting it be known he had money. "He hit on my girlfriend," he said. "I'm happy to say she was not impressed and used an unflattering comment about him." He added that Parsons was arrogant to other musicians and treated them badly. "I really have no axe to grind, other than I believe people should remember the facts. They don't."

In the spring of 1963, Parsons was in a romantic relationship with Patti Johnson. Not only was Johnson beautiful, for Gram there was the added cachet that he was dating a senior. The night before all the boys planned to make their annual trek to the Grand Prix race at Sebring, Gram skipped out early from a Legends' gig. Jesse Chambers took over lead-vocal duties and Jim Carlton was pulled out of the crowd to rejoin his old bandmates.

Word got around that Gram and Patti were planning to elope to Georgia, where underage kids could get married and laws regarding matrimony were more relaxed. According to Carlton, Patti's father intervened, giving some credence to the notion that the two did plan to run off together. Later that night Carlton saw Bob Johnson pacing in front of the young couple, "reading them the riot act."

For the next few days at school, friends kept coming up to Gram trying to draw the full story out of him, but he wouldn't reveal anything.

As if this wasn't enough drama, it was starting to become apparent around the Parsons and Snively households that Bob Parsons had taken more than a passing interest in the family's young babysitter, Bonnie Muma. If there were any thread of hope at all that Big Avis would curtail her drinking, rumors of an affair between her husband and the teenaged nanny put an end to that. Fueled by an alcohol-induced rage, Avis confronted her husband. Parsons tried in vain to maintain his devil-may-care, bon-vivant persona.

"I do think my father's inability to keep his pants on in the presence of an attractive woman who found him attractive was very deep-seated," surmised Bob's daughter Becky. She believes that paternal abandonment is the source of Bob Parsons's narcissism—much as it was in Gram's case.

Any hope Bob Parsons had of being perceived among the Snively clan as anything but a carpetbagging, lecherous slimeball was gone. The lawsuit he encouraged Avis to file against her own family members for mismanaging the Snively fortune had effectively made him persona non grata anyway.

Pictures of one of Diane's early birthday parties shows her surrounded by her babysitter Bonnie, half-sister Avis, and other little girls. Behind the children and presents is a row of black women in white uniforms, the maids. "They raised the children," Becky Parsons said. "They're the ones who got the kids dressed and took them to birthday parties, cleaned their knees, and loved and nurtured them." Absent from the photos were Diane's parents, Big Avis and Bob Parsons.

Some of Little Avis's fondest memories of childhood came when she got to stay with the family servants. "I wished very much that mother was poor," Little Avis wrote. "I spent a lot of time with our servants and their families for mother traveled a great deal. Their homes felt cozy and they had strange delicious things to eat; they had front porches with trellises of sweet potato vines."

Her daughter, Avis Johnson Bartkus says it got to the point Little Avis had to be told, "She was getting too close to the help." From "the help" came the love and nurturing often missing from parents in their children's lives.

The time had come for Gram to pay the price for neglecting his schoolwork: he flunked junior year. "I wasn't surprised at all," Donna Class remembered. Unlike most parents, Avis and Bob Parsons did not react as if this were a crisis. Jim Carlton said, "There was no overriding shame like in most households." But it did force them to act.

Gram's parents made the decision to send him back to the Bolles School in Jacksonville. They had their own issues to deal with, and Gram, at this point, was in the way. "They didn't do it for his welfare; they did it for their own," Gram's academic dean at Bolles, Rufus McClure surmised. "The real reason wasn't so that Gram would have a place to grow up or mature but to get him out of their way. Gram, I think, was a throwaway kid."

In the summer of 1963, two things happened that dramatically altered Gram Parsons's life. First, thanks to horseman Buddy Freeman's connections, Gram had a chance to participate in a hootenanny in South Carolina. And second, Parsons went back to Bolles to repeat his junior year. Fortunately, the academy was not the same rigid, constricting military school it had been before. Quite the opposite: the Bolles School was the best thing that could have happened to Gram given the deteriorating state of family life at home.

# 11

## Shilos and Bolles

Some of the venues tied to Gram Parsons's musical legacy in the South are gone forever.

In Greenville, South Carolina, helicopters whirred over Memorial Auditorium. Crews had finished placing 165 pounds of dynamite throughout the inside of the building. Outside, a ring of tractor-trailers was strategically parked to protect nearby buildings from flying debris. Police ordered people be kept at least 800 feet back from the place known as "the big brown box." It was September 20, 1997. As television cameras carried the goings-on live, at 8:00 a.m. the order was given to detonate. Within fifteen seconds, Greenville Memorial Auditorium collapsed into a pile of bricks, mortar, steel, and dust. Thirty-nine years of history that happened in the auditorium made way for the city's new and larger Bi-Lo center just a block away.

Now, when you drive by the vacant lot along East North Street, you have to imagine everything. Here in the "big brown box" with the cement floor, Gram Parsons took a new musical direction and a big step up. During a hootenanny concert there, he met the Shilos: three teenagers who would become the focus of his musical ambitions.

At the same time Gram was about to reprise junior year at the Bolles School in Jacksonville, family friend Buddy Freeman arranged for him to appear at the Coca-Cola Hootenanny in Freeman's hometown, Greenville.

It was September 1963, and despite Gram's poor academic performance, his parents continued to encourage and bankroll his musical ambitions. In Greenville, Freeman introduced Parsons to local disc jockey Johnny Batson. Greenville's answer to Dick Clark, Batson hosted the local Coca-Cola Hootenanny and liked what he heard in Gram. Since this folk version of a battle of the bands was limited to groups, Freeman arranged to have Gram sing solo at intermission and act as a judge.

The night before the big show, a three-piece folk group known as the Shilos was a member short. Guitarist George Wrigley had gotten into a fight at a party and ended up nursing a concussion. That left stand-up bassist Joe Kelly and guitar/banjo player Paul Surratt to soldier on as a duo. As they were warming up offstage Gram asked, "Are you guys going to do 'In the Hills of Shiloh?'"

Gram was planning to perform it the next night, and given the name of this band it was only natural Parsons thought the Shilos might be planning to do Shel Silverstein's ode to a Civil War widow. "That's how we happened to meet," remembered Joe Kelly. "I think he was impressed Paul was playing a Martin and I had a nice bass." The three boys decided to sing together, choosing "Run, Maggie, Run" by a group they admired, the Journeymen: John Phillips's pre-Mamas and the Papas folk trio.

"We hit that harmony right about in the middle and it was like we couldn't believe it," marveled Surratt. "Three of us sounded like six of us and we went *what*? We kind of looked at each other. You know how you know something special had just happened? And it had happened." Surratt added that if he could relive ten moments in his life, singing with seventeen-year-old Gram Parsons for the first time would be one of them.

"It was just really exhilarating," Kelly recalled. "Even at a young age you could feel when it clicked like that." The boys invited Gram to be in their band. As a reflection of his confidence as a front man, Gram took top billing. "I went home that night. . . . I remember I couldn't sleep," said Surratt. "All night long I tossed and turned and was hoping he really would call and we really would get together."

The next night, with Gram as their new member as well as judge of the contest, the Shilos won first place. Surratt laughed, "Here he is the judge, then he gets up and sings with us. I can't believe he had the balls to do that." The Shilos' new front man still had the issue of returning to the Bolles School 325 miles away to repeat junior year.

At first, Gram's new manager, Buddy Freeman, wanted nothing to do with the Shilos and didn't think it was the right move for Gram. Through the sheer force of his personality, Gram convinced him that's what he intended to do. "Buddy insisted we all go out and buy certain kinds of clothes," said Kelly. "He got us some pretty decent paying gigs around town." Thanks to Freeman, civic groups used to shelling out $100 for a full band paid $350 for "Gram Parsons and the Shilos."

Gram Parsons gave the Shilos a kind of pride they never had before: "The entire group was extremely confident and proud of our music," said Surratt. "We never feared playing against another group, we weren't afraid of anybody. It could be the Kingston Trio, we wouldn't care." To Surratt, their new level of talent was affirmation the Shilos would hit it big one day.

At the end of 1963, the Journeymen came through Greenville as part of a thirty-city "Hoot Tour." Besides Phillips's considerable songwriting abilities, the Journeymen featured Jacksonville native Scott McKenzie's soaring vocals along with folk purist Dick Weissman. After learning the five-string banjo in Vermont and New York City, Weissman bummed around New Mexico to better learn the instrument through the eyes of authentic rural folkies. Weissman propped up the Journeymen through what Phillips called his "dazzling musicianship."

The Hoot Tour had been hell. In the segregated South, anyone white riding a bus and playing music alongside black artists was immediately branded by some as a civil rights agitator. In Jackson, Mississippi, artists on the Hoot Tour boycotted the gig because the town's auditorium banned blacks from the building. Local rednecks responded by breaking the windows of their hotel and taunting them with racial slurs.

The Shilos were oblivious to racial unrest. The clean-cut, apolitical teen folkies were booked at hospitals, K-mart openings, high schools, charity functions for organizations like the South Carolina Teachers'

Association, and Coca-Cola shows. A photograph from Gram's scrap-book shows a marquee from the Greenville Memorial Auditorium: "Friday Coca-Cola Hi-Fi Hootenanny starring Gram Parsons." Pictures from that night show Surratt and Kelly dressed in white jackets and dark ties. Like the star of the group, Gram wears a contrasting dark sport coat and open-collared button-down shirt.

The most enthused member of the Shilos, Paul Surratt idolized groups like the Kingston Trio, the New Christy Minstrels, and most of all, the Journeymen. When musicians he admired came through town, Surratt would knock on the door of their hotel rooms and introduce himself. At a Journeymen gig about a hundred miles outside of Greenville, Surratt made his way backstage and forged a friendship with John Phillips. His idol even passed along a phone number if Surratt and his group ever made it up to New York City.

Gram was getting adept at courting the local press. In an article entitled "Recording Artist Likes Greenville's Folk Music," Gram fibbed about being with RCA records—Elvis's label. "Not only is Greenville a wonderful audience to play to, but I was astounded at the amount of fine talent in the area," Gram opined. "As you know, I plan to do some work with one of your groups." Gram went on to credit the local PTA as the primary force behind the spread of folk music's popularity among local students. "Whatever the reasons," he told the newspaper's reporter, "I'm delighted."

Also during this time Gram and the Shilos became regular performers on Greenville television WFBC's folk music show, *Shindy*. All of this presented a grand new distraction for Gram as he went back to boarding school. However, the Bolles School had changed since Gram's first stay. The school administration had voted to do away with the military training and adopt a more liberal approach to educating young people. Gone were the days of spending afternoons drilling and training. No more did students have to stand at attention in the dorm when a faculty officer walked by. In 1963, Bolles had transitioned to a college preparatory school for boys. JFK's Camelot was still in full swing, the Beatles had not yet stormed America, and campuses were not yet fomenting with antiwar sentiment. In this cloistered existence albeit not of Gram's choosing, he could further immerse himself in the arts, especially music.

"Gram demonstrated that from the moment he got here," remembered Rufus McClure. "And he had a huge amount of devotees who sat around and listened to him." One of them, a younger student named Roger Williams, had seen Gram around campus for about a week before meeting him in the snack shop.

"Where are you from?" Gram inquired.

"Waycross," Williams told him.

"Waycross, Georgia?" Gram perked up. "I used to live there. Who do you know in Waycross?"

"My sister just married Boo Clarke," Williams replied.

"Boo Clarke, that's Henry's cousin," Gram said. "Boo taught me my first guitar chords!"

Williams later realized he had known this guy as Gram Connor, the dark-skinned, good-looking kid who sometimes was a baseball teammate on play-out nights in Cherokee Heights. Now Gram was a worldly and confident musician who enjoyed being the center of conversation and attention. "He was on the fast track for sure," Williams said. "You can put a shirt on somebody and it would look one way but put it on him and it would look better. You know, he had a charisma about him." Gram inspired Williams to take up the guitar.

Gram educated a lot of new and less-cultured friends on what he liked to call simply "good music." A classmate from Miami named Paul Broder marveled at Gram's eclectic tastes: "He'd be just as likely to play Thelonious Monk or Jerry Lee Lewis or the Dillards or Dylan." Gram saw James Brown and Ray Charles in concert, and he was fascinated by Charles's landmark record, *Modern Sounds in Country and Western Music*.

If Parsons was conversational and outgoing in a group setting, he could be the opposite one-on-one. "I do remember him being moody and sullen," said Broder. "And he didn't really try to connect with people. You really had to kind of push your way into his life." Being a fictional recording artist spinning yarns for the press was one thing, but coming to terms with who he really was and why he was back at Bolles was quite another.

"He hid that he was running desperately psychologically," said McClure. "I don't think he knew it. I'm not sure many of the people around here knew." In the past five years of his life, Gram's father had killed himself, his distant and indifferent mother had descended deeper and deeper into "suicide by attrition," and stepfather Bob Parsons was having an affair with the family babysitter—a waif half his age.

Gram had plenty of distractions in Jacksonville and Greenville. He wrote for the school newspaper, took up acting, had his own hootenanny program at a Jacksonville radio station, and made new musician friends. And there were new girls to chase, woo, catch, and confide in.

In November, Gram decided to blend the old with the new by inviting his buddies from the Legends to play a school dance. When Jon Corneal and Jesse Chambers arrived on this particular November evening, the show did not go on. "We got there and they said 'Ain't gonna happen boys, here's your money,'" remembered Jesse Chambers. JFK had been assassinated. There was a pall over the campus. The two boys never even saw Gram that night. In a daze, they loaded back in the car and headed for home.

Meanwhile Stafford had been making the drive in a friend's beat-up old car that kept stopping. By the time he arrived at Bolles, the president was dead. "I don't know why we're here; they're not gonna have a dance," he told Gram. "Oh yeah," Gram replied, not yet grasping the gravity of the day's events. "They won't have the football game, but they're gonna have the dance."

It was the end of an era of innocence for most, but not for Gram Parsons. The idea of sudden death by gunshot was all-too-familiar to him. The evening of JFK's assassination, Gram played to a group of classmates in a boathouse alongside the St. Johns River. Those who were there recalled Gram's soul-stirring version of the folk standard, "You've Heard My Voice (and You Know My Name)."

The Bolles School's laid-back dorm supervisor, Joe Dyess, became a father figure to Gram, as did English teacher Robert Hubbard. An omnivorous reader, Hubbard modeled scholarship to his students. He introduced Gram to the avant-garde writings of Beat Generation writers like Jack Kerouac and Lawrence Ferlinghetti. Coincidentally, when the Legends played the Orlando Youth Center in 1962, Kerouac was living only a few miles away in a subdivision called Kingswood Manor.

"Bob Hubbard became the most profound influence in Gram's life," McClure believed. Gram did well in class but didn't put himself out—making a few A's but mostly B's and C's. Gram even joined the football team. Bolles re-engaged Gram academically and artistically; his performances reflected his confidence and focus on becoming a full-time musician.

Gram, Roger Williams, and a group of other students in the "smoking circle" liked to sing, play, and hold court in the campus's picturesque stone gazebo. "I would every now and then go by his room. He'd be playing. One or two times I'd catch him by himself," Williams remembered. "He liked to do the Kingston Trio, 'Bells of Rhymney,' 'Four Strong Winds,' 'Scotch and Soda,' and 'John Riley' by Joan Baez. When he hit the high notes on that, the hair would stand up on your arms." At a hootenanny in Jacksonville, one of the judges evaluating Gram's performance wrote on his clipboard in letters big enough for Williams to see: "PROFESSIONAL."

As in his early days in Waycross, Gram's growing renown struck some students the wrong way. "There was no real gray area; either they liked him or they really didn't like him," said Williams. "You'd hear stupid things like 'he can't play guitar very well but he's got that good voice.' Then you'd hear people say, 'he plays guitar real well but he can't sing.' I thought he played well and sang well myself. I loved his voice." Classmates recall that Gram was allowed to grow his hair longer than most. Under the more relaxed regime at Bolles, Gram had more latitude as an artist.

When Gram drove back up to South Carolina for a series of Valentine's Day concerts with the Shilos, his persona far exceeded that of the average seventeen-year-old. Singing with the Shilos in these concerts was Marilyn Garrett, Buddy Freeman's cousin, and one of two singers he brought in to give Gram a break on vocals and extend the length of the Shilos' concerts. Freeman patterned the Shilos after the co-ed ensemble the New Christy Minstrels, featuring, in various incarnations, Gene Clark, Barry McGuire, and Gram's future friend and bandmate, Bob Buchanan. Freeman micromanaged details down to hand gestures, clothing, and costume changes.

Garrett had met Gram Parsons for the first time at a radio station in Charleston. While most of the young men in the station had short hair, shirts, and ties, Gram appeared in boots and a cowboy hat, hair in his eyes, looking like an early manifestation of the cosmic hipster he would become. "I said to myself I have never in my life seen anything like this," Garrett recalled, "I was just totally blown out of the water."

Despite the country attire, in his performances Gram and the Shilos played all folk music. During warm-up sessions, Gram might pull out his Ode banjo and play an old bluegrass tune called "Grandfather Clock." However, at this stage in his career, he often looked down on bluegrass and referred to "couuuntry" with a derisive drawl. He had not yet discovered its deeper, authentic, and soulful side. "That twangy country thing later, I never saw that side of him," Garrett said. What she did see was a mesmerizing young performer who "was the only breath in the room; he could take over completely."

This was vintage Gram: clear-eyed, driven, focused, in full voice—aiming to be a star without the baggage of addiction undermining those efforts at every turn. He could have chosen any number of musical paths; it all seemed so effortless. Thanks to having structure and management, his grades were good and career on track. "We were so young and innocent," remembered Paul Surratt. "We thought all you had to do is be good and you'd make it. What's funny is we almost did." He credits Freeman for giving Gram a springboard: "Buddy was instrumental in bringing Gram a step closer to what he became."

The three-day engagement in South Carolina was a considerable success. Gram's performance at the Citadel's beach club is burned in Garrett's memory: "I can still in my mind's eye see him in the lights singing in his cowboy hat and thinking, 'My God, how talented is this kid?'" During dinner at her uncle's house, Gram pulled out his guitar and sang a parody song he'd made up, "The Twelve Days of Khrushchev." Gram told Garrett he'd written a more thoughtful and touching tune for her called "The Hand within the Glove." After decades she could still sing it from memory.

On February 17, 1964, Gram had returned to Bolles after the concerts and felt deflated. "The sun is setting over the river and I'm depressed. When I'm depressed I have to talk to someone. You're elected!" Parsons wrote Garrett. "I just called home and found out my two best friends are married. I know it can't be from their own choice and I feel sorry for them. Well, that's the sort of town I live in. Really, Cypress Gardens is the personification of Peyton Place." The two friends to whom he was referring is unclear.

He included some flattery for his new friend. "You're the Shilos' type of girl and it's nice to have you in the group," Parsons wrote. "I think the future is looking bright for the Shilos now and I'm happy. They're really great people (even Paul)." Gram went on to lobby against the guy Garrett was going out with, laying the groundwork for something more than a friendship when the two reconnected in Greenville.

The melancholy aspects of Gram's life were reflected in his singing. "His voice just had a sadness," said Garrett. "When he sang you could almost feel his soul." In letters to her, Gram confided some of the issues in his life. "I think he needed the attention and affirmation of other people; I think he needed that badly," Garrett surmised. "I think it came from confusion more than anything else; a kid thrown into all of this wealth and around a mom not very loving, now drinking all the time and apathetic." Gram told Garrett it was rough being away at school and he'd rather be home, but the ones who mattered back home didn't want him there. "And that hurts when you're a teenager," she said.

At school Gram showed considerable promise in acting. Items from his high-school scrapbook include a certificate of recognition from the National Thespian Society's regional conference in Jacksonville. Dated March 14, 1964, Gram's dramatic interpretation merited a rating of "good," and the judges found Gram's humorous interpretation "excellent."

His home life problems notwithstanding, when Gram returned to Winter Haven, friends welcomed him back as if he'd never left. In Jim Carlton, Gram still had a friend with whom he could find a laugh in absurdity, irony, or even on the highway. Gram borrowed one of the maid's cars and along I-4 tried to master driving a foreign stick shift. With all that going on, the boys simultaneously noticed an ad on the back of a Colonial Meat truck they'd pulled up behind: "You Can't Beat Our Meat."

They laughed all the way to Tampa.

Marilyn Garrett was too young to travel out of town with the boys; her parents wouldn't allow it. The Shilos decided it best if they continued on as a quartet. After four or five performances alongside Gram Parsons and the Shilos, that's as far as it went for Garrett: "I never had dreams of being a big star." She continued to exchange letters with Gram into 1965 and watch his star rise.

In the spring of 1964, the Shilos had a chance to travel to Chicago to record some songs in honor of an upcoming visit to Cypress Gardens by King Hussein of Jordan. For Gram and his bandmates, it was the first of two unforgettable trips out of the South that year.

With the benefit of hindsight, by 1964 the Shilos should have known that folk music as an avenue to commercial success was over. The Beatles' coming to America forever ushered in the era of groups writing, playing, and performing their own electrified rock. It would be another year before former folkies Jim (later Roger) McGuinn, Gene Clark, and David Crosby merged the styles of Dylan and the Beatles into what became known as folk rock.

It took working-class kids from the streets of Great Britain to import and embrace the struggle and pain of southern blues and bring it right on back to America. Groups like the Rolling Stones recorded and popularized the work of America's great blues artists without the political and racial overtones. Even the British invasion had roots in the American South.

# ❧ 12 ❧

# Chicago Surfinanny

In the spring of 1964, the Shilos had a chance to do more concerts in Greenville, South Carolina. Gram's fondness for Marilyn Garrett deepened, causing a rivalry with bandmate George Wrigley. "George almost had a stroke when I told him I was taking you out on a 'real date,'" Gram wrote Garrett. "He was so afraid that I was going to hurt or upset you that I had to convince him I'm not really the villain he thinks I am."

Wrigley was the group's pessimist who always felt resentment toward Gram: "Gram and George were always arguing," Paul Surratt remembered. "Gram was good-looking and got more girls, and that bothered George."

The band's performances at local steakhouses, store openings, and charity events left Gram wanting more. With his growing romantic interest in Garrett, each return to Bolles became more difficult. His grades were suffering too. "I've been staying here on the weekends to catch up on my studies," Gram reported. "You'll never see any place as dull as a prep school on a weekend. I'm about to go crazy. I'm not used to this servile life." He also confided: "I've been writing a lot of poetry lately to get rid of tension. That and my guitar are my emotional outlets."

Cypress Gardens' legendary owner Dick Pope, bankrolled a Chicago trip for the Shilos in April to make some promotional recordings for the park and to honor an upcoming visit from Jordan's King Hussein. This trip north gave the band their first opportunity to record together.

The bandmates' trip also gave Gram and Joe Kelly a chance to get to know each other better. "He went to that fancy Bolles School down there and we were just ordinary public school runabouts," said Kelly of Gram. "And he would be a little elitist around us sometimes. But I think he let his hair down a lot with us. He seemed to have a whole lot of fun just goofing around." Buddy Freeman put the boys up first class at the swank Palmer Hotel. Like real celebrities, the band ate at five-star restaurants.

"Here we are in a fancy hotel, gonna record the next day, and we're doing 'Railroad Bill' all night," Surratt laughed. "People were beating on the walls." The boys couldn't have cared less; they were having too much fun. It was a scene reminiscent of Gram's first out-of-town gigs with the Legends.

Surratt remembered the Shilos recording five or six songs in Chicago, including "Julie-Anne," a New Christy Minstrels song Gram convinced his confederates he'd written. There was also a jaunty tune Gram actually did write as a kind of Cypress Gardens theme, "Surfinanny," patterned closely after a song called "Raise a Ruckus Tonight." It kills Surratt to this day that the other songs recorded were left at the studio and apparently lost to history.

During the Chicago trip, Buddy Freeman passed on a chance for the Shilos to audition for the Ed Sullivan show. According to Surratt, he didn't think they were ready. "I wish we could have done that," Surratt reflected. This would not be the Shilos' only brush with the big time that year.

To Freeman's chagrin, Gram blew six hundred dollars on cowboy clothes: boots, jeans, and a fancy buckskin jacket with fringe all over. All the boys bought jeans and hooded jackets. The clothing choices reflected a growing mood within the band to abandon Freeman's insistence on formality for a more relaxed, countrified feel. Thanks to his spoiled upbringing, it didn't occur to Gram that charging several hundred dollars in clothing to his manager's account could be a serious financial hit. Gram grew up feeling entitled to the best clothes, schools, girls, and instruments; he took for granted living like a star.

Gram enlightened Kelly on why money would never become an issue. "I have a trust fund from my grandfather's estate and I'll get millions when I turn twenty-one," he confided. "But I really don't expect to live all that long after that anyway." Gram said he planned to take the money and do with it what he could while he could and that was it. Perhaps that was just Gram spinning a yarn for the sake of melodrama, but Kelly didn't take it that way. "It was a premonition of his own demise," Kelly believed. "It was kind of odd to me. We were only seventeen or eighteen years old and people that young usually don't think about death."

Parsons's correspondence with Marilyn Garrett reflects a lighter and more optimistic mood: "The Shilos mean a lot to me, and whenever I can be with all of you I'm as happy as the buffoon in a catsup factory," Gram joked. "Chicago was great. I wish you could have been there. We could have gone out and really 'raised a ruckus.' Paul was in rare form and kept me in stitches. George (naturally) was upset at the fact that I wear jeans, boots, and a sheepskin-suede jacket."

On April 19, 1964, the young monarch of Jordan visited Cypress Gardens. The *St. Petersburg Evening Independent* described the event: "After a 21-firecracker salute, inspecting a line of bathing beauties and launching, the young monarch donned red swim trunks and a yellow life preserver to spin around the lake." The newspaper featured a picture of the king waving to the crowd, apparently so sure of his waterskiing abilities he didn't even bother to take off his wrist watch.

In May Gram wrote to Garrett, "We're now beginning our last month of school. Emotions are running wild and pressure's building up. The whole school's like a bomb ready to go off." For Gram that pressure included unrequited feelings for Marilyn Garrett. "Every night I go to sleep listening to Ian and Sylvia and fall asleep thinking about you. I have the most beautiful, vivid dreams of you singing their songs." Gram made it clear he was interested in more than friendship:

"I can't live by 'ifs' and 'maybes.' I've never been too adept at concealing myself. This isn't a spur-of-the-moment decision. I've thought about you since the weekend in Charleston."

As Gram's second and more successful try at junior year came to a close, Bob Parsons rented a beach house near Jacksonville in Ponte Vedra Beach. To blow off steam Gram and his buddies loved to take girls out to the beaches and party. Beachside coffeehouses were great places to hone his chops as a solo act as well. "He would show up and they would make a place for him immediately," remembered classmate Paul Broder.

The most striking series of pictures of Gram Parsons during this period were taken at a club known as Café Espresso. Some photographs show him performing; one depicts Gram flashing a million-dollar smile as he perches on a stool with an acoustic guitar in his lap. Gram later used the photos for publicity.

His friends say Gram already showed a remarkable tolerance—and appetite—for booze. In a gag picture from the Bolles yearbook, Gram pretends to be feeding his teddy bear from a whiskey bottle. "We got really hammered except for Gram," said Broder. Despite a considerable intake, Gram could still find time and a way to make it to one of his favorite beachside clubs for a late-night, fully functional performance.

After school was out, Buddy Freeman arranged a Shilos gig at Fort Caroline, a resort near Myrtle Beach, South Carolina. In the small oceanside resort town, the Shilos played seven half-hour shows a day, seven days a week. The demands were grueling, but as a result, their playing and singing tightened. The quartet sounded far more professional than a bunch of still-underage kids. Unfortunately, none of the shows was recorded.

The band's off hours consisted of smoking, drinking, and chasing girls. When the prim, proper, and controlling Freeman showed up and saw what was going on, he tried to clean house. The Shilos would have none of it.

On their own, the band managed to turn their engagement into a month-long gig. Even though he'd been in Greenville while the boys were fulfilling their breakneck performing schedule, Freeman still wanted a full cut of the proceeds. "There was a falling out," remembered Kelly. "He had introduced us to these people in the first place, but we'd gotten the follow-up gig on our own." Finally, the band gave Freeman his money and told him they were going to go their own way. To some, Freeman's ouster showed how easily Gram could drop someone from his life once he or she was no longer useful.

Not long after returning home to his family, Joe Kelly got a phone call from Gram suggesting the Shilos come down for a long weekend at the Ponte Vedra beach house. "We were gonna sing for a couple parties Bob was hosting," Kelly said. "We rode the train down." At the beach house, Bob Parsons had a home base to do business in Jacksonville and a place where he didn't have to hide his romance with the children's former babysitter, Bonnie.

One of Surratt's most vivid memories of Gram is riding around Ponte Vedra Beach in a station wagon, having a "long talk" about their mutual ambitions, their pursuit of musical glory. "We're the only two who are going to do something with this," Gram said. Joe and George were resigned to pursuing education and pleasing their parents: "They don't care like we do, they don't feel the same as we do." With his bandmates assembled once again, Gram hatched a grand plan; he wanted the Shilos to head straight from Ponte Vedra Beach to Greenwich Village—folk music's mecca.

Kelly's conservative mother in South Carolina recoiled at the notion of her boy on his own in the big city. "Oh, you can't do that!" she told him. But his father's response surprised Kelly. In 1921, Kelly's father and uncle had taken a summer road trip to Oklahoma to work as migrant laborers picking beans. That experience opened his mind to the idea of his son's New York trip. "If you want to do it, go ahead and do it," replied Kelly's father. With all the other Shilos parents amenable, the ever-accommodating Bob Parsons rented the boys a 1964 Chevrolet.

The next day, after playing one of Bob Parsons's cocktail soirees, the Shilos loaded up their luggage, four guitars, and a bass fiddle. They pointed the Chevrolet north on U.S. 17 out of Florida for the bright lights and glamour of the Big Apple.

They drove through the night, ending up back in Myrtle Beach long enough to grab some breakfast. From South Carolina, Gram and the Shilos motored until the madness known as rush hour in Washington, D.C. The band stopped at a National Airport Marriott where they cleaned up, changed clothes in a hotel restroom, and headed north. At three a.m. the next day the band arrived in Greenwich Village, exhausted and content to crash on the floor of an apartment small enough to fit in Gram's living room.

To say that the center of New York's folk scene differed from life in the South is an obvious understatement. "That was my first time to New York and being from bible-belt South Carolina there's a whole lot of strange things going on," remembered Joe Kelly. Nonetheless he said, "We survived quite well." Soon the boys felt so comfortable in the scene they joined a picket line of union entertainers striking for better wages.

In the Village, Gram ran into one of his idols, John Phillips. "I had met Gram years earlier backstage at some of the Journeymen concerts down South," Phillips recalled. "Then he found Mitch and me on Charles Street and stayed on our floor for a couple weeks." "Mitch" was John's young wife Michelle Phillips, whom he'd tried to insert into a new conjugation of his folk band renamed the New Journeymen. While Gram and friends slept on his floor, Phillips was writing some of his best-known songs, which would propel the Mamas and the Papas to the top of the charts in 1965 and 1966.

Phillips helped the Shilos get an audition for Albert Grossman. If there was a definitive folk power broker in the 1960s, Grossman was it. In 1961, he assembled Peter, Paul and Mary. He signed Bob Dylan the following year and was instrumental in guiding him to superstar status. The Shilos so impressed Grossman he was ready to add them to his roster of artists. Surratt remembered: "We played live and blew everyone in the agency away. They were going to put us in at the Bitter End [one of the important Greenwich Village folk clubs of the era]."

That is, until Grossman and company found out the boys were minors. "You're still in high school?" asked an incredulous Grossman and gruffly sent them on their way. The boys wondered if having Buddy Freeman to run interference for them could have helped. But it was too late. The Shilos had to be satisfied with knowing Dylan's agent thought them talented enough to cut it alongside big-time artists.

The Shilos still became regular pass-the-hat acts at famed Village clubs like Folk City and the Night Owl. After one performance, the boys got a note from someone in the crowd. "We really enjoyed your set," read the message from Eric Burdon. Gram responded, "I wonder who that was?," wadded up the note, and threw it away. Two months later, Burdon's group the Animals' signature song, "House of the Rising Sun," topped the British and U.S. charts.

Gram made a point of seeking out Fred Neil. Already a legend in the Village by 1964, Neil paid his songwriting dues in the late fifties at New York's famed Brill Building. As emcee at Café Wha?, Neil introduced, or perhaps unleashed, Bob Dylan to a New York audience for the first time in 1961. There's a famous picture of Neil performing with Dylan and blues singer Karen Dalton. In 1964, Neil recorded his acclaimed solo album *Bleecker and MacDougal*, named after a famous Greenwich Village intersection.

Parsons biographer Jason Walker reported that a "respected folk singer" introduced Gram to heroin. Neil's addiction issues are well documented. Among many jazz and folk artists of the 1950s and 1960s, heroin was a ubiquitous scourge. Given the addiction issues in Gram's own family, introducing him to smack added a new and dangerous layer to the level of abuse already going on in his life.

Paul Surratt and Jim Carlton say they saw no evidence during this period Gram was using hard drugs, let alone becoming addicted. According to Carlton, Gram preferred to smoke hashish, because pot "was messy." When psychedelic drugs like LSD became part of the scene, Gram charged into those with abandon. "His drug use was no doubt a way of exploring other psychic arenas as opposed to being an escape," Carlton believed. "Pioneers such as he by nature, by definition, seek what's new and different." Carlton recalled how he and Gram used to climb on top of a boat house, get high, and indulge Gram's fascination with the cosmos.

In the Village, Gram fell for a dark-haired singer he met while staying at the apartment of an aspiring folk singer from Texas, Jack Estes, a woman named Zahariah. His new love interest inspired Gram to write a song, called "Zah's Blues." In Joe Kelly's estimation, it was his "wooing song." While Gram tried to squire around a new girlfriend, the rest of his bandmates shopped and took in ball games. Gram took on the persona of a serious artist. "Gram always had a notebook . . . and was writing stuff down," said Kelly. "He was driven. He really decided that's what he was all about. Music was kind of his identity."

Parsons also reached out to another member of the recently disbanded Journeymen, Dick Weissman. "After the Journeymen, I was interested in doing as much producing and studio work as possible," Weissman recalled. During that summer, Weissman played and recorded with Parsons.

"There were two sets of demos. One was recorded in my living room on a Uher tape recorder," Weissman said. "The second set of demos was recorded at a studio called Musicmakers on West 57th street." During those sessions Weissman recalled: "Gram didn't say much. . . . I thought he was talented, young, with kind of a romanticized view of life. I felt as though his songs might be too abstract for the commercial marketplace."

That second set of songs, like the Shilos' recordings in Chicago, are lost to history. "Gram played and sang, and I played guitar on most if not all the songs . . . five songs. I don't remember what they were." As fate would have it, the tape box was located by Mitch Myers, Shel Silverstein's nephew. The discovery was even documented in an NPR story. But alas, the sounds on the tape were not young Gram Parsons.

"It had been recorded over!" Weissman lamented.

Even if Gram had found a new urban-folkie identity to which he wanted to dedicate himself, senior year awaited. For Joe Kelly it was no big tragedy that the band was too young to be signed by Dylan's agent. "My mindset was if we do make it, how am I going to work this out with going to school?" Kelly said. "It was never that burning thing." In contrast, Surratt said he hoped a career in folk music was right around the corner.

Back home, some of Gram's musician friends and peers from the youth center circuit felt similar pangs of wanderlust. On July 5, 1964, Jon Corneal and Jim Stafford headed off for whatever fame and fortune they could find in Nashville. A couple months later, Bobby Braddock and his new bride did the same.

Had Gram been a little further along on his own musical journey— and a little older—he might have joined them on the road to Nashville.

# ❧ 13 ❧

## Senior Year and the Derry Down

Right in the middle of downtown Winter Haven sits a small, vacant building. Most people passing by have no clue this empty building represents another historic link to Gram Parsons's past. In 1964, this warehouse across the street from Carlton Music came alive with the sounds of Florida's folk era. If there's another definitive place to remember Gram Parsons in the South, it's here in this building once called the Derry Down: a club his parents opened so when Gram was home he and the Shilos would have a place to play.

It's easy to imagine this place being reborn as a performance hall or club dedicated to Parsons and the many musicians and entertainers who came out of this area. It's surprising there isn't already a more permanent memorial here. For fans of cultural tourism, the corridor between Winter Haven, Auburndale, and Lakeland would be an ideal place to create some sort of tribute to all the musicians who called this area home in the 1960s. There's already a beautiful array of old-school Florida tourist attractions here, but their quiet charm is often drowned out by the mega theme parks ensconced along I-4 in southwest Orlando.

When Parsons returned to the Bolles School for senior year, the news of his New York exploits caused quite a stir among his peers. In the cloistered world of pressed pants and blue blazers, the stories of Gram dating exotic women and trying forbidden substances enhanced his mystique. In the gazebo at twilight, Gram shared stories with his "smoking circle" buddies. In their rooms, Gram and his classmates had to learn the night watchman's routine: "He'd see that little red glow from a cigarette and figure out what room it was and report you," said Roger Williams. "You'd get demerits. Fifty and you'd be confined to campus and couldn't go out on Saturday."

The contrast couldn't be more striking: to the lily-white, provincial children of staunchly conservative moneyed parents, Gram brought tales of singing alongside the messengers for integration and civil rights. Classmate Frank David Murphy, nicknamed by Bolles friends as "Murph the Surf" after the infamous jewel thief, remembered Gram taking a stand in favor of President Johnson's Great Society. "It wasn't that he got huffy or anything. He'd just say 'you guys got this all wrong,'" Murphy said. "He was more enlightened than the rest of us."

But Gram still got into more than his share of mischief.

On weekends, buses ran from campus to downtown Jacksonville, where students could scatter and do whatever they wanted. A couple of guys bought a 1953 Ford and kept it at a girl's house alongside the St. Johns River. During free time they reclaimed the wreck, drove it to the package store, and hoped they could convince a wino to buy them booze. "Then we'd go to the Mayflower Hotel and party," remembered Williams. Gram was in on plenty of those sessions, bringing a guitar along and jamming all weekend.

When his accident-prone, science-geek friend Murph the Surf had to spend some time in the hospital, Gram hatched a plan to cheer him up. Seeing Gram arrive with his guitar in one hand and the guitar case in the other, Murphy knew something was up. Gram and two buddies had loaded the case full of beer. Two older patients in the semiprivate room joined in the party, as did some of the staff. "We had a real hootenanny right there in the hospital," Murphy laughed. "Nurses were coming around and hanging at the door listening to Gram singing and playing. We were all drinking beer and having a great time until the doctors came in."

Gram shared the good news of his Greenwich Village trip in a letter to Marilyn Garrett. "As you, no doubt, already know the boys and I had a fairly successful summer," said Gram, trying his best to feign modesty. "I am back at Bolles doing post-grad work for some extra credits and will probably attend either Harvard or Columbia next year." Gram was still an undergrad and perhaps used the "post-grad" line as a cover for the fact that he had had to complete a second junior year of high school and was only now a senior.

In light of the enthusiastic response from New York audiences, he thought the Shilos were on their way. "All future plans may be postponed," Gram wrote, "should success become a reality." He recounted how the Greenwich Village crowds reacted warmly to the song he sang for her, "The Hand within the Glove": "That was a big favorite with some of the Village folk this summer." Gram added a variation to a line he used on many girls in whom he was romantically interested. "You inspired that, you know. Even before I met you."

*   *   *

The biggest musical event to hit Jacksonville in the fall of 1964 came by way of Liverpool, England; fans were thrilled to learn the Beatles were booked to play Jacksonville's Gator Bowl. Earlier in the year, the Fab Four were the first to occupy all five top spots in the Billboard charts. In recent memory, only Elvis had caused a sensation big enough to be booked into the city's football stadium.

On September tenth, Hurricane Dora roared ashore between Jacksonville and St. Augustine. Twenty beachside houses were washed out to sea, and forty-three others inland destroyed. Flooding and damage were everywhere. To Beatles' fans all over the southeast, the storm threatened an even bigger calamity: there was talk of canceling the concert.

Thanks to the resolve of the Brennan brothers, who owned WAPE-AM, alternately known as "the Mighty 690" and "the Big Ape," the show went on as scheduled. Because of the storm, the Beatles' flight had to be diverted to Key West. They arrived in Jacksonville only to learn they had no rooms at the Hotel George Washington. During a press conference in the lobby, they endured silly questions from a reporter who henpecked John about being away from his wife so much.

The Beatles finally took the stage Friday evening, September 11, 1964. Damaged roads and bridges left thousands of out-of-town fans, who had paid five dollars per ticket, unable to get to the stadium. While the Beatles did their best to play on in the whipping wind, President Johnson was in town assessing storm damage. It was one hell of a day in Jacksonville, Florida.

Normally, Gram would want to be front and center such a musical event, especially if it involved thousands of screaming girls. At this stage, though, he was still very much dedicated to making a career out of folk music. Like Dylan, he had not yet plugged in. "I don't know how he felt about the Beatles," Paul Surratt observed. "He loved them later, but I don't know about then."

Frank David Murphy said it was likely Gram was not able to attend the show even if he wanted to: "September of '64 there's a good chance he was confined to campus." Gram and four of his close friends were so often before the disciplinary committee that year they became known as the "DC Five." Murphy recalled: "They got in so much trouble they came as close to getting dc'ed as anybody ever did without actually getting thrown out." They were practically in a constant state of lockdown. Then came the stunt that nearly pushed Gram out of Bolles for a second time.

In December, the "DC Five" checked into a motel near campus under fake names. The party came to an abrupt halt when a teacher busted them. School administrators ordered the parents to come back after Christmas break and explain why their sons should not be expelled. That didn't faze Gram; he had big plans waiting for him back home in Winter Haven.

Like Gram's flunking junior year at Winter Haven High, this issue didn't register as the crisis one might expect; it was just another PR problem Bob Parsons was good at smoothing over. Still enthralled with his experiences in Greenwich Village, Gram convinced his parents to buy him a place to perform in Winter Haven. The Parsons were preparing to welcome Gram and the Shilos for a series of holiday engagements once the new place was finished and staff hired. Bob Parsons was about to become proprietor of the town's newest teen club.

Parsons found a midsized warehouse on Fifth Street next door to the Gilmore Pontiac dealership. Gram came up with the name "Derry Down" after Greenwich Village clubs like the Bitter End. They set about renovating the place in an Old English theme, though Gram soon realized that sort of thing might go over people's heads. "We were really going to go Old English," Gram told a reporter for the *Tampa Tribune*, "but the trouble is nobody here understands it."

Undaunted, the Parsons's came up with a menu of Derryburgers, Downdogs, and nonalcoholic drinks like a Wales Sunset or Midsummer Night's Dream. They set up a small stage near the back. A bearded disc jockey, Jacquee Phillips, spun records. A grand opening was set for December 20, 1964. Big Avis set about drawing up an invitation list for the country-club set. Bob Parsons paid Jim Carlton ten dollars to record albums for use as background music. Family members were enthused to have such a grand distraction from their problems, especially Gram, who took refuge in his hopes for a career with the band.

Early that afternoon, a local radio station, WINT, signed on to cover the festivities surrounding the club's opening. The Shilos caught a train in from South Carolina. With all four boys back for their first string of gigs since the Village trip, they played live on the radio to promote the grand opening later that night. Gram used the opportunity to get a few digs at his bandmates: "Hi, my name's Gram Parsons, and to my left is George Wrigley. George is what we call the genius of the group. He writes his own songs and steals everyone else's. The man on the bass about seven feet tall, we call him Little Joe. . . . Paul on the banjo, he's a good guy to travel with. . . . we have Paul here to remind us that mental illness strikes one out of every four people."

The Shilos shined with the first song of their live set, a traditional number, "Oh Didn't They Crucify My Lord." The next tune paid homage to their mentor Dick Weissman. Gram tells the radio audience that Dick's group, the Journeymen, showed a great deal of promise but ended up "a great big flop." In an attempt to revive their music, the Shilos played Weissman's "I May Be Right." As much as Gram comes off as a good-natured smart-ass, the group's tight musicianship and excellent harmonies in this radio recording reflect why they drew such strong interest from Albert Grossman.

Jim Carlton sat at the side of the stage recording the Shilos' performance "just for the hell of it." He recalled, "The Shilos were very, very good, just kids with a considerable amount of talent and a front man who was exceptional." As the band played on, more and more kids showed up.

That night, the Derry Down's opening became the big social event Bob and Avis anticipated. Jim Carlton's mother showed up wearing a fur stole. Like a trendy Greenwich Village musician, Gram wore black. "It was pretty austere," Gram's old girlfriend Donna Class said of the Derry Down. "Just the stage and tables and that was about it." The warehouse came alive with acoustic guitar, banjo, standup bass, and harmonies that could raise the rafters. Gram Parsons brought a bit of the Village scene to Polk County. "It was a big success," Jim Carlton said of opening night. "The Shilos did very well."

During the rest of the Shilos' stay in Winter Haven, the band was feted at the Snively mansion, which Joe Kelly described as "high cotton." Bob Parsons arranged for the band to have publicity pictures taken in the home on Piedmont Drive. Kelly remembered Bob as "very appreciative" and encouraged the band, allowing them to rehearse in the family room. The series of color photos from that session can only be described as joyful.

Surratt said the photos are indicative of the band's chemistry: "There's a certain strength to the group . . . a camaraderie that's wonderful." Big Avis showed her softer side when Surratt suddenly came down with a serious case of tonsillitis: "Avis was wonderful to me, she nursed me back."

Bob Parsons's first order of business in the New Year was to travel to Bolles and convince the hierarchy not to boot his stepson out of school. Ever the charmer, Parsons pulled it off. But the net result for Gram and his friends was confinement to campus. In early January, a surprise letter from Marilyn Garrett lifted his spirits. Gram wrote back to Garrett telling her he was glad she'd parted ways with her boyfriend: "I'm glad you are rid of Keith. He was rather a pain in the ass."

In that same letter, Gram showed his sharp sense of humor in addressing Paul Surratt's zeal for music: "Honestly, some day I'm going to lose control and violently murder that child. The only problem is I like him too much, and I'm afraid I'm going to be responsible for him till the day I die. The Chinese have an old crusty proverb about that. Something about if you save a man's life you're responsible for it. Nice." He ended his correspondence to Garrett with this quote: "'Till my eyes again meet yours I remain a ghost within a ghost.' Sound as ever, Gram."

During his senior year, Gram brought his Miami buddy Paul Broder for a weekend in Winter Haven—a sadly memorable one. Like so many of Gram's friends over the years, Broder found Avis's behavior disturbing. "She was eating ice cubes and trying not to drink," Broder recalled. He was there the night Bob Parsons, dressed like a bourgeois dandy, escorted his girlfriend Bonnie to the dinner table.

"You could tell Avis had a serious problem," Broder recalled, "She was dropping nouns like crazy and not making a lot of sense. She was very sentimental and crying at the drop of a hat." Avis was suffering from withdrawal and watching her husband move on with his life. Gram appeared tired of seeing Big Avis embarrass herself and him in front of his friends. "Gram was not very kind to his mother," Broder said. Parsons was barely eighteen and fed up with the years of his mother's alcoholic behavior. "What seventeen- or eighteen-year-old understands that kind of angst anyway?"

In one of her diaries, Little Avis recalled Bob Parsons holding her severely inebriated mother by the hair. To her reflection in the mirror Bob roared, "Could you love this?" While Gram was away at school, Little Avis witnessed her parents' marriage falling apart. "They were cruel, ugly fights from which there was no escape," Little Avis remembered. "I remember locking myself in the bathroom for protection and crying and crying."

"The saddest part, and perhaps the hardest confession I'll ever make," Little Avis confided, "Is that Gram and I totally sided with Bob. If he had taken a lover it was only because mother had become so disgusting." Big Avis's health was deteriorating, and all her loved ones could do was watch and recoil.

\*   \*   \*

In early 1965, the Shilos came up with the idea of making a demo recording. They found a studio back in Greenville, at a radio station located on the campus of ultraconservative Bob Jones University. On March 20, Paul Surratt's father put up $33.70 for the group's session. Without state-of-the-art facilities or overdubbing, the boys took turns stepping up to a single, omnidirectional microphone. Their months of playing produced a sound of which the surviving band members are still proud. Said Joe Kelly: "I can still go back and listen to that tape that was on the first record and go 'That was pretty damn good harmony.'"

Encompassing the full range of folk influences and his own writing to that point, the recordings are a testament to Gram's youthful confidence. His tenor is strong and dramatically different from the frayed, fragile, and substance-scarred delivery on his later solo records with Emmylou Harris. Gram's vocals on "Big Country" reflect far more maturity than the acetate recorded at Ernie Garrison's home studio two years previous. In a 1979 album produced by Paul Surratt, he notes the band arranged their version of Pete Seeger's "Bells of Rhymney" in Ponte Vedra. Commenting that the band could not practice in motel rooms, Surratt wrote, "Luckily, no one minded in the laundromat." Parsons included his own composition, "Zah's Blues," written for the singer he'd met the previous summer.

In hindsight, Surratt regrets not having had the time to perform more songs during what turned out to be the band's final recording session together: "If I had any idea, I would have begged my father to pay for two or three hours."

Surratt considered Gram a far more experienced and worldly big brother. It didn't matter that Gram once slept with a girl Surratt had been seeing: "She wasn't good enough for you," was Gram's flimsy excuse.

What remains with Surratt are the nights of intense conversation with Parsons about their love of music. "I'd give a thousand dollars to hear Gram perform those songs again," he said.

The Bob Jones recording session produced a "demo" the boys could send to record companies. Surratt, Wrigley, and Parsons composed an accompanying letter: "We would greatly appreciate your giving the enclosed tapes your most careful consideration. We believe we have the newest and freshest style to come along in the folk field for many years. . . . We feel that we could be of significant value to your company." Unfortunately for the naive southern boys, at the same time they were shopping their folk songs, a fresh new wave in folk was hitting Southern California.

On April 12, 1965, the Byrds topped the Billboard charts with their electrified version of Bob Dylan's "Mister Tambourine Man." Jim (later Roger) McGuinn's distinctive twelve-string electric guitar and lead vocals, coupled with the harmonies of Gene Clark and David Crosby, ushered in a new genre known as folk rock. All were former folkies: the Byrds' blend of Dylan's lyrical sensibilities and the Beatles' electric guitar hooks became their formula for commercial success. Couple the music with the Byrds' pre-hippy fashion style, and a new era in rock quickly started to evolve.

Back at the Bolles School, Gram was enamored. "He submitted 'Mr. Tambourine Man' as one of his own poems," Paul Broder chuckled. "Bob Hubbard busted him on it." In Gram Parsons, Hubbard had a willing young protégé, which would explain why Gram would never get into a lot of trouble for trying to plagiarize the Byrds or Lawrence Ferlinghetti. "I think Bob Hubbard really turned him around in terms of appreciating literature and music," said Broder. "Hubbard, I think, really gave him hope."

Gram's thoughts were turning toward what to do after graduation. He intended to go to college but only as a means to further his artistic pursuits and get out of Florida. He sat down for a long talk with his academic dean, Rufus McClure.

"Do you think Harvard is a place for me?" Gram asked.

"It could be if you are really committed," McClure cautioned.

Gram assured his advisor of his commitment to pursuing an Ivy League education. In those days, Harvard had a kind of mystique for Bolles students and their parents. The Bolles School made a tradition of taking out an ad in the Jacksonville paper trumpeting all the prestigious institutions to which their graduates were headed.

"If you give me your commitment you'll try your best, I'll write a letter of recommendation on your behalf," McClure offered.

In retrospect, McClure thinks he did not read Gram correctly. With the benefit of decades of hindsight, he concluded Gram wanted to get into Harvard simply to prove to his parents and himself he could. "Gram is a capable student," McClure wrote in his letter. "Capable of doing the work . . . but there is some likelihood he will not because he is so engrossed in his music." He concluded in his letter that Harvard should consider Gram Parsons a "calculated risk."

While he waited for a decision on his Harvard application, Gram pondered the Shilos' future. On May 27, 1965, he typed a letter to Paul Surratt. "We're going to have to do some serious rearranging," Gram explained. "The people want a different sound, and ours isn't different enough yet." Gram wanted the band to start doing serious rehearsals, performing all new music and working on his material. "I know it will sell," Gram assured. "I know my music's going to be as big as Dylan's."

He told Surratt the Shilos needed to "cash in on this thing Dylan's started, and like it or not we'll be associated with him." Gram assured Surratt he still wanted "very much to make it with the Shilos, I always have."

In March of 1965, with the release of "Highway 61 Revisited," Dylan was including electric instruments. His monster hit that summer was a six-minute masterpiece, "Like a Rolling Stone." Dylan drove a stake through the heart of folk as most knew it by playing electric at the old-school Newport Folk Festival. "Gram was really blown away by Dylan and played his songs," Paul Broder said. At this prolific point in his career, Bob Dylan was America's most influential artist.

Thanks to McClure's letter of recommendation and no small amount of string-pulling from Bob Parsons, Gram was accepted to Harvard. "He got a letter asking if he wanted white, pinstripe, or Harvard crimson sheets," Jim Carlton remembered. As his graduation gift, Gram received an Austin Healey 3000 from his parents. Back in Winter Haven, Gram was happy to lend Carlton the car. "I want you to play around with the electronic overdrive," he said. In return, Gram and his date had Carlton's house to themselves.

Below Gram's senior picture in the Bolles School yearbook was this caption: "Bolles noted singer/songwriter plans to go to Harvard and study psychology. Noted for his prolonged stays at Bolles over the week-end. Best course at Bolles was Advanced Composition. One of his hobbies was arranging 'social functions.'"

Paul Broder was accepted to Boston College. In his yearbook, Gram wrote this inscription: "I suppose looking in to the future we'll both do a lot of changing. I just hope we don't have a lot of influence on each other. But I'm glad we'll have the chance anyway. See you in Boston."

One of Gram's final performances as a Bolles student was the Spring Jubilee choral concert at Bartram, the nearby boarding school for girls. Backstage, fifteen-year-old student Karen Johann realized she was "being observed quite attentively" by Gram. "I quite properly was quietly coy," Johann said. "Because Margaret Fisher had been telling everyone how gorgeous he was and how everyone would be falling in love with him."

During Gram's solo performance, Johann and the other girls starting drifting from the third row to the front. "He really seemed to be singing to me," Johann recalled. "Right then and there he was the very first love of my life."

After another Bartram concert a few weeks later, Gram struck up a conversation with Johann, and she learned they had both grown up in wealthy families just one hundred miles apart. "His father also married the boss's daughter, as did mine," she wrote. The two voiced a shared sense of not belonging in the "oppressive boredom" of the small towns where they grew up. Johann was one of the few peers in whom Gram confided the sadness in his life.

"I thought it was the most tragic thing in the world for his father to have died when he was so young, and he told me that his mother was quite sick too." When Gram wondered if it might be a good thing to invite Coon Dog's parents to his upcoming graduation, Johann told him, "Of course your grandparents should be there."

Gram showed her a few chords and his Gibson guitar and told Johann she could keep it for a while to practice. "So I did," she recalled. "And you can be sure I did sleep with that guitar. I was afraid one of the other girls would take it!" That's how she came to be known as the girl who slept with Gram Parsons's guitar. But more than that, Parsons "made a positive influence on me with regard to my total outlook toward my own future. I had finally found a true, kindred spirit."

*    *    *

Back in Winter Haven, Big Avis experienced a serious health crisis. One morning, she woke up with no ability to move and no control of her bodily functions. Bob Parsons rushed home from a business trip and immediately had her hospitalized. For a time, her health improved. "We talked woman to woman for the first time," Little Avis wrote. "She would divorce Bob as soon as she got well. In her eyes I could see an eagerness for life that had not been there before."

But there was no way around the hard reality that Big Avis's liver was failing and there was nothing the Snively family's connections and wealth could do to stop it. Despite her death sentence, just as a smoker suffering from emphysema will die for one last cigarette, Avis asked Bob to bring her some booze.

In a move that would forever rain controversy upon him, Bob Parsons obliged. To the Snively clan this was nothing short of a man's homicidal intentions. To those sympathetic to Bob, Avis was holding a gun to her own head—Bob Parsons just supplied the bullets.

*  *  *

Back at Bolles, Gram had helped organize entertainment for graduation festivities. According to Paul Broder, Gram hired the Dillards to play at the senior breakfast. Lead by Doug Dillard on banjo and Rodney Dillard on acoustic guitar, the legendary bluegrass group from the Missouri Ozarks already had a pair of albums under their belt on Elektra Records. But everyone knew them better as the fictional Darlin' boys from the *Andy Griffith Show*.

Graduation day was a typical hot and steamy affair. Little Avis traveled to Jacksonville with their beloved maternal grandmother, Nancy "Hainie" Snively. Their paternal grandfather, Ingram Connor, accepted Gram's invitation and came in from Tennessee. Gram's classmate Murph the Surf noticed Gram appeared to be going through the motions, disconnected. "I turned to somebody and asked 'Hey why is Gram acting so weird?' And they told me his mother had died."

Earlier that day the phone call had come in from Winter Haven. His dorm supervisor and close friend Joe Dyess broke the news to Gram: Big Avis had died. In an emblematic family photo taken that day at Gram's graduation, the grandparents are somber. Gram looks bewildered; only Little Avis appears to be oblivious to the dark cloud hanging over Gram's special day.

Earlier in the year, Gram had published a poem called "Prereminiscence" in the Bolles School's literary magazine. The words mirrored a song Gram wrote later about losing his mother, "Brass Buttons." Now Gram was on the precipice of seismic change. The summer of 1965 would be a decisive turning point.

# ❧ **14** ❧

## "A Country Beatle"

Some images and memories seem to come sprinkled with stardust, as if they'd been waiting years for just the right moment to reveal themselves. That's the only way to describe the photo Jim Stafford had loaded onto a laptop. Standing in the middle of his parents' old living room, he pulled up and enlarged the image of four boys—bandmates. Stafford pivoted and turned the computer toward the very spot the picture had been taken two generations before, likely 1961.

From left to right, Stafford, Gram Parsons, Lamar Braxton, and Bill Waldrup, one of the earliest incarnations of their garage band, the Legends, are immortalized in black and white. Unlike so many other pictures from his teen years where Gram is somber or trying to look cool, his smile here is unabashed and bright. He had joined a fraternity of young teens who loved their guitars, and with each chord, each hour of practice, the guitar was loving them back. It's a quintessential photo of Florida's garage-band days, and to see it for the first time with Stafford in his old living room, in the very spot it was taken, made the experience far more moving.

"Now here I am flipping the bird," said Stafford, pointing to himself in the photo playing guitar with his middle finger extended on the neck. "That was always my little way of saying 'howdy.'" Maybe that explains why all the boys in the picture are laughing.

Off Snively Avenue on Fifth Street in a working-class enclave called Eloise, due south of Winter Haven, Jim Stafford stopped in front of that tiny shotgun home where his earliest memories revolve around his father Woody playing guitar on the front porch to gain the attention of passersby. In this uncommonly musical corner of Florida, Stafford remembered the neighbor who wrote a song recorded by Chet Atkins. Even when he became a recording star himself, Stafford said, "I kept running into people who were from here."

We pulled up to the old building that had housed the family business, Quality Cleaners. Now rows and rows of mattresses were being sold there, only no one seemed to be minding the store. "The layout is still the same," said Stafford, walking toward the back. In an alcove, Stafford pointed out an area that used to be the front counter: "I remember playing the guitar right here with the clothes right back here." He pointed out the lobby space where the Legends once rehearsed.

Just a block behind the old dry cleaning store, Stafford directed us to the middle-class ranch home where his older sister still lives.

Stafford sat on the bed in what appeared to be a guest room. "I spent three months sitting on the edge of that bed working on 'Spiders and Snakes,'" Stafford said of his 1974 top-five hit record co-written with David Bellamy. "So many of us who grew up playing guitar spent a lot of time like this, sitting on the edge of their beds working on stuff." On a wall in the dining room is Stafford's gold record indicating sales of 500,000 copies of the single.

The youthful partnership between trust-fund teen Gram Parsons and working-class kid Jim Stafford was an early manifestation of Parsons's idea of Cosmic American Music. Their mutual love of the guitar spanned what were clearly defined socioeconomic classes in Winter Haven. Talent was Jim Stafford's equalizer.

Stafford pointed to a spot in the living room where he "made a little history" through nothing more than a conversation with Gram Parsons. It was Parsons himself who told friends this was a turning point in his career path, during his 1965 summer of change.

For Big Avis's funeral, childhood buddies Henry Clarke and Dickey Smith made the trip from Waycross. They found Gram lounging on his bed in the Piedmont Drive home. He greeted them with a smile, shook their hands, then lay back down on the bed cross-legged, "drinking Jack Black straight." Jim Carlton said the best thing he could do was offer to get Gram out of there. Jim dropped Gram at Donna Class's house.

Little Avis was fourteen when her mother died. "Why should I cry?" she wrote. "Mother would be much happier in heaven." Diane and Little Avis soon came under the care of their great aunt's maid, Erka Lee Lewis. Hers is another example of the sacrifices domestics were expected to make for their moneyed employers: "She had left twelve children home with her husband," Little Avis marveled. "She was the first strong woman I had ever known."

Gram's ultimate escape was, as always, the music. After all the mourning, he hit the road for his creative center: New York City. On the way, he stopped in Myrtle Beach for some postgraduation, much-needed good times with the Shilos. "We went down and played at a place with a bunch of girls," Joe Kelly remembered. "We had thirty people in this beach house and put on a show for our friends that night." It was the last time Gram and the boys from South Carolina were together as the Shilos.

"I'm headed north and I'm never comin' back south again," Gram said, shaking their hands. "Good luck to all the rest of you." As expected, Joe Kelly and George Wrigley ended up going off to college. For Paul Surratt, Gram's departure meant the loss of a friend and all the ambitions they shared. "That's the first time I'd ever been really depressed and stayed like that for days," Surratt remembered. Shattered at the prospect of not achieving musical success alongside Gram, Surratt joined the Navy. The Bob Jones University recordings remain a legacy to the band's talent and potential had the boys been older and their timing a little better. The summer of 1965 was a natural time for all of them to move on.

Gram was on his way to the Village and a studio apartment just off Bleecker Street. Dreading the prospect of summer in Miami, Paul Broder told his parents he needed to take a college Spanish class and instead hooked up with Gram in New York. "It was a really enlightening experience," Broder recalled. "One day we went to a bunch of folk clubs, where he was sitting in with different people." The next day they went to a Dodgers-Yankees old-timers game with Fred Neil and Dave Van Ronk. Sitting in the stands, the group swilled beer and smoked joints.

Raised in St. Petersburg, Neil started out writing songs for the likes of Buddy Holly and Roy Orbison before becoming a revered member of the Greenwich Village folk scene. In the liner notes to Neil and Vince Martin's 1964 folk album, *Tear Down the Walls*, John Sebastian said of Fred Neil: "Fred was a natural linkup of various musical styles. The thing that was so different about Fred was that he had not only a southern background, but was one of the first guys that was crossing racial boundaries in his style in a sense."

Through Fred Neil's records, Gram could also put a voice to the pain in his life. Neil's song "A Little Bit of Rain" is considered a folk and blues classic. With its soul-stirring richness and depth, Neil's voice has been described as a "healing instrument." Neil achieved fame as the man who wrote "Everybody's Talkin'" from the film *Midnight Cowboy*.

In the Village, Gram was impressed by Native American singer-songwriter, Buffy Sainte-Marie, one of the first artists to write a protest song about Vietnam. After a throat infection, Sainte-Marie became addicted to painkillers. Gram later did his own "cover" version of her stark, autobiographical song about the odyssey, called "Codeine." In New York, the drug culture was coming on and Parsons was now at the forefront.

"Did you like that pot we smoked last night?" Gram asked Paul Broder, "Because I've got this stuff called Owsley."

"I had never even heard of LSD at that time," Broder recalled. "We dropped some acid and he invited some girlfriends over. We had this great party and I was tripping for days. Every time I would take a shower and move my hand, there would be trails . . . it had to be a massive dose."

Gram played for Broder the poem he turned into a musical homage to his mother, "Brass Buttons":

Her words still dance inside my head
Her comb still lies beside my bed
And the sun comes up without her, it just doesn't know she's gone
Oh, but I remember everything she said

One of Gram's neighbors that summer was another guitarist from the Florida youth center days, Stephen Stills, and his future Buffalo Springfield bandmate Richie Furay. The trio jammed and talked about the possibility of forming a folk rock band. Gram also met up in the Village with former child star and budding musician Brandon De Wilde. At the time De Wilde made a name for himself playing Joey Starrett in the 1953 western, *Shane*. And it was De Wilde who uttered those unforgettable words at the film's end: "Come back, Shane!" De Wilde would later prove instrumental in convincing Gram to move to California.

On August 23, 1965, as reported by biographer David Meyer, Parsons and De Wilde saw the Beatles at Shea Stadium. Surely the sound of 50,000 screaming girls had to evoke—if not eclipse—the experience of seeing Elvis in 1956.

That summer, his adventures into drug use cost Parsons an important career contact: would-be music producer Dick Weissman, who had already recorded two sessions with him. While Parsons was in New York, for a short time he shared an apartment with Weissman's brother-in-law. The scene Weissman walked in on one day left a lasting and unsavory impression:

"It appeared to me that Gram was cooking up heroin," Weissman remembered. "This was a shock to me. The smell almost made me sick, and left me with no desire to have anything to do with Gram again, I didn't."

The Village scene as Parsons had known it the past two summers was changing. Fred Neil headed to Coconut Grove, Florida, for refuge from his own struggles with hard drugs. Stephen Stills went off to Southern California to join the likes of David Crosby and John Phillips. In June 1965 the Byrds hit number-one with "Mr. Tambourine Man." And there was Gram—the urban folkie, the schoolboy still looking for a direction. He would find it in a fateful conversation with an old friend back home in Florida.

"He was a little disenchanted. He was in a turning point clearly," recalled Gram's big-brother figure Jim Stafford. "He was seeing that the folk thing wasn't gonna happen." A year after leaving for Nashville, Stafford was back home. Gram was back from the Village preparing for his move to Harvard. It was summer of 1965 and the two were sitting in Stafford's house in Winter Haven. Stafford recalled what he told Parsons:

"I just blurted it out without thinking about it at all. I just said 'Why don't you just let your hair grow long and do country music? And you could be'—I remember saying the words—'a country Beatle. You could be a country Beatle.' I think I was thinking more of a gimmick for him. It never occurred to me that you could change music. You could do rock plus country. There wasn't an ounce of that. There wasn't anything about what he ended up accomplishing. But I did say let your hair grow and you'd be the first long-haired country guy."

Gram did not react as if this were some revelation. But, "he kind of perked up. I think he liked it," Stafford said. He never wanted it to appear he was trying to claim credit, because his idea at the time was not in the same context as Gram's eventual move to so-called Cosmic American Music. "He may have had a little more vision at the moment than I did," Stafford said with a laugh. Stafford was simply trying to think of a gimmick for Gram to sell records

Gram later told Jim Carlton that his move to country started with that advice from Jim Stafford.

The Beatles had dabbled in a little country music that year. Included as the B-side for their hit "Yesterday" was a toe-tapping cover of Buck Owens's 1963 hit "Act Naturally," featuring Ringo on lead vocals. After seeing the spectacle at Shea, the words "country Beatle" had to take on a special resonance. Gram took Stafford's advice and ran with it. Within a span of less than three years, Gram and his country vision would join forces with the most important and influential American band of the 1960s: the Byrds.

But first, Gram had to follow through on the promise he'd made to Rufus McClure and his commitment to pursue an Ivy League education.

# ❧ 15 ❧

## The Polumbaum Photos

It was one of those rare moments that makes the heart of a writer and researcher race: a cache of rare images of Gram Parsons was on the way, and what arrived did not disappoint. The twenty-seven contact sheet pages and roughly five hundred images are without doubt the most complete photo essay on Gram Parsons. Of an artist, by an artist, the photos document the life of an emerging musician, half boy and half man.

What makes the photos even more important and intriguing is the man who took them: a courageous and accomplished photojournalist named Ted Polumbaum. In 1964, the year before taking these pictures of Gram Parsons at Harvard, Polumbaum risked his life to document the so-called Freedom Summer in Mississippi for *Time*.

Before Polumbaum came into his life, Gram Parsons's experiences with racial inequality were rather benign. He grew up with black housekeepers and their families and considered them close friends. At the Bolles School, Gram tried to enlighten classmates based on what he'd learned in Greenwich Village. However, Parsons and the Shilos never picked up on the political aspects of folk music or endured the kind of hostility encountered by their mentors the Journeymen, who toured the South with black musicians.

Polumbaum suffered his own social injustice. Fresh out of Yale University and working as a television news writer in the 1950s, he was forced to defend his collegiate associations before the House Un-American Activities Committee. Polumbaum's refusal to name names left him blacklisted. He was fired from his job as a news writer for United Press International. At the height of its golden age, Polumbaum turned to photojournalism.

"Stringing for *Life* occupied most of my Dad's working hours," said his daughter Judy. "And he was on call for the entire *Time-Life* stable, including *Time*, *Fortune*, *Sports Illustrated* and *People*."

Volunteering to shoot the Freedom Summer in Mississippi was the kind of venture that easily could have gotten Polumbaum a bullet in the head. He once said: "I'd never been so scared and sometimes wondered why I volunteered for the assignment. That's why I was so interested in why these young people had come."

Polumbaum's widow did not recall her husband mentioning why he chose to photograph Parsons and his new band. Polumbaum was living and working in Boston at the same time Parsons and his bandmates were generating local newspaper coverage in and around Cambridge.

Parsons's former roommate Larry Piro remembered: "There was all this talk that a photographer from *Life* magazine was coming. Gram was whisked away and photographed all over campus. It was a big deal."

The result was a remarkable collection of images taken around the time Parsons turned nineteen. It took almost half a century for them to see the light of day.

In early September 1965, Gram Parsons left Florida for Harvard. He would make plenty more historic stops in the South, including getting married, performing pivotal concerts, and making important recordings with the Byrds. Arguably, it took leaving the South for Parsons to fully embrace his country roots and music.

For the next year he would split time among Cambridge, New York City, and his stepfather's new home in the Orlando suburb, Winter Park. He also made a series of recordings in central Florida that document the end of his brief urban-folkie period.

Larry Piro arrived at Harvard's Pennypacker Hall two days before his roommate. He staked out room 22 and wondered when this guy from the South would arrive. He cracked open the freshman guide to see the person with whom he'd be living for the upcoming year. "He looked like a normal high school kid, anybody I might have known from a little prep school." Piro recalled, "Nobody arrived. I registered with everyone else at Memorial Hall."

With barely fifteen or twenty minutes to spare before registration was over, Parsons arrived. Or perhaps it's more apt to say he made his entrance. "All of a sudden, he appeared, top-down in this green sports car, looking at least five years older than his picture . . . zipping up in the Austin Healey 3000, tearing off to Memorial Hall to see if he can register, just getting in under the wire," said Piro. "That turned out to be typical Gram Parsons. He was like that: a lot of flourish, a lot of unusual."

"Gram immediately wanted to find other musicians here. He wanted to play. He wanted to write songs in the wee hours of the morning," Piro recalled. In their minimally furnished dorm room, he watched Parsons's method of songwriting: "What he would do was write words first sitting cross-legged. He would write a verse, then just strum through the keys and chord changes and get something to meld into something with which he was comfortable. This was the basic process he would use." Piro kept some of the notebook pages on which Gram wrote lyrics.

Parsons also began to surround himself right away with new musician friends, including Ian Dunlop, a young British ex-patriot bass and sax player. Dunlop wore his hair in a pageboy like Rolling Stones' scenester Brian Jones, cutting a swashbuckling image, sometimes even wearing a cape. "We got together because Gram wanted to do demos of his own songs," Dunlop recalled. "So he was trying to work out an arrangement." The two became fast friends playing folk-influenced songs inspired by Gram and his romanticism. In their down time, they listened to albums like the Beatles' *Rubber Soul* and *Ray Charles Live*.

Dunlop recalled Parsons still working on an early version of "Brass Buttons," an up-tempo tune called "I Just Can't Take It Any More," and songs like "Wheel of Fortune" and "November Night." Gram was still looking for some style to embrace and make his own.

His old girlfriend Donna Class was "so surprised" when Gram made it into Harvard. Up for a weekend visit at nearby Wellesley, Class hung out with Gram and zoomed through town in Gram's sports car just as in the old days before he flunked out of Winter Haven High. What a difference two years had made. "I was riding around in the back of the convertible with him," Class said, "in the freezing cold, top down." Class wondered whether Gram would embrace the intellectual challenge Harvard presented.

Around that time, Gram stopped in a Cambridge antique shop and told the woman working there about his musical ambitions. She invited Gram over to meet her sister and the musician with whom she was staying. "He had an acoustic guitar there. He whipped it out and played a tune or two," said guitarist John Nuese. "I had a very good musical rapport with him from the very outset, and bang!"

Parsons, Nuese, and Dunlop recruited a talented drummer named Mickey Gauvin from Boston's rough-and-tumble downtown bar scene. At the outset, the group was known as "Gram Parsons and the Like." Gram had a new and exciting creative outlet to go with his challenging new academic environs.

"I am now officially a Harvard freshman," Gram wrote proudly in a September 26 letter to his sister Avis. "This school is really fantastic. I never dreamed that college could be so interesting. All of the advisors and profs are brilliant." Gram told his sister about his twenty-seven-year-old advisor, a Baptist minister, who lived next door.

This advisor, the Reverend James Ellison Thomas—or Jet, as he has come to be known—was one of the most important friends Parsons made at Harvard. Jet became a mentor and older-brother figure in Parsons's life. The two spent hours in Thomas's apartment in deep discussions about songwriting, religion, and the typical young-adult questions about life. It was clear to Thomas that Parsons was far more interested in playing music than in his studies.

"He easily could have done well at Harvard," Thomas surmised. "He was intellectually capable, but his real interest was his music." Jet was someone in whom Gram could confide his concerns about Avis;

she was living in a new home and new town without her mother or brother. To hear that Gram was having the time of his life without her had to make a tough situation for his litter sister more difficult.

Cambridge in the mid-1960s was a heady cultural change from sleepy, sun-drenched central Florida. Clearly Parsons was intent on drinking it all in, especially the music scene. Before long, he had a dozen songs of his own that he would sing and perform regularly. In October, Parsons brought his group publicity by making some outrageous claims in the school paper.

In an article entitled "Yardling to Rock, Signs RCA Contract," Parsons dusted off an old fish tale that he and his band, the Like, had just signed with RCA. But that wasn't enough: Parsons also claimed they were given "the second-highest promotional contract in RCA-Victor's history—exceeded only by Elvis Presley." The paper reported that a dozen other companies were vying to sign Parsons and the Like. According to the article, "thirty-six songs of Gram's have already been published."

The *Boston Globe* reporter William Fripp picked up on the story and allowed Gram to embellish further. In an article that was pure puffery, entitled "Will Harvard Spoil Gram Parsons?," Fripp reported that Ed Sullivan was calling Parsons's new manager, Marty Erlichman. Parsons said he'd spent time doing a dance called the Frug with the Beatles. That came about, he claimed, while making the New York scene with the Fab Four at the chic nightclub Arthur and at a party thrown by Broadway producer David Merrick.

In the article Parsons acknowledged that he was into Dylan, but with a caveat: "Bobby asks questions and hints at emotion. I want to answer some of the questions teen-agers ask about love, to describe the gamut of feelings and how to deal with them."

"It's not that Gram Parsons can't adjust to the freshman grind at Harvard," Fripp wrote. "It's all these other things. . . . They keep a boy busy, on edge." Parsons concluded, "If it gets too complicated I'll just have to get a leave of absence from the college."

The following week, the *Tampa Tribune* picked up the story and repeated much of Gram's propaganda in an article entitled "Havenite Brings Go-Go to Staid Harvard Yard."

During this period, Gram and his new band had been making side trips to New York City backing another aspiring musician, actor friend Brandon De Wilde. Parsons biographer Jason Walker reported the discovery of a lost RCA demo recording made in New York on October 28, 1965, by Gram Parsons and the Tinkers—a name the group used for the occasion. On the reel were early versions of "Just Can't Take It Anymore" and "November Night."

On November 10, Parsons appeared at a Students for a Democratic Society benefit at a local high school, singing mostly Dylan-type folk songs.

Thanks to his ability as an unabashed confabulator combined with frequent appearances in and around Cambridge, Parsons caught the eye of *Life* magazine and a Boston photographer who worked for the publication, Ted Polumbaum. A dedicated photojournalist, Polumbaum followed Parsons everywhere: on and off campus, the lunchroom, locker room, jam sessions, quiet times, late at night, early in the morning, sober, and otherwise.

From an especially intimate perspective, thanks to the Polumbaum photos we can see the young artist and visionary songwriter emerge before our eyes. The series marks a line in the sand where Gram Parsons gives up a southern boy's fantasy of becoming some Ivy League intellectual. That was just all for show anyway. It's obvious in these photos: music was Gram Parsons's essence.

Parsons's hair hangs low over his right eye, as if he'd just walked off the cover of the Beatles' *Rubber Soul* album or the Byrds' *Mr. Tambourine Man*. One lengthy part of the shoot shows Parsons in a room filled with bandmates; graffiti on the wall suggests they celebrated Gram's nineteenth birthday on November 5, 1965. Gram holds an acoustic guitar, singing and playing with abandon. John Nuese plays left-handed a Fender Stratocaster. Ian Dunlop and Mickey Gauvin appear to be following Gram's lead in a raucous jam session.

Seeing the photos for the first time decades later, Dunlop struggled for any recollection of being in them. "We barely look old enough to have a driver's license," he remarked. "Were we ever that young?"

Someone had drawn a large "19" on the wall. There are slogans: "Gram Parsons is outta sight, Be Hip, Ruth Loves Gram, I love Lu-Lu."

But the stirring thing about the photos is the dichotomy between Gram the slightly lost-looking student wandering around campus and Gram the self-assured artist and songwriter. In the months since his graduation from Bolles, his hair is longer and wilder. Something about the experience of living in the Village and moving to Cambridge changed him. He appears more mature and passionate; in these photos he's becoming Gram Parsons the free and unbridled artist.

Another series of photos shows Gram and the band at a late-night jam session in his room. They're passing around a jug of cheap wine. Then, when the bandmates have gone, Gram sits on the floor strumming by candlelight and jotting something in a notebook. Another image shows him bent over his desk writing, a stack of albums at his side. There's a lighthearted moment where he's sharing a laugh with Piro.

Each contact sheet is dated December 10, 1965. By that time, Parsons's flirtation with Harvard was over. His academic dean at Bolles had been right: the pull of the music and easy access to a bohemian lifestyle was too much to pass up. "Suddenly the world turned 180 degrees for him and college no longer meant anything," Rufus McClure said. Instead, Parsons dedicated himself to serious rehearsals, songwriting, and numerous gigs.

From Jacksonville to Greenville, Waycross to Winter Haven, with his wealth and talent, day in and day out Gram Parsons was used to being the center of attention. The self-possession and confidence he had at nineteen to be photographed by Polumbaum in nothing but a towel clowning around with his straitlaced ROTC roommate shows why Parsons later had enough moxie to front one of America's most influential bands on the most important stage in the South.

Up to that point Gram and the other band members had some peripheral knowledge of Buck Owens. Then along came Merle Haggard and George Jones. "When I turned them on to these singers, they all liked it very much and were caught up," Nuese said, "totally hooked on the music." Hardly the work of stereotypical hillbilly bumpkins, these songs about love lost and opportunity missed had the emotional depth Gram found in the music of Bob Dylan and Fred Neil.

Ian Dunlop explained that after his first meeting with Parsons, "it was probably four or five months later that we started singing country and listening to country music more." Parsons was in a position and place to act on Jim Stafford's "country Beatle" advice.

With no high school "lights-out" orders, no night watchman, no curfew, and no disciplinary committee, the jamming, partying, drinking, and smoking could go on and on. There was no way for Parsons to meet Harvard's considerable academic challenges by blowing off classes and trying to sway people with his endless supply of bullshit. The Harvard experience ended with a thud. After flunking or failing to complete his classes, Gram was asked not to return by administrators. The time, effort, and money spent by the likes of Bob Parsons and Rufus McClure lobbying to get Gram into Harvard could be chalked up to the notion that he'd always wanted to be an artist. Harvard was nothing more than the means to get him out of Florida; it required far more commitment and discipline than Gram was prepared to give. "Mainly I was turned off by the fact that I had to study all these things I didn't understand," he rationalized.

Just a few months after he said he was moving north for good, Gram headed back south—to Florida.

# ❧ 16 ❧

## Orlando, New York City

Down a tree-lined avenue of magnificent homes and ostentatious wealth, there's a driveway that appears to go nowhere. For the first time in decades, Bob Parsons's daughter, Gram's stepsister Becky was returning to see the suburban Orlando home she visited when she was thirteen. At the end of that long and winding driveway, you finally get to it: the place Bob Parsons rented after the death of his wife, Big Avis.

"This looks nothing like I remember it," Becky exclaimed.

Both the guest house where Gram used to stay and the home on Lake Maitland had undergone a massive renovation. The structures are more stately and impressive, but any of the Old South character is gone. The sleepy neighborhood of the 1960s is disappearing, giving way to McMansions and ever-creeping elegance.

Around back, down by the water, Becky finally started to get her bearings. The soaring cypress trees bathed in Spanish moss appeared to stand guard over a neighbor's aged boathouse. The slick and stumpy cypress knees threatened to send you tumbling.

It was on this expansive and glassy lake Becky remembered teaching Gram's bandmate Mickey Gauvin to water-ski. "Gram had just had his wisdom teeth pulled. His jaws were swollen and he could only bear the sunlight about twenty minutes at a time," she remembered. "Mickey was bored."

Becky is one of two children from Bob Parsons's first marriage. Once Bob remarried, Becky and her sister Jan took a backseat to Gram, Little Avis, and Diane. Though Becky acknowledges Bob Parsons's philandering and alcoholism, she remains steadfast in defending her late father.

"He was so proud of Gram and it didn't matter what he did," she recalled. "I think he married Avis because he loved her and they fell into a self-destructive, drinking lifestyle." Bob later told Becky that Avis was jealous of the fact that he had two children from a previous marriage: "People marry for the second time and they wish their spouse didn't have children to deal with."

In this home Bob Parsons was a new widower. Bonnie Muma took an apartment nearby. The home is just up U.S. Route 17/92 from the old Orlando Youth Center where the Legends and other youth-center circuit bands used to perform. The time Gram Parsons spent in Winter Park represents his final transition from student to urban-folkie to fulltime artist and musician.

Harvard had been a whirlwind of new friendships, bandmates, songwriting, and partying—with perhaps some study thrown in. Gram's adoptive father's new suburban Orlando home provided the perfect place to enjoy some lakeside tranquility, sunshine, and a chance to dry out. The guest house gave Gram room to be alone, write, and play. It also helped diffuse the tension in the home, as his personality was opposite from that of outgoing Bob Parsons.

The only child from Bob and Avis's marriage, Diane, was only four years old when her mother died. Little Avis absorbed a double hit: the loss of her mother and moving away from the familial and familiar in Winter Haven. The Snivelys believed Bob Parsons was trying to isolate Big Avis's children from them for financial reasons. Ever since Bob had helped Avis salvage money from the estate, the two sides had been at odds. The Snivelys blamed Bob for Avis's death, but truth be told, she came from a long line of hard drinkers. What happened in the hospital was the sad final act of someone who had been killing herself for years. It foreshadowed Bob's own death barely a decade later.

At Winter Park High, Little Avis gravitated toward a pair of outsiders: John Clark and Dan Jovi. The two best friends rode the biggest motorcycles of anyone at school and considered stupid all the preppy activities that occupied most young residents of this upscale Orlando suburb. Avis could escape all of the turmoil in her life on the back of John Clark's motorcycle or water-skiing on Lake Maitland.

"There was a deep well, a very deep well in her of unhappiness," Dan Jovi remembered. "I felt like if I ever said the wrong thing there would be hell to pay, so I always walked on eggshells around her." Avis was beginning to blossom into an attractive young woman. However, with all the changes in her life, there seemed to be very few good times: "I don't think I ever saw her laughing or smiling," said Jovi.

Bob Parsons reacted to Little Avis's unhappiness by abandoning whatever attempts he'd made previously at discipline. "Bob kind of released the reins on her," said her daughter Avis Johnson Bartkus. "He became more of a friend than a father."

"In this strange, amoral household, I was free to do as I pleased," said Little Avis. "I did so, with a vengeance. But I must say that all the while I did I was screaming inside." In high school, Little Avis excelled in journalism and liked to sing and play guitar herself.

Dan Jovi's buddy John Clark became Avis's boyfriend. She often had both boys over to her home to ski or hang out. "The first time we were in the house she introduced us to her brother," Jovi recalled. "I do remember him not making eye contact and not being engaged socially in any way whatsoever." Jovi remembered the "omnipresent" sound of Gram's guitar, which the trio could hear even when he was in other parts of the house. "I remember him being extremely unusual looking," Jovi chuckled. "His hair was bold at the time."

"The Beatles were a big deal," said Jovi of their impact on American style and customs. "People were still freaking out over that. For us to go to school with hair over our collar, you'd get sent home." Gram's style and reclusiveness sent a clear message that he was an artist. In the mid-1960s, that kind of nonconformity in the South was often greeted with open hostility.

Bob Parsons coped with the loss of his wife and resentment toward his children's family as he always did. "I never saw him without a drink in his hand, even if it was 9:30 in the morning," said Jovi. It's astonishing when you consider Parsons had just witnessed his wife die an agonizing drunkard's death. Jovi and his friend also picked up on the "bizarre" dynamic of Bob's much younger girlfriend, Bonnie. Gram started using sarcasm to describe his "parents."

After Big Avis's death, Bob waited until 1967 to marry Bonnie. According to Becky, Avis cut him out of her will. The notion that Bob Parsons planned to have some wealthy dream life after Avis was gone is untrue, Becky claims. Though Bob had helped Avis reclaim her inheritance, his exclusion from that money was her rebuke for his philandering.

Little Avis did not share Gram's casual attitude toward Bonnie, to whom many still referred to as "the babysitter." Despite the fact that Bonnie was warm and loving toward Bob's children, Avis made it clear she would never replace her mother. When Gram wasn't around, Little Avis felt terribly isolated. They'd hung a portrait of Big Avis in the house, which undoubtedly exacerbated the pain. Bob's daughter Becky remembered, "Avis hung a picture of Bonnie in the closet and used it as a dart board." In early November, Avis shared those feelings with Gram. In his response, Gram tried to address her issues and at the same time, offer some advice:

> They're not just your concern, they're our concern, yours mine, and Diane's, and I'm afraid they will continue for some time yet. The best thing we can do is learn from the past and live our lives the right way so, in time, when we can do something to change things, we will be real people, not sick or haunted by what life has done to us.

Gram joined his family for the Christmas holidays at the Ponte Vedra beach house, inviting a couple of Harvard friends. One of them, Tony Hendra, edited the school's renowned humor publication, the *Harvard Lampoon*. Gram's friend from the Bolles School, Frank David Murphy, joined them for a fun-filled weekend. "Everybody had to get the most obscure information and concepts," Murphy remembered, "then sit and twist them together and bounce them off each other." While Bob and Bonnie passed in and out of the beach house, Gram and his friends spent much of the time swilling absinthe and champagne. "It was a pretty blitzy week-end," Murphy concluded.

Gram spent his first Christmas without his mother at the Snively mansion. On December 26, 1965, he paid a visit to his old Winter Haven buddy and bandmate Jim Carlton. In the afternoon Gram picked up a Gibson acoustic guitar and played a collection of songs into Carlton's Sony 500 reel-to-reel machine. Thanks to that machine, Carlton preserved the songs Gram wrote and performed during his brief days as an urban folkie.

The songs gave Gram an opportunity to show Carlton some of the influence he'd picked up from his Greenwich Village trips. "Wheel of Fortune" was a new tune Gram had written while still attending Harvard. "Another Side of this Life" and "Candy Man" were Fred Neil covers. And Gram recorded his own simple and moving version of the poem he'd started at Bolles before his mother's death, "Brass Buttons."

The year of such dramatic change in Gram's life, 1965, was coming to a close. He had lost his mother, graduated from high school, and seen his immediate family move away from the home he'd known since childhood. He had broken up with the Shilos, spent another summer in the Village, and seen the Beatles. He enrolled in Harvard and dropped out, and had been encouraged to consider country music and started down that road.

For Gram Parsons, 1966 would be all about the music. Gram and his musician friends set their sights on New York City, the place that held their dreams. "We went to New York as economic migrants," said Ian Dunlop. Gram rented a house in the Bronx at University and 195th Street big enough to provide a rehearsal space. Gram's old Winter Haven girlfriend Donna Class moved in with them for a short time. Gram was no longer the clean-cut kid she'd met in the country-club teen room. "I didn't like the lifestyle," Class recalled. "I wasn't into staying up all night and doing drugs."

Despite being abruptly dumped as the Shilos' manager, Buddy Freeman also made the trek to the Bronx during a horse show trip to New York City. "This place was dreary, cold and dank," said Freeman. "Gram came downstairs with no shirt. He looked a mess." It was the equivalent of a rock-and-roll fraternity house with all the decadent trappings.

Still unknowns in New York City, the group managed to land a tour outside of New England. Where better to play than Gram's old stomping grounds in central Florida? Now calling themselves the International Submarine Band, the boys were booked to open up for Freddy "Boom Boom" Cannon, whose hit "Palisades Park" Gram used to play on the youth center circuit.

Gram and Ian Dunlop made the long drive south. "I remember it was the first time I had been in Florida," Dunlop recalled. "It was my first exposure to the Deep South and I found it terrifically exotic." The journey had the opposite effect on Gram; he became more remote and withdrawn. Dunlop reflected, "I think he was revisiting some memories, you know?"

The band warmed up with a homecoming gig at the Derry Down. Their first show opening for Cannon came at the Peabody Auditorium in Daytona Beach. The crowd was young and receptive, thanks to the strong teen music scene on the beach.

At places like Club Martinique, the City Island Recreation Center, and the Wedge, kids had a place to play and see live music. Bernie Leadon and Don Felder played the beach in their British Invasion-inspired group, the Maundy Quintet. In 1966, Jesse Chambers was in the Starfires and lent his new Bassman amp to a kid who'd asked to play during the band's breaks. He proceeded to crank it up to eight or nine and play wild blues completely different from the pop stuff Chambers was playing.

"I told him, don't ever turn my amp up that loud again," Chambers recalled. It was his first meeting with an apologetic Duane Allman. In 1966 Duane and his brother Gregg were fixtures around Daytona Beach as the Allman Joys. Even at that early stage, both the Allmans and the ISB, also known as the Sub Band, were trying to stretch the traditional boundaries of contemporary rock and roll. While most young bands were trying to imitate hit makers, these bands were carving out their own sound. The ISB's flamboyant costumes at that time looked to be right out of the Byrds' hippie-chic fashion.

The next gig in Cocoa Beach had to be completely deflating. This was a town known to cater to Apollo astronauts, not hybrid rock and rollers. Somehow the band ended up in a parade that climaxed at a local Holiday Inn. That night, the ISB and Freddy Cannon played at the Carriage Inn Restaurant and Lounge for twelve people. "It was a very, very funny experience," recalled Ian Dunlop. "We had to laugh, we didn't care. Gram and I had a very exaggerated perception of irony. It was the perfect farce and we were enjoying it." To top off the night, the tour promoter didn't pay for the band's rooms. They were encouraged to take their gear and scatter.

On the drive back to Winter Haven that night, Gram and Ian stopped at an old southern drive-in for a bucket of fried chicken. Even in winter, with the top down, the drive through the pitch-black central Florida night was warm and humid. As the boys passed through the desolate, starlit wetlands, they made a discovery: "We drove back inland eating this chicken and listening to this wonderful, wonderful music," Dunlop recalled, his memory of that night still vivid. "It was a mixture of black rhythm and blues and country and western music and we thought we had gone into the twilight zone. . . . we were like 'God this is great.' Every one of them was a killer, one killer song after another."

They'd driven back into the heart of Cosmic America. That fact was not lost on Ian Dunlop: "The South is rich in that heritage, the musical heritage, all the important forms of music." It was exactly the kind of mix the ISB was playing. During rehearsals they might start off with a Buck Owens tune and move into something by Wilson Pickett or a longtime Gram favorite, Little Richard.

Gram showed the band around the Snively mansion. John Snively Jr. welcomed them with an obligatory cocktail party. To kill some time, they went four-wheeling in the woods in pursuit of armadillos. They paid a visit to Jim Carlton, whose father seemed solicitous, offering beers. "I think because of Nuese's little glasses he thought they were the Lovin' Spoonful," Carlton joked. "He mistook Nuese for John Sebastian."

The band took in a cocktail-lounge performance by Gram's friend Jim Stafford. "I was really quite impressed," said Dunlop. "He had a keyboard and a guitar across his lap and he'd jump back and forth between them in the same song." Gram had grown up idolizing Stafford, and now he had to watch Stafford using the instrument in some sort of comedy act. "You know he really shouldn't be doing that," Gram remarked, implying Stafford deserved better. In time, Stafford rode his considerable musical abilities, natural comedic talent, and strong work ethic to national stardom.

From Winter Haven it was on to Winter Park. Bob Parsons threw a party to welcome Gram. Bob had been buzzing with the news that Gram was getting the chance to make a record. While the audition sessions in New York failed to impress RCA executives, the band's new managers, Monte Kay and Dick Lewis, arranged for the ISB to record its first single for an upcoming Norman Jewison feature film called *The Russians Are Coming*. Bob Parsons's daughter Becky remembered, "When they did *The Russians Are Coming* it was the big talk."

Also at that party was Jim Carlton, who remembered one of the guests being none other than Domingo Samudio, better known as Sam the Sham, who was in town for a gig. In 1965 and 1966 Sam the Sham and the Pharaohs scored huge hits with "Wooly Bully" and "Lil' Red Riding Hood." According to Carlton, "no one paid unusual attention to Sam the Sham." Bob's older friends drank; Gram and his bandmates spent the evening smoking hash. Carlton was so stoned it took him forever to get to the main road four blocks away. He missed National Guard training the next morning.

Gram made another eventful trip to central Florida in April recording the final few songs Carlton later assembled for the album *Gram Parsons, Another Side of This Life*. On April 18, 1966, the tunes included a cover of Fred Neil's bluesy "That's the Bag I'm In."

These final few songs effectively mark the end of Gram's urban-folkie period; they were also his last known recordings in Florida. By the spring of 1966 Gram immersed himself fully in country. Back in New York, Barry Tashian of the group the Remains hung out with the Sub Band at their house in the Bronx. "I remember Ian actually had a motorcycle in his room," Tashian recalled. He also remembered how the band lined their small rehearsal room upstairs with egg cartons. "I thought it was great they were playing country," Tashian said. "They introduced me to the notion that country was cool." The chord changes to Dave Dudley's "Six Days on the Road" stuck out: "It was a refreshing thing for me. I was about at the end of the Remains."

The Remains went on one last, memorable tour. They never had a hit record, but they will always be remembered as the group that opened for the Beatles on their final American tour. Their last show came at San Francisco's Candlestick Park on August 29, 1966.

On July 5, the Sub Band opened for the Young Rascals in Central

Park. The festival crowd of 15,000 was by far the largest group Gram had ever performed for—and a big leap from the audience of twelve in Cocoa Beach. They also had a chance to go back into the studio.

Although *The Russians Are Coming* failed to make a commercial splash, the Sub Band's management lined-up an opportunity to record a single for Columbia records. The resulting "Sum Up Broke" and flip-side "One Day Week" sound far more like the Beatles than a group becoming deeply immersed in country music. Nonetheless, both songs reflect Gram and the band's pop sensibilities. Nothing happened with that single either. A three-week visit with his buddy Brandon De Wilde in Los Angeles whetted Gram's appetite for another permanent change of scenery.

In 1967, Gram would relocate to California and start to realize his musical vision. He'd get a chance that year to make his first full-length record. To do it, he called on a couple of old Central Florida bandmates for help. One accepted Gram's invitation and traveled west; the other didn't trust Gram enough to go.

Diane Parsons's birthday party, circa 1963. Her sister Avis was advised she was getting too close to "the help." (The Estate of Robert Parsons)

*Above:* Bob and Bonnie Parsons undated photo. (The Estate of Robert Parsons)

*Left:* Marilyn Garrett, Shilos backup singer, circa 1963. (From the personal collection of Marilyn Garrett)

The Shilos photographed in the family room of the Parsons's home on Piedmont Dr., Winter Haven, Fla. (The Estate of Robert Parsons)

The Derry Down building in downtown Winter Haven, Fla. (Michael Robinson)

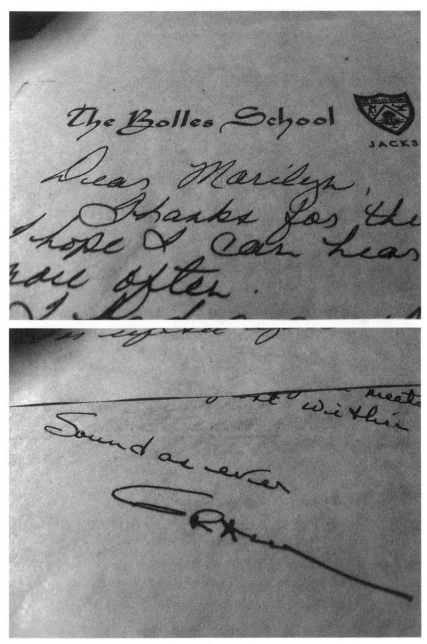

Gram Parsons's letter to Marilyn Garrett. (From the personal collection of Marilyn Platt)

Jim Stafford photographed outside what was Quality Cleaners, Winter Haven, Fla. (Michael Robinson)

The Legends circa 1962, photographed in Jim Stafford's living room, where he later gave Parsons advice to pursue country music. (Jim Stafford)

Photographer Ted Polumbaum with Senator Ted Kennedy, undated. (Judy Polumbaum)

Gram Parsons and the Like at Harvard, 1965. (The Newseum, Ted Polumbaum Collection)

Gram Parsons jamming 1965, nineteenth birthday graffiti can be seen on the wall. (The News-eum, Ted Polumbaum collection)

A lighthearted moment between Gram Parsons and roommate Larry Piro, Pennypacker Hall, Harvard. (The Newseum, Ted Polumbaum Collection)

Gram Parsons clowning around in a towel with his ROTC roommate Larry Piro, Pennypacker Hall, Harvard. (The Newseum, Ted Polumbaum Collection)

Gram Parsons outside the Music Building, Harvard. (The Newseum, Ted Polumbaum Collection)

Gram Parsons looking slightly lost on campus, Harvard 1965. (The Newseum, Ted Polumbaum Collection)

Gram Parsons Songs

*[signature]*

November Night
I can't make it any more
Zah's Blues
Small Boy's World
Some Blues Thing
Pam
That Kind of Living
A Place to be going
Apple Tree
Brass Buttons
Night Walk
Between Your Hands and Mine
A River is made out of Raindrops
Don't ask Me
Big Country
Rollin' Stone
The Hand Within* the Glove
The Rains came down
Honda Rider
The Darkest Years
Run little boy run
My name—it is the Wind

Gram Parsons handwritten list of "Gram Parsons Songs" circa 1965. (Courtesy Lawrence Piro)

## Will Harvard Spoil Gram Parsons?

# Singer Makes Scene Twice: Student, Performer

**By WILLIAM FRIPP**

It's not that Gram Parsons can't adjust to the freshman grind at Harvard.

It's all these other things, like calls from Ed Sullivan, frugging with the Beatles at Arthur, wrapping up that contract with RCA Victor.

Rarified things like that, they keep him busy, on edge. Gram's made most of The Scene. He's been rolling, has carried him in front-page Variety, coupled him with the elegantes in whispery gossip columns, propelled him under the kleigs.

But he's only 19, and Harvard with its hour exams and labs and reading lists is awfully demanding.

"If it gets too complicated, I'll just have to try to get a leave of absence from college," drawled Gram of Winter Haven, Fla.

Lolling around his Pennypacker Hall digs with his shaggy main, jeans and tennies, Gram is the quintessence of the cool cult. But while they dream, he's arrived.

Like in a few days he'll take his group, The Likes, down to Nashville to cut a record for RCA. The other four likes, like Gram, are established professionals. They rehearse almost daily in Cambridge.

Just a few weeks ago Gram signed his RCA contract, and its reported that the promotional package is second only to that of Elvis Presley.

His manager, Marty Erlichman, also manages Barbra Streisand. Success doesn't seem to have spoiled Gram Parsons. Classmates boggle when he describes the Beatles' antics at producer David Merrick's bash, how they moved the furniture and Picassos around, but it's all done in a boyishly offhand manner and no one is offended.

Lanky Gram plays the steel string guitar, sings and composes Bobby Dylan-style songs. His music, he says, draws on Bach, is rhythmically like the Beatles, and makes the new noise, thanks to the band's electric organ.

He admires Dylan, but doesn't think he goes far enough in trying to reach his teen-age audience.

"Bobby asks questions and hints at emotion. I want to answer some of the questions teen-agers ask about love, to describe the gamut of feelings, how to deal with them."

It all started in Waycross, Ga., where Gram sang country and western ballads over local radio at age 10. Later he sang blues at Southern night boites, then turned to rock 'n roll and success.

He bounced around "six or seven" Southern schools before finally graduating. Acceptance at Harvard?

"Mark me down to the clerical error portion."

Hanging fire are a possible Ed Sullivan show appearance, a contract with the Beatles to handle two of his songs, and hour exams.

*Boston Globe.* William Fripp, "Singer Makes Scene Twice: Student, performer," October 31, 1965.

# Yardling to Rock, Signs RCA Contract

OCT 21 1965

Some people at Harvard spend their time studying and don't worry about making money. Others worry about money and don't study. GRAM PARSONS doesn't worry.

A Harvard freshman has signed the second largest promotional contract in RCA Victor's history — exceeded only by Elvis Presley's.

Gram Parsons, 19, of Pennypacker Hall and Winter Haven, Florida, came to terms with RCA two weeks ago, after considering offers from MGM, Capitol, and nine other smaller studios. His first record, "November Night", will make its national debut in Boston in six to eight weeks.

Gram and his group, "The Likes", play a new type of music. It supposedly blends sounds of the Beatles, Byrds, and Dylan. Each member of the five piece band is an established professional.

Before coming to Harvard, Gram attended "six or seven" different schools in Florida and South Carolina before settling down for his last two years at Bowles Academy near Jacksonville.

He was surprised about his admittance to Harvard —"mark me down in the clerical error portion."

Gram's manager, Marty Erlichman, looks for an appearance on the Ed Sullivan Show and a possible television "Special" next year. Erlichman is also Barbra Streisand's agent. Gram himself admitted that the Beatles are interested in two of his songs for their next album.

Thirty-six songs of Gram's have already been published. His
(Continued on page eight)

## Harvard Teen Rocker
(Continued from page one)

professional career began at the age of nine in Waycross, Georgia, where he sang country and western music on a local radio station. Since that time Gram has been playing rock 'n' roll, folk, and blues in night clubs from Florida to New York. He began composing seriously at sixteen. His lyrics are typified in this excerpt from "November Night":

"I'll just remember a November night
When the dawn on your doorway
Shone white with frost,
And the soft love that always began
With the touch of your hand,
And recalled the mornings
That tossed your hair in the wind."

"Gram Parson and the Likes" will be practicing in the Freshman Union nightly for the next week and a half. They are flying to Nashville on Saturday, September 30, to record their first single.

Unknown publication, "Yardling to Rock, Signs RCA Contract," October 21, 1965. An example of Gram Parsons's tendency to exaggerate or make up stories about musical accomplishments to garner publicity.

Jamming with John Nuese, Pennypacker Hall, Harvard. (The Newseum, Ted Polumbaum Collection)

Gram Parsons writing at Harvard, 1965. (The Newseum, Ted Polumbaum Collection)

Gram Parsons in gym class, Harvard 1965. (The Newseum, Ted Polumbaum Collection)

# Wheel of Fortune

I. Fingertips — "rainbows for rings light
my way
Circles carved in my hand
Magic trips to gather stars in the daytime
Look here and there and we may find
them blinking in the sand.

II. Wave your wand—to stir the stream of my
thinking —
Let me know where it winds—
Pastel dawns — show searching nights without
armor — Casting cards on the water while
they tell me what they find.

Chorus
Wheel of fortune keeps on turning
Everyday that I've been learning
Where I stand and what I want to be
You see.

III. In the sky — words appear without meaning
Making shadows on the sun.
You and I can snap our fingers and
leave them we don't have to believe them
When we're back where we begin.

Gram Parsons's handwritten lyrics, "Wheel of Fortune." (Lawrence Piro)

Becky Parsons Gottsegen in the backyard of her father's former suburban Orlando home. (Michael Robinson)

The suburban Orlando home Bob Parsons rented after moving from Winter Haven. Gram's guest house is pictured at left. (Bob Kealing)

Jesse Chambers, the first musician to sing "high lonesome" harmony with Gram Parsons, holding the bass Parsons helped him buy. (Michael Robinson)

Vince Martin's cottage
in Coconut Grove, Fla.
Notice the mooring rope
railing. (Bob Kealing)

The Byrds on stage at the Ryman Auditorium, original home of the Grand Ole Opry, March 1968. (Les Leverett)

The Byrds recording *Sweetheart of the Rodeo* in Nashville, 1968. *L–R:* John Hartford, Gram Parsons, Chris Hillman, Roger McGuinn. (Neil V. Rosenberg)

*Above:* The author with Roger McGuinn in the Folk Den, Orlando, Fla. (Michael Robinson)

*Left:* Jon Corneal photographed in the Nudie jacket he received during his work with the Flying Burrito Brothers, Auburndale, Fla. (Michael Robinson)

Gram Parsons photographed by Eve Babitz at the Chateau Marmont hotel in Los Angeles, early 1970s. (Courtesy Eve Babitz)

But these Record Company thugs are the ones most responsable for what goes down.

Somehow I'm getting thru' it now. Yer right – I do love the album – and all the guys (& 1 girl, Emmy Lou Harris) I'm workin' with now. My old friend – I couldn't fool you Could I? Lost & refound. Bulls-eye. Thanks to Love – its real self. And I'm always searching for ways to communicate it. Even down in the depths you certainly must have sussed me to be in – I suppose my Social concience grew alot, when after going "through it" too many times, almost, to stick around much longer – I found it! It seemed easy! & others have asked and had the same results. Only disappointment is – . . .

We got to stop this ramblin' even tho' I really mean it – The guy I want to play drums – N. D. Smart, fer real, is coming by so I gotta clear out a few Xmas piles.

Mo' later, baby! ——

——→ 1/14/73/A.M.(L.A.)♀ I really mean it. I wuz 'specialy glad to hear from you t'day! It'll be a gas when we get t' see you – come march. I HATE to get on your colorin' case but I sure would dig one. OH! the (my) platter is taking right off. Thank magik! Art, music – Are coming Back. GOT TO SPLIT. KEEP COLORIN'. LOVE US! TO YOU

※ NOT TO BE TAKEN LIGHTLY. G.P.

Gram Parsons's 1972 letter to Frank David Murphy. (Frank David Murphy)

Gram and Gretchen Parsons on 1973 sailing trip. (The Estate of Robert Parsons)

Gram Parsons photographed in the Grenadine Islands, 1973. (The Estate of Robert Parsons)

Gram Parsons gravesite, New Orleans, La. (The Estate of Robert Parsons)

Bob Buchanan and Charlie Louvin at City Auditorium, Waycross, Ga. (Michael Robinson)

# ❋ 17 ❋

## Staying Behind, Safe at Home

"I have strong opinions about Gram and they are probably not popular," warned Gerald "Jesse" Chambers.

From his home in Auburndale, Chambers noted with a self-deprecating laugh he's now old enough to be invited to the senior center near the auditorium where many years ago he, Parsons, and Jon Corneal met. Like many of the musicians who were Gram Parsons's peers in Winter Haven and Auburndale, they're not buying into the hero worship that has overshadowed Parsons's legacy as a music pioneer.

Chambers still owns the bass Gram Parsons helped him buy. It's mounted on the wall of his office along with other cherished instruments. "I don't know if I'd have gone in that direction had it not been for him," said Chambers. There was another direction Parsons offered to take Chambers: west to California. It was 1967 and Gram was looking to round out the roster of players for his upcoming album. "I wouldn't go," Chambers said flatly. "I was twenty-two years old. I had bills." He also had a young wife and wanted some guarantees about what would happen if he went. "What was okay for Gram," Chambers said, "would not be okay for me."

But the issue was more than money: what concerned Chambers was the possibility of going west and getting stranded without a way to support himself or his young family. He wasn't about to take such a long leap of faith based on the word of someone he felt he couldn't trust.

Without offering specifics, Chambers added: "There were things I saw Gram do and promises he didn't do that involved friends and family and girlfriends." His critics have said Gram was capable of dropping associates like Buddy Freeman or the Shilos as soon as he felt he no longer had a use for them. Chambers was also referring to Parsons's own personal vices when he was back visiting Winter Haven in the spring of 1967.

"That's when I was aware there was such a thing called marijuana," Chambers said. "My involvement ended there. It's certainly not for me. I hated that about Gram, I really did. Gram was a talented kid, talented person. Nasty sometimes with the way he lived, the way he treated people. But he had talent."

Chambers had talent too. Despite his decision to pass up the opportunity to go to California to record with Parsons, Jesse, like his cousin Carl, had a long and successful career as a backing musician. When that came to an end, he prospered in the business world as a salesman and has not looked back—very often. He holds a sincere appreciation for the entertainers with whom he worked, such as Ricky Skaggs and the Bellamy Brothers. Chambers has few regrets except that he spent a lot of time on the road when he should have been home helping raise his family. His decision to tell Gram Parsons "no" is not one of those regrets.

"It was a good decision on my part not to do that," Chambers said of his choice not to play on the International Submarine Band's historic and some say archetypal country-rock record. It could have opened other doors: "Unfortunately, I missed some of the things like Chris Hillman and all that. But I'm here and Gram's not."

Despite Chambers's rejection, Parsons's Central Florida recruiting trip in 1967 did yield one youth center circuit player with enough stars in his eyes and ambition in his belly to go to California: Jon Corneal.

Parsons's love of music wasn't the only reason he relocated to the city of Angels. During his visit with actor Brandon De Wilde, Gram had met a dark-haired beauty named Nancy Ross, who resembled Ali McGraw and Natalie Wood. At the time Ross was happily ensconced with the Byrds' wild child and onetime South Florida folkie, David Crosby.

"I was secure and happy and fulfilled with David," she remembered. "When I saw this guy who looked like a coon dog/drowned water puppy come up the driveway, it was not in my mind to be unfaithful." Like something you might hear in a movie, Gram told her, "I've been looking for you for a long time and I'm going to take you with me," and that's exactly what he did. Gram took Nancy back to New York to meet his band, and then he sold the band on moving out west.

Gram moved into an apartment with Nancy on Sweetzer Avenue in Los Angeles. The rest of the Sub Band occupied a house in Laurel Canyon. A few weeks later in early 1967, fresh from his breakup with the Remains, Barry Tashian followed. Brandon De Wilde introduced Gram and the ISB to Peter Fonda, who helped them get a bit part in a party scene of his film *The Trip*. Fonda, like De Wilde, had designs on a recording career. To Gram's delight, Fonda asked to record one of his compositions, now called "November Nights."

Tashian was there the morning Gram announced he'd completed one of his most memorable tunes from this early country period: "I remember him doing 'Luxury Liner' on that little Martin New Yorker guitar." The song's train motif —"I've been a long lost soul, for a long long time"—evokes images often used by one of Gram's literary influences, Jack Kerouac.

Not everyone in the Sub Band was buying into Gram's vision. Mickey Gauvin and Ian Dunlop remained interested in playing the kind of rhythm and blues they performed in their live shows. The man who played such a big role in turning Gram onto country, John Nuese, wanted to continue in that direction.

Another issue dividing the band was disagreement about a work ethic. Gram was spending more and more time with Nancy and less in serious rehearsals like they'd had in New York. The Sub Band got off to a fast start in LA, opening up for emerging bands like the Doors, Love, and Iron Butterfly. However, their lack of rehearsal showed, creating more tension within the band. In Gram's world, annual five-figure trust fund payouts meant he didn't have to worry about being a *working* musician.

In the spring of 1967, Gram received some jolting news: Ross was pregnant. He was forced to make a choice. Ross said, "I was actively fighting for this little soul in my belly, because Gram's manager wanted me to have an abortion on my very own bed. Gram didn't know what to do. He was so young, so scared and so confused. A baby wasn't part of his vision for us."

Nancy refused to end the pregnancy, pitting her against Gram's notion of continuing on as a freewheeling musician. "He had to choose and that's where the pain started," Nancy surmised. Just like any other time when family dramas heated up, Gram could always throw himself into the music. He renewed ties with John Phillips, who was basking in the glory of his post-folk super-group, the Mamas and the Papas.

At the home of Phillips's bandmate Denny Dougherty, Gram ran into none other than Fred Neil, who'd been coaxed out of his comfy South Florida environs to record a new album, *Sessions*. That reunion opened the door for Gram to make another important contact.

"Fred and I always hooked up and hung together," remembered former New Christy Minstrel Bob Buchanan. "One day I come back and there's this young-looking fella with a guitar and they're just jamming away." Buchanan introduced himself.

"Fred wandered off and Gram started playing an Everly Brothers song and just knocked me down," Buchanan marveled. He had fallen in love with the Everly Brothers songs as a child in Michigan. "This was taking me back home. Hollywood isn't exactly the warm place you think it is." Gram and Bob started playing and singing like Phil and Don Everly.

Neil, a musician whom Gram revered, struggled with heroin addiction. "Fred would hurt himself too much and have to fly back to Coconut Grove," Buchanan remembered. Bob and Gram were hurting themselves with hard drugs too. When Gram made opiates a regular part of his life, friends say the clarity, drive, and ambition he'd had dissipated. On smack, Gram's soft, southern drawl often slowed to a crawl. A prime example of this came in a later interview Parsons did with Dutch journalist Jan Donkers; listening to a recording of it, one might expect Gram to nod off at any minute.

Opportunity came from an unlikely source, Lee Hazelwood. Best known as the impresario behind Nancy Sinatra's smash, "These Boots Are Made for Walkin'," Hazelwood was looking for a project his girlfriend, Suzi Jane Hokum, could produce. "It was kind of her little toy to do Gram's album," Buchanan said. After some false hopes with major labels, the ISB signed to Hazelwood's label, LHI Records. Dunlop and Gauvin exited, preferring to pursue a new band with Tashian they were calling the Flying Burrito Brothers. Gram would later hijack that name for a project of his own.

To find Gauvin and Dunlop's replacements, Gram and Nancy headed back to Florida. In the spring of 1967 Jon Corneal was back home from doing session work with Doyle and Teddy Wilburn in Nashville. In the 1960s they had their own syndicated television show and a string of top-40 country albums. The Wilburns gave Corneal a chance to learn how to play real country.

Gram told Corneal he'd come back to Winter Haven to collect his $30,000 trust-fund payment. Not remembering where Corneal had been the last two years, Gram told him, "I've gotta play you this stuff I've discovered!" He invited Corneal to the Snively mansion and flipped on his tape recorder. "Loretta Lynn, Buck Owens, Merle Haggard, George Jones, you know *he's* discovered," Corneal said with sarcasm. It had only been two years before that Gram was chiding Corneal: "Jon, as good as you are at playing drums, why are you playing country?" Now, Gram extolled country as the next big thing.

What piqued Corneal's interest in doing the International Submarine Band's album with Gram, though, was his promise they would do some of Jon's songs and let him sing. Corneal was not content to stay in the background; he felt he had what it took to be a star and have his own recording contract. "I was writing songs in Nashville; I thought eventually it would happen." After two years of barely making ends meet, Corneal was single and ambitious. He likened it to walking right into the record deal he couldn't get in Nashville.

When Jesse Chambers visited with Gram in Winter Haven, he couldn't believe what he was hearing. "We'll get country people to like rock and roll," Gram said. "And we'll get rock and roll people to like country." This was still Polk County in 1967 and Chambers told Gram his idea was ridiculous: "Are you crazy? You can't do that." He didn't buy into Gram's vision and worried he would end up stranded out west, another throwaway bandmate.

Spurned by Jesse Chambers, Gram offered a place in the Sub Band to Bob Buchanan, who readily accepted. Unlike Jon Corneal, Buchanan fostered no illusions about who the star of the album would be: "I suspected this was a tool for Gram to make a record, and it was." But that was fine with Buchanan. He could make good studio money and rub elbows with "some heavyweights" Gram planned to bring in: Jay Dee Maness and session guitarist Glenn Campbell, on the verge of stardom himself.

While staying at the Snively mansion, Gram met up with his old bass-player buddy Jim Carlton. The two jammed in the home's spacious foyer and marveled at the Beatles' *Sgt. Pepper's Lonely Hearts Club Band.* "Gram would play 'With a Little Help from My Friends,'" Carlton recalled. "Gram loved that song."

Carlton also recalled Gram's interest in metaphysical energy and psychic exploration, which expanded during that time due to Nancy's influence and encouragement. Carlton said he regarded all that as bunk but never called his friend on it.

In Los Angeles, Gram had a music enclave around his apartment at 821 Sweetzer Avenue. Buchanan rented a downstairs place, and soon after Fred Neil reappeared. Corneal flew out for the first ISB session that summer, crashing at Gram and Nancy's. "I was sleeping on the couch so I was getting on her nerves," Corneal said.

Another concern Parsons faced, along with other American pop-music artists, was Vietnam. During the historic Summer of Love, almost 2,700 American soldiers lost their lives, and many more were maimed. Protesters marched on the Pentagon. The prospect of involuntary conscription scared the hell out of young men bent on making music, getting high, and loving the ones they were with. Important bands across the country broke up as some musicians went to college or looked for ways to avoid the draft.

"I was eatin' like a pig cause I wanted to weigh-in too large to go to Vietnam," Corneal confessed. "I weighed-in, my porkage was too much." Gram's strategy was to get so stoned they'd never take him: "Now, Gram, he dropped acid. That's how he kept from going. He was just crazy acting. He got out on a psych deferment. It worked for him." With a cherished "4F" rating from the military, that meant the war worries were over and the party could go on and on.

Corneal and Buchanan were witnesses to the tension between Gram and his pregnant girlfriend. "He and Nancy were up and down and going crazy," Buchanan recalled. According to John Nuese, this time of impending fatherhood was the heaviest emotional period he'd seen Gram go through: "It was tearing him up constantly."

At night, the guys would convene in Buchanan's downstairs apartment across the courtyard from Gram's. Corneal admitted he was hitting the bottle pretty hard: "I was probably drinking large jugs of wine." He doesn't know if Gram was trying to counsel him on the dangers of drinking too much or was just having his own moment of catharsis. There in the darkness Gram said to his friend: "I'm not gonna drink myself to death like my Mom." Corneal knew Big Avis had a problem, but this was the first time Gram actually told him she died of alcoholism.

After one year in Winter Park, Bob Parsons relocated Gram's sisters and Bonnie to his hometown, New Orleans. He flew to visit Gram in Los Angeles and meet Nancy. According to Corneal, Gram never had a cross word to say about Bob. "He never spoke about Coon Dog as his real Daddy. He saw Bob as a father figure." Gram was the only son Bob ever had. Corneal was witness to the ways Bob indulged his son: buying a touring van for the Legends, opening the Derry Down, helping pull strings to get Gram into Harvard.

The musicians assembled for the first Sub Band recording session in July 1967. According to liner notes written by writer/musician Sid Griffin, the session started as an audition of the new International Submarine Band for their producer, Suzi Jane Hokum. The first two cuts recorded were Gram compositions, "Blue Eyes" and "Luxury Liner." The rest of the album would get made in late 1967.

Making a record is often a nerve-wracking, intense experience. For Gram that anxiety was magnified because Nancy was due to deliver in early December. Their baby, Polly, born on December 1, 1967, is Gram's only known child. For Nancy, trying to help Gram fulfill his dream and meet their child's needs pulled her in opposing directions. "For me it was Gram and his happiness or Polly and her life," Nancy told Pamela Des Barres. "I knew he was going to split apart from me and what we represented and make his music happen."

In the studio, Gram and John Nuese were at odds with Hokum and her deliberate, piecemeal method of recording. To Buchanan, it was a simple case of Hokum "not knowing what she was doing." But slowly, it started coming together. Two years after Jim Stafford encouraged Gram to take this new musical direction, there was Gram surrounded by people making what is arguably the first full-length country rock record. Four tracks on the album were written or co-written by Gram Parsons; the others range from covers of Merle Haggard's "I Must Be Somebody Else You've Known" to Johnny Cash's "Folsom Prison Blues."

"The main thing about Gram was his feel for country music," John Nuese said. "For him the ISB was a reintroduction, a reawakening in him of the emotional thing which produces country music." Gram had no problem singing with authenticity a song like "Do You Know How It Feels to Be Lonesome?"

Did you ever try to smile at some people
And all they ever seem to do is stare

As the album began to take shape, Jon Corneal came to the realization he'd been brought to California under false pretenses. "It was all Gram's show," Bob Buchanan said. "Jon was very mad about it."

Corneal felt used: "Gram led me to believe we could do some of my tunes and I would get to sing, which is not what he really had in mind. He just wanted me to be his drummer. It wasn't supposed to be that way from the story he told me to get me out there." The International Submarine Band was merely a backing outfit for Gram Parsons. Corneal should have known, he said, given all the money Gram was shelling out of his own pocket to make it happen.

Corneal got in his face, forcing Gram to tell him what he really thought of his music. "You don't write very good songs," said the ever-direct and opinionated Parsons, "and you can't sing."

Corneal exploded, shoving him into a chest of drawers, "You ly-ing son of a bitch, you got me to come out here for nothing!" Gram had misled him, but Corneal was getting his first chance to make a record—that opportunity opened other doors down the line, and he was getting paid. Corneal wanted to share some of the spotlight and it wasn't in the cards for him. Weighing in at a meaty 230 pounds, he could have kicked Gram's ass.

"I just backed off. There was no use to go any further," Corneal said. "We were living in the era of peace and love."

By Christmas, there was much to celebrate. Nancy had given birth to "Pretty Polly" and Gram had fathered his first country rock record. Gram's days of searching for a musical direction were over. In less than a year, he had moved to the West Coast, met his first intense love interest, turned twenty-one, became a father, put his band back to-gether, and made his first album titled *Safe at Home*.

Recording wrapped up just before the holidays. When it came time to think about a cover, band members realized they had no suitable photographs. An artist named Frank Morton was brought in to sketch a cover drawing based on a photograph of Nuese, Parsons, and Cor-neal sitting on a couch resplendent in Old South regalia. Through the magic of Morton's pen, a nonplussed-looking Buchanan appeared on the couch with the rest of the band.

Gram Parsons was positioned to ascend to much greater heights musically. He was rubbing elbows with important Hollywood players and music-industry heavyweights. Thanks to the ISB's early opening gigs and Gram's friendship with Brandon De Wilde and Peter Fonda, he was developing a buzz around LA. The ISB should have been happy, but according to Sid Griffin, storm clouds were forming: "The band knew trouble was brewing. Gram shared the same business manager as the Byrds, and he'd even visited several sessions for *The Notorious Byrd Brothers* album."

The making of this album had increased conflict among the Byrds, and the band was falling apart. The Byrds' chief songwriter, Gene Clark, had already departed. The remaining members reached their limit with Crosby's antics and told him to leave. A slot in America's most important band was open, and Gram happened to meet band member Chris Hillman in a bank line. The two struck up a conversation and formed a fast friendship through their mutual love of country music.

With his bank account depleted from laying out so much cash to make the record, Gram headed back to Florida for a vacation and another trust-fund injection. Bob Buchanan departed for Coconut Grove to hang out with Fred Neil. Gram would soon follow.

# ❦ 18 ❦

# Vinny's Place

Since the early 1960s, a vast collection of musicians, poets, and writers have called Coconut Grove home. Bordered by Biscayne Bay's restless waters, few places outside New York City have nurtured the careers of more important folkies than the Grove. When he wrote the immortal lyrics to "Everybody's Talkin'," Fred Neil was referring to this unique part of old Miami:

> I'm goin' where the sun keeps shinin'
> Through the pourin' rain
> Goin' where the weather suits my clothes

In the mid-1960s, Fred Neil and Vince Martin occupied neighboring homes at 3026 and 3028 Aviation Avenue in the Grove. Martin's picturesque cottage was a way station for famous musicians passing through and making history: John Phillips, David Crosby, Gram Parsons, Stephen Stills, John Sebastian, Phil Ochs, Tim Hardin, and many others. In these neighboring homes, Martin and Neil composed their 1964 collaboration, *Tear Down the Walls*. And Neil wrote his solo follow-up, *Bleecker and MacDougal*.

Vince Martin's old place is completely obscured from the road. To get to it, you follow a narrow stone walkway past an explosion of tropical bougainvillea. Beyond a high fence, the intimate cottage features pecky cypress paneling, a fireplace, a steep staircase and hand railing made of thick mooring rope, a loft bedroom, and a kitchen resembling a ship's galley. This small home was the scene of countless all-night jam sessions featuring some of the most important musicians of the 1960s.

Though Coconut Grove has fallen prey to sprawl and overdevelopment, the locale is still exotic enough to see why it draws musicians looking to drop out for a while and get in touch with a creative muse.

Robert Frost and Tennessee Williams wintered here. Jimmy Buffett played the same coffeehouse where an unknown Joni Mitchell was discovered by David Crosby in 1968, the Gaslight South. The Grove is a veritable food court with a wide selection of restaurants reflecting the area's ethnic diversity. It's an eclectic feast of art, music, sunshine, and tropical scenery with a slower pace of life. At the beginning of 1968, Gram Parsons paid a visit to Fred Neil, Vince Martin, and Bob Buchanan, kicking off one of the most important periods of his career.

Parsons couldn't have found a better place for a respite from the pressures of making a record, dealing with bandmates' egos, and coming to terms with fatherhood. In Coconut Grove, he settled into a lifestyle and music scene revolving around South Florida folk gods Vince Martin and Fred Neil. For folkies, their neighboring homes were like Greenwich Village south. Musicians were welcome to show up at any time and crash wherever they could find room. It didn't matter that folk was no longer as commercially viable as it had been at the beginning of the sixties. The Grove's folk scene continued to thrive.

During the Byrds' chart-topping years of 1965 and 1966, David Crosby brought his bandmates to Coconut Grove to meet Fred Neil. Prior to that, Roger McGuinn had only admired him from afar: "I saw Fred Neil in Greenwich Village and I remember him walking down MacDougal Street with these white pants that were all sooty from being in New York and a leather gig bag on his back and I thought 'this guy is pretty cool.'"

Vince Martin recalled Crosby's days in the Grove after he was ousted from the Byrds. "He would show up in his Borsalino hat and his leather cape, crash on the floor and eat my grapefruit and oranges," Martin said. According to Martin, the first vestiges of Crosby's post-Byrds super group took shape in his Aviation Avenue cottage: "Crosby and Stephen Stills sat on my floor and told me about their new idea." They sang together for Martin, then went next door and performed for Fred Neil. Another occasional Grove-ite, Cass Elliott, introduced them to Graham Nash back in California.

Like Crosby, Parsons stayed at Vince Martin's place, jamming virtually 24/7. "We played all the time!" Martin gushed. "All day and all night, fueled by my first wife Christina's freshly baked chocolate-chip cookies and iced tea and coffee by the pail full." Even when the people inside were sleeping, the door was open for more pilgrims. Martin and Neil were the musical gurus. Their acoustic performances around Coconut Grove are still recalled with great reverence.

"I think what Gram found in Fred was a real down-to-earth guy," said Bob Buchanan. "And Gram deep down was that kind of guy." Fred Neil was another mentor who preached the merging of musical styles and, above all, originality. In a 1966 interview, one of the few he ever gave, Neil talked about a kind of artistic nonconformity Parsons had already started to follow. "In pop music there's too much imitation; songwriters continually try to come up with something that sounds like a record in the top ten," Neil commented. "A lot of record producers are still trying for the same baloney sound. They're reluctant to try something new. I think they should let the music happen the way the new songwriters and singers are creating it."

The Grove's relaxed and exotic atmosphere was evocative of Parsons's days in Greenwich Village. With an album of country and rock in the can, it didn't matter that folk no longer held the key to his future. Since his family life was often a mess, these artists and their music offered him a sense of roots—the feeling of home.

Rejuvenated by his stay in the Grove, Parsons invited Bob Buchanan to accompany him to Winter Haven. This trip was the last time Jim Carlton saw Gram in person. He had just collected a trust fund payment and sat in his Cypress Gardens motel room, thousands of dollars in cash spread out on the bed. Carlton's old 1957 clunker wasn't running, so Gram picked up a twenty from the stack of cash, handed it to him and said, "Go get yourself another battery."

To some, the episode is evidence of Parsons's generosity. To others, it shows his inability to claim the essence of what it takes to be an authentic country musician: coming up the hard way, playing dives to scratch out a living, and using experience as inspiration. For Gram, subsistence was always within arm's length, a short grab from an ever-flowing river of family money. Yet, the spate of family addictions and tragedy gave him plenty to say about common themes in country music: loss, heartache, and alienation.

Parsons and Buchanan boarded a north-bound train to begin the trek back to Los Angeles. Buchanan planned to show Gram around some of the Chicago folk clubs he played before earning a spot in the New Christy Minstrels.

Riding the rails through the South was a tradition Gram Parsons had known since childhood. The summer after Coon Dog killed himself, Big Avis boarded the children on a train trip across America. From the safety and comfort of a softly swaying luxury liner, sadness could give way to a kaleidoscope of passing scenery fading into nighttime darkness as the train clickety-clacked down the line.

Nine years later, Parsons rode the Santa Fe Chief in a private car and started to strum a melancholy song he'd been working on since being back in Florida. He came up with a first verse:

In South Carolina, there are many tall pines
I remember the oak trees that we used to climb
But now when I'm lonesome, I always pretend
That I'm gettin' the feel of hickory wind

Buchanan recalled he had been down at the dining car and came back to find Gram working on his new song. "Hey Bob, can you help me with this?" he asked.

"Ya, what's going on?" Buchanan asked.

"I need help. I can't get some lyrics to this song. I only got this one verse."

Buchanan joined in, "We both had a lot of home in us at that time, and here we are headed back to what you might call 'the bullfight.'" Even if home was just a feeling of being away from all of the pressures and temptation of Los Angeles, neither of the two men was in a big hurry to get back. They already looked at Tinseltown with world-weary, jaundiced eyes: greedy record company executives, pressure to produce, fair-weather friends, and the siren's song of drugs and alcohol.

"I was not a happy camper at the time I'd been out in Hollywood," Buchanan reflected. "I had sports cars, I had money. I lost it. I made some more, I lost that. You make it, you spend it, you make it." From that state of mind, lyrics to the second verse of Gram's song started to flow:

I started out younger, had most everything
All the riches and pleasures, what else could life bring?
But it makes me feel better each time it begins
Callin' me home, hickory wind

"So I came up with the second lyric and then Gram came up with that beautiful one at the end," Buchanan recalled:

It's a hard way to find out, that trouble is real
In a faraway city, with a faraway feel
But it makes me feel better each time it begins
Callin' me home, hickory wind
Keeps callin' me home, hickory wind

Fresh from a trip to Cosmic America, two friends composed what many consider to be Parsons's most memorable and evocative song. To some, "Hickory Wind" is Gram's paean to the better days of his southern childhood. To others, it's a dirge lamenting his feelings of rootlessness; the only solace is something elusive and impossible to hold onto.

"If you don't have a little bit of sympathy in there or understand where he's coming from in writing that song, then you don't know him" said his childhood bandmate Jesse Chambers. "What a killer song."

Gram Parsons was on a train ride to the most important career move of his life. Now he had a great song to take with him. It was 1968, a year of tumult and turmoil. In a period of six months, Parsons would experience the equivalent of a musical moon shot and then come crashing back to earth through his own immaturity and impatience.

# ❧ 19 ❧

# A Country Byrd

On the walls of Roger McGuinn's Orlando office, a row of guitars hang like great artwork. Among them is McGuinn's own model twelve-string Rickenbacker like those he played on the Byrds' biggest hits. McGuinn's blending of Bob Dylan and Pete Seeger's acoustic folk with the Beatles' electrified rhythms ignited America's "folk rock" era, catapulted the Byrds to international stardom, and earned them a place in the Rock and Roll Hall of Fame in 1991.

Also on the wall hangs the lyrics to Seeger's timeless "Turn! Turn! Turn!"—a monster chart topper for the Byrds in 1966. In another place of honor, something unexpected: a songwriting award for "You Showed Me," a top ten hit for the Turtles.

"It was the first tune Gene Clark and I ever wrote," McGuinn revealed. "It was rejected by the Byrds; they didn't think it was any good." Now it's a million-seller.

From his home office in Orlando, McGuinn plays, records, and uploads to his computer a variety of traditional folk tunes: sea chanties and cowboy songs, lullabies and other obscurities. In 2002, McGuinn's songs from the Folk Den section of his website earned a Grammy nomination. More important, they've kept him engaged in a lifelong passion for his roots—folk music.

The name Folk Den is a tip of the hat to a room of the same name at the Troubadour nightclub in Los Angeles. Fresh from Greenwich Village in 1964, McGuinn was there playing his blend of folk to a Beatle beat before a curious and not altogether appreciative crowd.

In the audience was Gene Clark, a young folkie who'd been plucked out of obscurity in Kansas City by members of the New Christy Minstrels. After months of touring the country, Clark was anxious to step out of the background and become a star. Clark was impressed with the Beatles and liked what McGuinn was doing.

That historic meeting with McGuinn in the Folk Den changed the course of popular music. From 1965 to 1973, a roster of visionaries passed through the Byrds: Gene Clark, Roger McGuinn, Gram Parsons, Clarence White, David Crosby, and Chris Hillman. The earliest, "classic" incarnation of the Byrds included the interpreter McGuinn, the main songwriter and heartthrob Clark, the essential voice and mad-hatter Crosby on rhythm guitar, brooding bluegrass scion Hillman on bass, and drummer Michael Clarke, a ringer for Rolling Stone Brian Jones.

The Byrds' sound, embracing folk, country, rock, bluegrass, even jazz, inspired many important hybrid bands. The early line-up, rife with egos, jealousy, and very little chemistry led Parsons biographer David Meyer to call them "a nest of vipers, *Lord of the Flies* with guitars."

The Byrds' first incarnation came to an end in February 1966. Freaked out by the pressures of fame, flying, and the band's internal strife, Gene Clark departed.

"Gene had a problem with success," McGuinn reflected. "Whenever he got successful he had to go drown his sorrows. It bugged him to no end to be successful." That psychological fragility combined with heavy substance abuse became malignant problems the rest of Clark's career. A handsome, brooding, cerebral kind of guy, Gene Clark was the Jack Kerouac of rock and roll.

After McGuinn and Hillman fired Crosby midway through 1967, Clark tried one more time with the Byrds to no avail. His second departure paved the way for Parsons to join and spearhead the Byrds' most historic period: their transition to "country rock."

I handed McGuinn a photograph of the Parsons-era Byrds performing on the stage of the Grand Ole Opry on March 15, 1968. Gone were McGuinn's "granny" glasses, the hippie chic clothes, and any suggestion of "Eight Miles High." The baby-faced new guy standing stage right, Gram Parsons, looks clean-cut and right out of college.

"I felt like I was in a movie when I was with Gram Parsons," McGuinn remarked. "It was surreal in a very disturbing way. It was almost like you could feel his impending doom coming on. Like life and death. I got that vibe a lot when I was with him."

At this snapshot in time, fate had shined a kind light on Parsons. He was making music with the most influential band in America. He'd sold them on his country vision. The Opry's long-time photographer, Les Leverett, captured in black and white the most historic performance of Gram Parsons's career. And it came on the most famous stage in the South.

*   *   *

Back in Los Angeles in early 1968, Parsons started sending signals the International Submarine Band was no longer a top priority. Bob Buchanan knew it was coming: "I was kind of indifferent, I didn't suspect a (touring) band was gonna happen anyway." Jon Corneal was revved up to take their work on the road and start making some money: "We would have made fifteen grand for a tour with the Turtles." Nuese claimed his guitar needed work and it just wasn't the right time. Feigning loyalty to his fellow country connoisseur, Parsons told Corneal, "John's the guy; if he can't do it, I can't do it."

Corneal knew what Gram was really up to: "He was already starting to shop out as a sideman for the Byrds."

It wouldn't be as easy for Gram to drop the Sub Band as it had been to drop his previous two bands, the Shilos and the Legends. Lee Hazelwood was a formidable player on the LA scene. With a yet-to-be-released album in the can, which was effectively a Gram Parsons solo record, Hazelwood wasn't going to just let him walk away. In a 1973 interview with Michael Bate, Parsons talked about their acrimonious meeting: "I picked up every single that his label put out and I listened to every one of them. Every side of them," Parsons said. "I took all the singles and laid 'em on his desk and said listen, man, I've listened to every one of the singles your company's put out and they're all garbage and I want off."

According to this account Hazelwood shot back, "You don't know anything about making singles; you never had a hit record in your life. You can get off but I'm keeping the name."

This exchange cleared the way for Parsons to move on, but he had to renounce rights to the International Submarine Band name. He also left the remaining members with no way to tour the record or put any money in their pockets. For the second time, Gram had discarded Corneal like yesterday's news. Corneal realized: "I allowed the silver-tongued devil to talk me into this stuff." It had happened in 1963 when Gram went off to Bolles and the Legends had to find his replacement. This time it was far more complicated, and Corneal was stuck in LA without steady work.

When *Safe at Home* was released in 1968, a few reviewers took notice, but nothing happened commercially. It took another decade for the album to be recognized as groundbreaking.

At the beginning of 1968, Gene Clark had departed the Byrds for a second time, David Crosby had been fired, and the group was running on fumes as a trio.

"It was just not happening," McGuinn remembered. "There was not enough going on to make it a band." Parsons's encounter with Chris Hillman in that Beverly Hills bank line was fortuitous. Hillman invited him over to a Byrds rehearsal. "I wanted to do an extension of 'Eight Miles High' to a sort of jazz-fusion thing we were into," McGuinn remembered. "I sat him down . . . and he played a little Floyd Kramer-ish style piano. I figured this guy's got talent, he's in."

Parsons had moved in on David Crosby's girlfriend; now he was more or less filling Crosby's shoes in the Byrds. In February 1968, Parsons was hired as a salaried side-man. Of course, that's not how he put it when he called up old friend Jim Carlton: "I'm a full-fledged Byrd now," Parsons announced. He marveled at the electric eye McGuinn had installed at his house for security and his Moog (pronounced

MOGE) synthesizer about as big as a sofa. Once again Gram had moved on to the next phase of his career without a great deal of effort or hardship.

Parsons brought a new energy and vision at a time when the Byrds had very little left. By their own admission, McGuinn and Hillman had no original songs to bring to whatever record would follow up *The Notorious Byrd Brothers* album.

"We had a commitment to do two albums a year for Columbia," McGuinn said. "We were touring and it was a pretty hectic pace." Gram Parsons was ambitious and about to have the platform to take his Cosmic American dream to the world. "He was just an evangelist for country," said McGuinn. "And then I fell in love with it."

Chris Hillman was a willing ally, having grown up in Southern California playing bluegrass and plucking the mandolin. His early band, the Scottsville Squirrel Barkers, featured a teenaged Bernie Leadon before he moved to Gainesville, Florida. Before long, Corneal would cross paths again with Parsons. Corneal also hooked up with Gene Clark and banjoist Doug Dillard to play on their groundbreaking collaborations of the late 1960s.

Parsons would never be happy as a sideman. Being from money brought with it an inherent star status that had translated to every one of his musical endeavors. Besides, Gram brought to the Byrds two killer original songs: "Hickory Wind" and "One Hundred Years from Now."

Parsons's first concerts with the Byrds in early February featured traditional Byrds material and no country. He dutifully sat in the shadows and tried to integrate keyboards with their guitar-driven sound. That changed at a University of Michigan tour stop on February 23, 1968, when Parsons took the stage and for the first time performed "Hickory Wind." The set that night also featured Porter Wagoner's "A Satisfied Mind," covered by the Byrds in 1965.

McGuinn, Hillman, and their new side-man discussed the idea of doing a full-on country record as part of a double-album exploration of the history of music. In the end, they decided to go to Nashville to record a single country album. "We could pull that off," McGuinn explained.

In 1968, country was generally thought of as un-cool and reserved for hicks, squares, and hillbillies. In that sense, this new direction by such a recognizable and established rock band was far more risky than their earlier folk-influenced offerings—and far ahead of their time.

Being on Columbia Records helped; by 1968 artists of many different genres were starting to come to Columbia's Nashville studios to cut their most celebrated work. In marathon sessions in 1966, Bob Dylan laid down many of the tracks for his milestone, *Blonde on Blonde*. His follow-up, *John Wesley Harding*, is widely considered a hybrid country milestone.

Never mind the electrified folk the Byrds played, this was still a rarity for a rock band to record in Nashville. After having achieved commercial and critical glory blending folk and rock, they hoped having top-notch country studio players might help them again catch lightning in a bottle.

McGuinn said the Byrds decided to cut their hair, but not as an attempt to assimilate with Nashville. "I think we were just tired of long hair and psychedelia," he offered. "It was like folk rock had peaked and it was embarrassing to be part of." McGuinn went to Nudie's Rodeo Tailors in Hollywood and invested in cowboy clothes. He also bought a black Cadillac El Dorado, "just to sort of fit in with the scene."

Nashville was known for rigid, workmanlike recording schedules and glossy Chet Atkins-type production; the Byrds were two thousand miles and even further, stylistically speaking, from the laissez-faire recording they were accustomed to in California.

The Byrds weren't just taking a new creative direction; they were flying into a different world. The same week they were making music history in Nashville, Bobby Kennedy trumpeted civil rights nearby at Vanderbilt University. In less than three weeks, Martin Luther King would be doing the same in Memphis. In two months' time, both would be assassinated, throwing the country into despair.

In 1968, all of America seemed to be forced to choose sides, watching political turmoil in the streets and pointless death in Vietnam— and looking for some way to escape. Yet many artists and musicians picked up on America's emotionally heightened state and turned out their most important and unforgettable work. Even Parsons's childhood hero Elvis Presley, who had spent the decade making forgettable films, roared back musically with a critically acclaimed television special.

Vanderbilt disc jockey Randy Brooks was another wannabe songwriter who liked to hang around the halls of Columbia records. A fellow DJ at Brooks's college radio station, Earl Scruggs's son Gary, tipped him off when there was something interesting going on. Around the time the Byrds were beginning to lay down new tracks there, Brooks got a tip Simon and Garfunkel were also recording at Columbia. He headed down to check it out.

"I guess it was a simpler time," recalled Brooks. "Because you could go over at midnight and walk in the back door of the studio." That night Brooks witnessed music history taking shape right in front of him: "Paul Simon was standing in the hall teaching Charlie McCoy the bass harmonica part he wanted for 'The Boxer.'" McCoy is a studio legend who played with Dylan, Elvis, and Roy Orbison. Brooks would soon have a front-row seat to watch the Byrds make history.

On Saturday March 9, McGuinn, Hillman, Parsons, and drummer Kevin Kelley began their historic sessions in Columbia's Studio A. The Byrds brought a case of Portuguese wine and enough pot to take the edge off the tension their presence created. "That was the first time I saw the studio lit up with marijuana smoke," recalled steel player Lloyd Green. At 10 a.m. the Byrds came in and broke the awkward silence by announcing the first song they planned to record: Dylan's "You Ain't Goin' Nowhere."

Green replied, "Great, great, how do you want me to approach it on steel? Where do you want me to play?" They responded in unison, "Everywhere." Green's joyful hook at the beginning of the song is one of its most recognizable aspects.

"You Ain't Goin' Nowhere" has become emblematic of the Byrds' country period. Many artists have covered it, most memorably McGuinn and Hillman themselves on the Nitty Gritty Dirt Band's transcendent 1989 tribute album, *Will the Circle Be Unbroken: Volume II*. This album embraces the idioms of traditional country, bluegrass, and other hybrid forms of music, with old-schoolers like Roy Acuff singing alongside so-called country rockers.

The Byrds' second recording was the wistful song Gram had written with Bob Buchanan on the train a couple of months previously, "Hickory Wind." It's Gram's debut as the Byrds' lead voice on record. The song features multi-instrumentalist and Grammy-winner John Hartford on fiddle.

Originally, McGuinn revealed, Gram's lyrics to the third verse of "Hickory Wind" included the line:

It's a hard way to find out,
The devil is real.

In place of "the devil" Gram substituted "trouble."

With the Byrds, on Saturday March 9, 1968, Parsons had recorded two country-rock classics in one day—not bad for a kid just four months past his twenty-first birthday.

Thanks to Columbia's influence, the band was invited to appear Friday night, March 15, at the Ryman Auditorium, home of the Grand Ole Opry. In the world of country music, it doesn't get bigger than that. Not only were the Byrds the first rock act to record in Nashville, they were going to be the first rock band to perform on its grandest and most revered stage. That day, the Byrds finished the last of eight songs they'd recorded in Nashville: "Nothing Was Delivered," another unreleased Dylan track.

Being from Chicago, McGuinn said the Opry's mystique was lost on him. The Grand Ole Opry, the mother church of country music, was "just another gig." But not to Gram Parsons. "He was blown away to be there," McGuinn remembered. "And his grandmother was listening to the show on the radio."

A Byrds fan and not much into country, college journalist Randy Brooks was disappointed to hear Gary Scruggs was going to interview the Byrds at their station WRVU, after the Opry performance. Brooks decided to get the jump on Scruggs, go to the Opry, and interview the Byrds for his school paper, the *Vanderbilt Hustler*.

That evening, Brooks and his photographer managed to muster enough credibility to get in the back door at the Ryman. In those days, security there was similar to Columbia's easy access. It wasn't unusual to run into one of the artists who slipped across the alley to Tootsie's Orchid Lounge. Back and forth was easy.

Before he knew it, Brooks was face to face with the new-look Byrds and their manager, Gary Usher. Brooks gravitated toward the two remaining original members: McGuinn and Hillman. When he asked them about Crosby's departure, both rolled their eyes and said "dear old David" was probably "out sailing" somewhere.

Brooks's recollections of then-unknown Gram Parsons remain vivid: "The endearing memory I have is this young, fresh-faced kid so happy to be where he was at the time. Talking to him, it was almost like he wasn't a member of the band. He was just another kid like me, easy to talk to, not pretentious." Gram could not contain the pleasure of performing on country's biggest stage in front of Coon Dog's family in Tennessee. "He just seemed like a kid that was just so thrilled with it all. It's like somebody making it through the first round of *American Idol*."

In the Ryman's dingy, unadorned backstage before the performance, Brooks watched Parsons hold court with three cousins. He was all smiles—and no wonder. He'd just wrapped up a week of recording at Columbia and was about to be part of the new "country Byrds" rollout. It was his vision that helped bring them to this new and historic stage in their careers.

With his pageboy haircut, simple long-sleeve sweater, and down-home way about him, Parsons looked more like Huck Finn living the dream of every young southern musician, standing in the shadows of Opry greatness: Hank Williams, Ernest Tubb, Johnny Cash, Roy Acuff, Loretta Lynn, Patsy Cline, Charlie and Ira Louvin, and country music's patron saints.

And here were the older Byrds who had topped the pop charts twice, only now without a hint of pretense, glitz, or irony, wagering their previous success to come here. For them it was all about showing respect for a genre of music most of their contemporaries still considered un-cool. There were no rhinestone suits to hide behind, no California coolness or attitude—just pure country.

To some in the audience, that was the problem: How did they know the Byrds weren't coming to the Opry as some sort of stoned-out hippie joke? And weren't they part of the Left Coast, draft dodging, drug taking, free-loving pinkos who were corrupting the country's youth?

"I picked up on a tension," Brooks said. "The audience was not into this at all."

At one moment they were cheering for the Glaser Brothers and the girl who caught everyone's fancy, Skeeter Davis. And the next moment the audience was stone-cold silent. Someone in the crowd muttered "tweet tweet" and others told them to cut their hair. WSM's Opry show was always well-planned and there could be no surprises. The Byrds told emcee Tompall Glaser they would cover two Merle Haggard songs: "Life in Prison" and "Sing Me Back Home."

The first song fell flat. This is Parsons's account of what happened next: "Tompall Glaser said, 'And now here's Gram Parsons singing Merle Haggard's famous "Sing Me Back Home."' And I got out and my grandmother was in the audience 'cause part of my family's from Tennessee right around there. And I said, 'Instead of doin' that song I'm going to do a song I wrote for my grandmother. It's called "Hickory Wind."'" McGuinn and Hillman fell in and did their best to remember the song they'd recorded just five days before.

Gram Parsons seized the moment; he had dared to break the Opry's sacred routine. Parsons recalled the reaction: "We did that and the Glaser Brothers just flipped out and they're yelling at us and Roy Acuff was having fits. Skeeter Davis ran up after it was all over and kissed us. She was so happy someone had blown those guys off."

Much has been made of Parsons's controversial ad-lib, which was nothing more than the brainchild of a headstrong college-aged kid feeling his oats. And the Opry was a perfect place to unveil a heart-felt country song about southern childhood. "What's the big deal?" McGuinn reflected. "It wasn't a bad song to do. We did it okay, I think."

The Byrds will go down in history as the band that jumped in with both feet to bridge the country and rock divide. With his actions that night, Parsons was true to the feelings of a legion of hybrid artists who have resisted the tried-and-true Nashville way of doing things.

The website http://www.opry.com ranks the Byrds' appearance as the Opry's thirty-third most unforgettable moment, one place behind Merle Haggard's debut. Gram's decision to sing "Hickory Wind" was nothing compared to Johnny Cash's rebellious turn. In 1965, Cash dragged his microphone stand along the front of the stage and broke out the footlights, earning him the boot from the Opry. Cash's foot-light stomp ranks two spots below the Byrds' appearance as most unforgettable.

Later that night, the group traveled to Vanderbilt's WRVU for an informal interview with Gary Scruggs. Curious students crowded into the station's small confines to watch the band answer questions and play disc jockey. A caller to the station accused the Byrds of being nothing but "dirty Commies." It turns out the prankster was Chris Hillman phoning in from downstairs—his way of flipping the bird to their closed-minded Opry audience.

Earlier that week, the Byrds had tried to get some airplay for their new single on Ralph Emery's radio show. Emery refused. McGuinn and Parsons later collaborated on a scathing song about Emery called "Drug Store Truck Drivin' Man."

In Brooks's piece for the college paper, Gram said the next big sound in popular music would be "an exploitation of country music." Brooks said: "It's almost like he was predicting the arrival of the Eagles."

Brooks's review of the Opry show was generous, accurately reflecting the Byrds' toned-down country direction and the audience's lack of interest. Whoever wrote the headline obviously didn't bother to read the story: "Soft-Singing Byrds Make Opry Debut Smashing Success Here."

Years later, Brooks made his own contribution to the pantheon of American pop culture by writing the novelty song "Grandma Got Run Over by a Reindeer."

The day after their Opry appearance, the Byrds flew on to the University of Virginia for a concert. Still basking in the glow of his accomplishments the previous week, Gram hosted some Bolles students backstage.

"Well, it was nice meeting you," Gram told the boys. "Tell everyone back at Bolles to—"

"Suck?" one replied.

"Uh yeah," Gram laughed, appreciating the kind of answer he would have given at that age.

After a few more shows, it was time to head back to LA for more recording—and some hard reality about the rock world's reaction to what the Byrds thought was a step forward in their evolution. On

April 2, "You Ain't Goin' Nowhere" limped to number 74 on the U.S. charts and failed to chart at all in the United Kingdom. Still the band moved forward, finishing off its purely country album with Gram taking lead vocals on Charlie and Ira Louvin's "The Christian Life." The album would be called *Sweetheart of the Rodeo.*

Later in April, *Safe at Home* was finally released and gave Gram cause for more celebration. Commercially, it sank like a brick, but influential publications like the *Los Angeles Times* gave Gram his first critical recognition: "His voice and pen seem meant for the medium. . . . he and his cohorts have produced a successful fusion of modern ideas and C&W sounds in this album."

Less than three years after Gram hired the Dillards for his highschool graduation breakfast, banjo virtuoso Doug Dillard signed on to play a series of European dates with the newly countrified Byrds. A well-circulated bootleg recording of their May 7 performance at the Piper Club in Rome reflected their evolving sound. A reviewer for the Dutch music publication *Hitweek* said the Byrds' bad reputation as a live band was unjust: "The close harmony vocals of McGuinn and Hillman as well as their backing for Parsons' solos are extraordinary."

Upon returning to the United States, the Byrds' new country sound was well received by New York audiences at the Fillmore East. Parsons's star was on the rise, and had this stellar line-up managed to stay together, the new-era Byrds just might have ridden the country-rock wave to the same type of success they had seen as avatars of folk rock. Photos of Parsons at the Fillmore East show him decked out in black, his hair and sideburns longer; he's smiling and appears perfectly lucid, vintage GP.

In June 1968, while the country grieved the loss of another Kennedy brother, Parsons received news he'd be playing in Europe for the second time in three months. The Byrds signed on to perform at a charity concert in London the next month called "Sounds '68." Once more Doug Dillard agreed to accompany the band on their European dates. Dillard had split off from his bluegrass group in favor of exploring more progressive sounds with Gene Clark. One can only imagine what a formidable Byrds line-up that would have been with both Dillard and Clark on the tour.

On Saturday July 6, the Byrds performed at London's legendary

Roundhouse. Built as a steamship repair shed in 1846, the building had been the site of many celebrated performances. In bootleg recordings, the band sounds well-rehearsed and their harmonies are tight. A medley of songs with Gram on lead vocals in "Hickory Wind" and "Sing Me Back Home" sounds like a harbinger of the country-rock wave soon to follow in the early 1970s. The songs are well received by the British audience.

On Sunday July 7, the Byrds played at another prestigious venue, London's Royal Albert Hall. VIPs like Paul McCartney and George Harrison of the Beatles and Keith Richards, Mick Jagger, and Bill Wyman of the Rolling Stones attended. After the show Gram began a historic, albeit self-destructive friendship with Keith Richards. Career-wise, meeting the Rolling Stones may have been the worst thing that ever happened to Gram Parsons.

# ❧ 20 ❧

## The Lost Burrito Brother

As soon as Jon Corneal stepped out of his small home in Auburndale, Florida, he'd been transformed into a cosmic redneck-hippie cowboy straight out of 1969. This was part of the reason we came: to get a look at his bright orange, rhinestone-studded Nudie suit he'd been given for participating in Gram Parsons's post-Byrds group the Flying Burrito Brothers, America's archetypal country-rock band.

Each member picked out certain motifs to have displayed up and down his suit. As a tribute to his Old South roots, Corneal chose an alligator, a paddle-wheel boat, and an American flag. For his now-famous ensemble Gram Parsons chose pills, poppies, marijuana leaves, and naked women. Fire runs up his leg and a cross adorns the back of his coat. Today that iconic suit sits in a display case at the Country Music Hall of Fame in Nashville.

"By the time I got out there they had spent most of the money," Corneal said of his trip to Los Angeles in 1969. "But I did get this suit."

Why would Corneal once again follow the guy he knew would end up dropping him? It was all about dreams and money. Corneal was back in Polk County trying to make a go of community college when the call came from A&M Records to play on the Burritos' classic debut album, *The Gilded Palace of Sin*. For Corneal, the Burritos gig provided another chance to get signed as a solo recording artist. He took his first-class ticket and boarded a plane in Tampa for the West Coast. On board, Corneal set about getting crocked and preparing to chase his rock star dreams all over again.

After 1968, most of Gram Parsons's music was no longer written or recorded in the South, but it was still very much *of* the South.

Being near such a wildly famous band as the Rolling Stones turned Gram into a sycophant. For buying in to his risky musical vision, Parsons thanked the Byrds by giving in to naked ambition, immaturity, and a common lust for booze and chemicals he found in his soon-to-be-countrified soul brother, Keith Richards.

After the Byrds' Royal Albert Hall concert, Parsons seized on a chance to party with British rock-and-roll royalty. "Mick and Keith take us out to Stonehenge and we're all hanging out. It was fun," remembered McGuinn. "Went out there in their Bentleys and Rolls Royces and had to walk around in the mud. Mick pulls over in some little town and buys us all new socks and stuff. It was a really fun time." As they watched Gram following the Stones around like an enamored schoolboy, McGuinn and Hillman realized he was up to something.

Two days later, when it was time to leave on the next leg of the Byrds' tour in South Africa, Parsons informed them he wasn't going. He claimed to be taking a moral stand against apartheid: "I knew right off when I heard about it I didn't want to go. I stood firmly on my conviction." McGuinn and Hillman believed Parsons's motives to be less idealistic and more about his desire to nurture his new friendship with the Stones.

Parsons's performance at the Royal Albert Hall proved to be his last as a country Byrd. His relationship with America's most influential band of the 1960s was over almost before it started. That morning in England, the Byrds fired their headstrong sideman and flew on to Africa without him.

When the Byrds limped down to South Africa, the audiences were segregated and the tour did not go off well. "I was naive in thinking we would get to play before mixed audiences," McGuinn admitted. "We went to the press and blasted apartheid and were given death threats and everything."

For the second time in less than a year, Parsons managed to find his way out of a group before the release of the record he'd made with them. Before *Sweetheart of the Rodeo* came out, their attorney got wind of Gram's contractual issues with Lee Hazelwood. Fearing a lawsuit, the band had most of his vocals erased except for his lead on "Hickory Wind." Many years later, these vocals got restored on reissues of *Sweetheart*.

McGuinn explained that in addition to the possibility of a legal entanglement, he thought it misleading to have so many vocals on the album by someone who was no longer in the band and was only supposed to have been a sideman. The issue was not Gram's singing: "I'm the first one to say Gram sang that stuff better than I could. I didn't think I could do it better. That wasn't the motive behind it."

Released three weeks after Gram's departure, *Sweetheart* made it to number 77 in the Billboard charts. Through the passage of time, the Byrds have come to be recognized as the first major rock-and-roll group to do a full-on country record. In 2003, *Rolling Stone* ranked it number 117 of its top 500 records of all time. Fans can only wonder what more would have come from this collaboration if Parsons could just have been more focused and patient.

McGuinn acknowledges the value of Parsons's vision and the record that came from their short, historic collaboration: "I'd say *Sweetheart of the Rodeo* is the most revered Byrds album ever."

That summer Parsons connected with Keith Richards in London and later in Los Angeles. Richards credited Parsons with turning him on to two schools of country: Nashville and Bakersfield. "Keith had an affinity for country music; he really loved it," Parsons recalled. In the early 1960s, Richards schooled himself on the blues from Cosmic America; later it was Parsons contributing the country soul influence you hear on such Stones songs as "Wild Horses," "Sweet Virginia," and "Country Honk."

Keith's romantic partner, Anita Pallenberg, told Parsons about a beautiful young photographer named Andee Nathanson. Soon Gram was going to her apartment along Santa Monica Boulevard asking for a place to crash, playing the part of sad-eyed puppy dog and never talking about his trust fund. In the era before digital file sharing, Gram traveled with an armload of albums and enthusiastically preached the gospel of country. "He was beautiful, sexy, poetic and complex," Nathanson remembered.

The two listened to records, talked all night, and in the morning headed out to swap meets. In a series of historic photographs, Nathanson captured Gram at a swap meet playfully trying on an old leather flying helmet and assorted clothing. There are also intimate photos of Gram playing piano and enjoying moments of introspection. "He was discovering his sound," Nathanson said of this period. "His real personality was internal."

Nathanson photographed Gram, Keith, and Anita on a trip to the vast desert country in Joshua Tree, California. At night, the hum of nature and endless starscape provided Gram the cosmic setting to connect with the inner spirit and rekindle his interest in UFOs and metaphysics. The group took over the Joshua Tree Inn, singing soul, gospel, and country under the stars.

Parsons and a bassist from Mississippi, Chris Ethridge, started sitting in with Leon Russell, who would later become an important player in Delaney and Bonnie's band. Russell stands alone as one of the great progressive soul men of modern rock and roll, having played on sessions and performing alongside the Byrds, Sinatra, B. B. King, Clapton, Joe Cocker, and Dylan. In the summer and fall of 1968, Gram Parsons was in very good musical company.

To hear Parsons tell it, the next step in his new musical direction came when Chris Hillman showed up back in LA after the Byrds' tour of South Africa. "Finally Chris Hillman came around and said 'I'm sorry, look I didn't want to go to South Africa either. It was the wrong thing to do and I think I'll quit the Byrds and join you guys,' and I said fine." The pair appropriated a band name Gram had always liked, and in the fall of 1968 their version of the Flying Burrito Brothers was born.

Hoping to capitalize on the nascent country-rock movement, and with a bankable name like Chris Hillman on board, A&M Records signed the Flying Burrito Brothers and gave them a $20,000 advance. Gram took the boys down to Nudie Cohn's rhinestone cowboy glam factory at the corner of Victory and Vineland in North Hollywood. Gram and the Burrito Brothers' suits are now among Nudie's most recognizable, along with Elvis's $10,000 gold lamé ensemble.

Parsons and Hillman moved into their cowboy crash pad in the San Fernando Valley they christened Burrito Manor. There the two embarked on one of the most fertile and creative periods of their careers. Both were in the process of extricating themselves from troubled relationships. And both had fathers who had committed suicide: Gram was twelve when he lost his dad, Hillman sixteen. From their shared sense of sadness, cynicism, and redemption came some of Parsons's best moments as a writer.

"I was blown away," Roger McGuinn said of his reaction to the new material. "I said 'You guys have got some really great stuff here.'"

During rehearsals at Burrito Manor, Chris Ethridge mentioned to Gram, "I've got these two old melodies that I wrote back in high school that I've had for a long time. Would you be interested in helping me?" After playing what he had, Gram's response to him was short and sweet: "Hell, yes."

Rock-and-roll scenestress Pamela Des Barres had become part of the action. She was privy to the first song Parsons co-wrote with Ethridge. "Gram took my roommate, Miss Andee, and me into a little room where he played us a bleeding ballad for Nancy called 'Hot Burrito #1.' As he looked at his exquisite hands on the piano keys, Gram said, 'Sometimes I wonder where these hands come from, I keep expecting to see stitches around my wrists.'"

"Hot Burrito #1" is widely considered Parsons's most heartfelt and soul-stirring recorded performance. There's a particularly spellbinding live version of the song on a posthumous release, *Gram Parsons with the Flying Burrito Brothers, Archives Volume I*, recorded in 1969 at San Francisco's Avalon Ballroom. To Nancy, Gram sings:

I'm your toy,
I'm your old boy,
But I don't want
No one but you to love me
No, I wouldn't lie,
You know I'm not that kind of guy

"It is a killer vocal, man. He *means* it. You got chills listening to it," Chris Hillman raved.

Gram had never officially broken away from Nancy and baby Polly, who were living in Santa Barbara. "One afternoon, Nancy gaily announced that Gram had proposed to her," Des Barres wrote in her memoir. Nancy followed Gram's direction to have a wedding dress made to match his own Nudie creation. To her sadness and humiliation, Nancy found out Gram planned the wedding as a publicity stunt he hoped would get the band some recognition. He never even bothered to pay for Nancy's wedding dress.

"It was a big, awful, horrible joke . . . this is the man I loved with my immortal soul," Nancy confided to Des Barres. To the mother of his only child, Gram showed how heartless he could be. Contrary to the words of his new Burrito love ballad, in this case he *was* that kind of guy.

That episode apparently did nothing to stop the flow of creativity, pot, and cocaine at Burrito Manor. After arriving in LA and getting outfitted with his own bright orange Nudie suit, Jon Corneal became immersed. "Before you know it, I'm sleeping on the couch at Burrito Manor," he recalled. "The scene was a little heavy. They got into some extracurricular drugs I was afraid of." Corneal played drums on five tracks from the Burritos' initial offering: "Christine's Tune," "Do Right Woman," "Dark End of the Street," "My Uncle," and "Juanita." Not wanting to graduate to hard drugs, Corneal claims he left the Burritos on his own. They plugged in another ex-Byrd, Michael Clarke, and played on.

The Flying Burrito Brothers concept was closer to the idea Jim Stafford had when he advised Gram to go country. This time there was no attempt to cut their hair or adhere to Nashville standards. The Burritos brought country music out of the confines of Cosmic America and dusty Bakersfield bars, applying a hip LA aesthetic and attitude. The band's secret weapon was "Sneaky" Pete Kleinow on steel guitar. Parsons, Hillman, and Ethridge wrote songs reflecting the band's expansive, genre-bending sound.

A decade before the Eagles' "Life in the Fast Lane" rebuked the shallow, drug-fueled, narcissistic West Coast lifestyle, Parsons and Hillman did the same in "Sin City":

This old town's filled with sin,
It'll swallow you in,
If you've got some money to burn

At the time, no one knew the hard reality of the rock-and-roll lifestyle better than Gram's buddy Bob Buchanan. By 1969, he'd gone all
the way up the substance abuse ladder. By his own admission, Buchanan was strung out on heroin and on his way to certain death.
"When you're going out to a cold city, you'd better guard your warm
heart," Buchanan reflected. "When you get that whacked-out you don't
know how to act. You're crying out for help, but nobody's listening."

At a party one night, Buchanan told Parsons he was leaving for good.
"Oh, okay, where you going?" Gram replied. "Saginaw," Buchanan told
him. Gram was so loaded all he could do was feign interest and stam-
mer back, "Uh, okay." Buchanan was no longer doing what Gram was
doing, so what was the point in their friendship?

Buchanan left the Chateau Marmont on the Sunset Strip, loaded
up his VW micro van, and bid an unemotional farewell. "The ego is
not that strong," Buchanan said. "It's survival and I can't survive out
here." Through a blizzard in the Rockies, Buchanan drove and drove:
"I about froze to death." Finally, he arrived at his Mom's home in Saginaw: "I was alive, barely. I slept for two days."

Buchanan was finally and truly, "safe at home." He explained,
"That's why Gram named the album that. But he had to get back out
there, people expected him to do stuff. He expected to do that. After
people started passing away I knew I'd made the right move." Among
old friends, Buchanan had to swallow his pride. "They said 'what are
you doin' back here? I watched you on TV, you had it made,'" referring
to his days with the New Christy Minstrels. "And here I am with the
needle barely out of my arm saying, 'Oh, I got tired of it.'"

*   *   *

Gram was only beginning to step out into that abyss. Bob and Bonnie
Parsons had settled in New Orleans, got married, and had to deal with
myriad family issues including a teen-aged wild child, Little Avis.

"She got pretty heavy into partying, the underside of New Orleans,"
recalled daughter Avis Johnson Bartkus. "Then she met my biological

father." Little Avis ran away with and married a man thirteen years her senior—a Tulane University professor who performed illegal abortions on the side. By the time Bob and Bonnie found her in Colorado, she was eighteen, pregnant, and hooked on drugs herself. In an attempt to save her, Bob had her committed to a psychiatric hospital. She was still there nine months later.

"Then one morning, I woke up in a different frame of mind," Little Avis wrote. "I went through the following event as if it were a dream." She sold her guitar to a boy down the hall for fifty dollars, asked to be let out to mail some letters, and headed for the bus station. Coon Dog's family in Tennessee was willing to take her in. She got off the bus hungry, poor, in labor, but most important—free. "I was home," she remembered. "Two days later my daughter, Avie, was born." Little Avis credited Avie for saving her from a life of addiction and despair.

Through all the turmoil, Bob's own drinking and partying had not subsided. Everywhere she turned, Bonnie Parsons had crisis and substance-abuse problems to deal with.

*   *   *

Gram turned a blind eye to family problems as he toured the Burritos' debut album on a cross-country train trip. In rare film footage from the tour, it's obvious the boys did more than their share of poker playing and drugs, showing up for gigs looking resplendent in their Nudie regalia and sounding woefully unrehearsed. *The Gilded Palace of Sin* only sold around 40,000 copies. Gram's vision was again too far ahead of its time. It didn't help that many of the group's live shows reflected his lack of discipline.

Frustrated by the album's lack of success, Ethridge departed and Hillman moved to playing bass. To fill in on guitar, Hillman lured back to California his old buddy from the Scottsville Squirrel Barkers, Bernie Leadon. In 1968, Leadon had co-written one of Gene Clark's most memorable songs, "Train Leaves Here This Mornin'," for *The Dillard and Clark Expedition*. He'd also done studio work with soon-to-be-famous, Linda Ronstadt.

Back in Florida, Bernie Leadon's younger brother Tom was in a band called Mudcrutch with future superstar Tom Petty. "We started listening to the first Flying Burrito Brothers album and just loved it,"

Tom Leadon remembered. "Nobody in Florida was doing anything like that. They didn't understand why these longhaired rock musicians would be playing this truck-stop country music." When Bernie was asked to join their favorite band, Tom Leadon and Petty were thrilled.

The Burritos' debut album drew positive feedback from Bob Dylan, who said the record "knocked me out." And fellow Waycross native Stanley Booth wrote in *Rolling Stone* that the album "is about the temptation of urban life and the suffering of a man who finds himself at home neither where he came from nor in the city he has escaped to." It was an apt description of guys who were chasing their ambitions at all costs, and in Gram's case constantly being derailed by the abundant temptations and his lack of professionalism.

Some of the negative feedback had to do with the Burritos' look. Who did they think they were wearing those sequined suits and strutting around like poseurs? Parsons lamented, "They're so uptight about our sequined suits. Just because we wear sequined suits doesn't mean we think we're great, it means we think sequins are great." At authentic country bars like the Palomino Club in North Hollywood, the Burritos' wardrobe would draw merciless heckling about the boys' sexuality.

Chris Hillman remembered meeting a most interested future Eagle, Glenn Frey, from an opening act, Longbranch Pennywhistle. "Frey was in awe of Gram. He learned from Gram," Hillman told Sid Griffin. "He learned about stage presence and how to deliver a vocal, and don't think Frey wasn't in that audience studying Gram."

On February 20–23, 1969, the Burritos were in Boston to open for the Byrds in a triumphant series of shows at another legendary venue, the Boston Tea Party. Roger McGuinn invited Gram on stage to sing "Hickory Wind." His performance was praised by Jon Landau in *Rolling Stone*: "Eyes closed, Gram seemed to be entranced and in touch with his music in a way he is not with the Burritos. . . . Gram Parsons with the Byrds was beautiful on *Sweetheart of the Rodeo* and was beautiful that night."

The beginning of the end for Gram came when the Rolling Stones returned to Los Angeles. In October, the band had come to America to mix *Let It Bleed*, their latest in a string of powerhouse albums that included *Beggar's Banquet*, *Sticky Fingers*, and *Exile on Main Street*. To

Mick Jagger's chagrin, Parsons and Keith Richards started hanging out together, indulging their shared passion for old-school country music. According to Hillman, it was more important for Gram to hang out with the Stones "and play rock star games than it was to do his own thing with the Burritos."

As if to prove Hillman right, Parsons and Andee Nathanson joined Richards and Anita Pallenberg on a junket to see Elvis in Vegas. Nathanson marveled, "Gram was so excited, he was like a little kid."

With Richards, Gram enjoyed seeing just how obliterated he could get. "Gram was as knowledgeable about chemical substances as I was," Keith said. "I don't think I taught him much about drugs—I was still learning myself, much to my detriment." Gram was intermittently doing hard drugs with the likes of Bob Buchanan and Fred Neil before he and Keith became track-marked brothers in arms.

Referring to Gram's increasing abuse of drugs during this time, Buchanan commented, "We lost him then, you know? There was no turning back. He wouldn't listen to anybody."

Just as Parsons didn't need to learn about drugs from Keith, he didn't need to learn how to dress cool and impress women from Mick Jagger. Gram was so instinctively stylish, Stanley Booth, who traveled extensively with the Stones, noted Jagger was jealous and slightly intimidated by Gram.

Yet, in his performances and persona, Gram was borrowing moves from Jagger evidenced by his sad attempt to imitate him in the Burritos' 1970 video, "Older Guys." This song from the album, *Burrito Deluxe* is a kind of pop number; the Burritos' outlaw country look and Cosmic American sound is gone. The band is on a yacht yukking it up for the camera, and it's obvious no one's really having a good time. Gram has that thin, junkie face and looks more like a character from a schlock sitcom.

The only song Gram brought to *Burrito Deluxe* that was anything like the first album came from the Stones themselves. Mick gave Gram his blessing to record "Wild Horses" as long as the Burritos didn't release it as a single. Many have speculated Parsons actually co-wrote this song. In his biography, Richards acknowledged he and Parsons did do some writing together, but he has denied speculation Gram actually penned the song.

Parsons was on his way to becoming the lost Burrito Brother, more likely to be found hanging around at the Stones' recording sessions than fulfilling his own obligations with the Burritos or advancing his Cosmic American vision.

It was during one of these Rolling Stones sessions that Gram met a sixteen-year-old aspiring actress named Gretchen Burrell, the daughter of LA news anchor Larry Burrell. Gram was smitten with her long, blond hair and waifish physique. "She soon took up residence with Gram at the Chateau Marmont, sliding comfortably into his chaotic, stoned-out life," Pamela Des Barres wrote.

In December 1969, the Rolling Stones offered Parsons and the Burritos an opening slot for their free show at California's Altamont Speedway. The Burritos are briefly shown in "Gimme Shelter," the Maysles brothers' documentary of the Stones' tour, adding a few peaceful early vibes to what turned into a violent, bloody nightmare. A gun-wielding man near the stage was bludgeoned to death by a member of the motorcycle gang Hell's Angels, who'd been brought in to provide of all things, security. True to form, Parsons escaped into an overloaded helicopter with the Stones and their entourage, leaving his bandmates to fend for themselves.

The new decade began as badly as the old one ended. After his old friend Peter Fonda's film *Easy Rider* became a hit, Gram and a generation of twenty-something males bought their own choppers and tried to imitate Fonda's Captain America character. "Gram's chopper was pure redneck—buckskin seats, fringe hanging down. The front fender was loose and he had rigged it together with a coat hanger," John Phillips wrote. During a ride with Phillips through Bel Air, Gram lost control and ended up splayed out on the street: "Blood was everywhere."

"I brought Gram flowers in the hospital and didn't recognize him," Pamela Des Barres remembered. "His face was a puffy, purple balloon. I worried hard that Gram was trying to keep up with his friend Keith and didn't have the constitution."

After Parsons's injuries healed, he took another half-hearted stab at rejoining his band. Gram's behavior led to a jarring confrontation: during a Burritos gig, at a place called the Brass Ring, bandmates Chris Hillman and Michael Clarke had had enough. "It got to the point where we couldn't work with him," Hillman recalled. "Michael and I said, 'Out!'" Hillman said he broke Gram's guitar in lieu of punching him in the face.

Parsons was thrown out of parties, pitied by his peers, and with less luck might have died even earlier. The sixties were over, and shooting stars were about to start falling: Janice Joplin, Jimi Hendrix, and Jim Morrison.

"It was peer pressure, a macho thing," Roger McGuinn explained about the prevalent drug scene of the late 1960s and early 1970s. "We all started fairly innocently with pot and then a couple of pills and then cocaine came along. And with cocaine you're into white powders." That's how they started snorting heroin too, McGuinn said.

In the notebook Parsons kept, he jotted down tunes he planned to record on a solo album. They included Roy Orbison's "Sweet Dream Baby," Phil and Don Everly's, "Sleepless Nights," and at the top of his list the song most true to where Gram's life was at that point, Hank Cochran and Harlan Howard's, "I Fall to Pieces." Thanks to his worsening substance abuse problems and devastating motorcycle accident, this first solo attempt was never completed.

Bob Parsons's wife Bonnie told *Crawdaddy!*: "Bob was one of those people who said 'If you need help, come home,' which Gram did at least once a year. Sometimes he'd come home to get the monkey off his back, as they say. He'd be so thin, with a stubble of a beard—which he never *could* grow—and I'd get him to bed and put good food in him."

\*   \*   \*

In 1971, to escape tax problems in England, the Rolling Stones relocated to the South of France. For the recording of "Exile on Main Street," Richards rented a sprawling chateau on the French Riviera, Villa Nellcôte, a former Nazi World War II headquarters. Having nothing better to do, Gram and Gretchen accepted an invitation to become part of the Stones' traveling circus.

Gram and Keith listened to country music, jammed, and grew closer. An only child, Richards said his friendship with Parsons seemed "ancient" from the beginning. "It was like a reunion with a long-lost brother for me," Richards wrote. Gram convinced himself Keith would produce his solo album for the Rolling Stones' new label.

The blossoming friendship bothered Jagger. Parsons's needling of the Stones' front man didn't help either. Photographs show Gram and Keith lounging like twin viceroys of music and overindulgence. Mick looks bored.

With Gram around and the heroin supply plentiful, Keith was often tempted to stay wasted and not work. The place was overrun with druggie hangers-on leaching off the Stones' fame. Tension was high while the Stones struggled to make their basement recordings at the villa take shape. Gretchen had been telling Gram to take the hint from Jagger and get out. Finally, the Stones left it up to their staff to let Gram know it was time to go.

The Stones were giving Parsons the same kind of treatment he was used to dishing out to those who were no longer useful to him. Rudderless and depressed, Gram returned to Britain, rekindling a friendship he'd made in 1968 with Ric Grech, former member of Family and Blind Faith whose own addictions had gotten him sacked.

At the time, Grech was making a record with Sam Hutt, a singing doctor whose real name was Hank Wangford. According to Wangford, Parsons was in the throes of a nearly lethal heroin addiction. "I'd be called 'round the house in an emergency. That happened three times. He'd be on the lav or sitting in a chair going blue. Once he was lying there with the needle hanging out of his arm, really terminal, really getting himself to the edge, and we'd always pull him back."

Slowly, Parsons began to come up with ideas for a new solo record. Ric Grech's wife Jenny described Parsons during this up-and-down period as "genteel, polite, well-mannered, well-educated, sympathetic, spiritual—and totally mad as well. He and Rick were a lethal combination."

Thanks to the Greches and Parsons's long-suffering friends from the Burrito Brothers, Gram ended his wandering in Europe and refocused on his Cosmic American ambitions. His attempt to get himself back on track started with a proposal of marriage to his young girlfriend Gretchen. His career would revive when he met another woman who became in every way his musical soul mate.

# ❧ 21 ❧

## Like a Bird

In South Austin, Texas, there's a sign commemorating a long-gone live music venue called the Armadillo World Headquarters. Located in a parking lot on South First Street and Barton Springs Road, the sign has pictures of what the old concert hall used to look like. It was nothing more than a cavernous old armory building with some very cool artwork and a beer garden. "Remember the Armadillo" the sign reads, "the music, art and spirit of Austin flourished here."

Beginning in August 1970 until its final show on New Year's Eve 1980, the Armadillo was home to an eclectic mix of cowboys and hippies, shamans and shit-kickers. Music legends and up-and-coming pioneers made the Armadillo a regular stop, among them Van Morrison, Frank Zappa, Commander Cody, Charles Mingus, Janis Joplin, Count Basie, Bruce Springsteen, and ZZ Top. The Armadillo was ground zero for Austin's emergence as a world-class live-music destination, manifested in later years by the *Austin City Limits* television show and the South by Southwest Music Conference and Festival.

It's also another historic stopping-off point in Gram Parsons's Cosmic American journey. He'd begun to cobble together a solo career thanks in large part to an unknown folk singer from Birmingham,

Alabama, named Emmylou Harris. The duo's live shows in Austin and Houston's Liberty Hall were the largest and best-received on their short tour in early 1973.

During a concert here at the Armadillo, Gram began to see that in this region, his idea of bringing together under one roof such disparate groups of fans could work; these artists didn't have to adhere to a set standard established by the power brokers in Nashville and Los Angeles. You might call them outlaws. They included a songwriter from Abbott, Texas, who'd been struggling to carve out his own identity as a performer, Willie Nelson.

"I started hanging out at the Armadillo—there was a lot of young people around," Nelson remembered. "I thought, listen, we can try out some Hank Williams here. So I started playing there and, sure enough, they were big country fans. There were guys doing it already, like Gram Parsons."

There's a strange duality about Gram's music at the time. Those who played with him on the tour insist it was much more genuine steel and fiddle country music than was coming out of Nashville. Yet because of Gram's lyrics and long hair, he was still considered progressive.

The Armadillo came down in the 1980s to make way for a giant complex called One Texas Center. But at least the people of Austin had enough foresight to commemorate the importance of what happened here.

\*　　\*　　\*

Gram and Gretchen planned a cowboy wedding for September 13, 1971, to be held at Bob and Bonnie Parsons's house on Pine Street in New Orleans. In a 1985 interview, Gretchen said New Orleans was "where we really wanted to make our home." One of the few friends Gram thought to invite was Reverend Jet Thomas from his Harvard days, who he asked to conduct the ceremony. Little Avis was there with her baby girl everyone called "Avie."

Gram's stepsister Becky attended with her husband and toddler. "I remember it being fun, but also feeling like Gram was not himself," Becky said. "I can remember talking about how bizarre it was that they planned to go to Disney World for their honeymoon."

In photos from the wedding, Gram has a mustache, wears a bolo tie, and looks like a heavier wax figure of himself. Gretchen is the beautiful young prairie bride. In the absence of many invitees from the bride and groom, Bob and Bonnie filled the place with their own family and friends. For the first time, Gram was a married man.

In a letter to his Bolles School buddy Frank David Murphy, Gram described Gretchen's sometimes mercurial personality: "She is a beautiful young blond girl I met while I was being a rock and roll star. She's in high school . . . what a drag! She still isn't 21 . . . fights with bouncers, bartenders, club owners. . . . These 'honks' are where I've been doing my research for some years now."

While Parsons was trying to get his life back together, Chris Hillman hired a singer out of Clearwater, Florida, Rick Roberts, to round out the Burritos lineup. During this period, the band became a better live act and produced some good songs. Former Byrd Gene Clark contributed a couple of radio-ready pop ballads with some nice harmonies called "Here Tonight" and "Tried So Hard." Bernie Leadon departed for a new musical venture.

At different periods throughout 1971, Leadon, Glenn Frey, Randy Meisner, and a Texas-born drummer named Don Henley had worked as backing musicians for Linda Ronstadt. In early 1972, David Geffen signed them to his new Asylum label as the Eagles. From that humble, country-rock lineup morphed the band that sold tens of millions of albums and conquered the world of arena and stadium shows.

Chris Hillman decided to team up with superstar Stephen Stills. Their band, Manassas, also pursued a more straightforward country-rock blend. Before the Burritos folded the tent, they had a couple more gigs along the East Coast. Once again showing his ability to forgive and forget, Hillman called Parsons in New Orleans and asked if he'd like to sit in.

"I said sure, why not, cause Byron Berline was there and a bunch of guys that played bluegrass and stuff and I thought it'd be fun," Parsons said.

Around that time, an old friend from Washington, D.C., called Rick Roberts who was in town with the Burritos, and told him about a female singer performing at a club in Georgetown. "When I heard her, I called Chris Hillman at the hotel and told him to get over there,"

Roberts recalled. Both shared with Parsons their impressions about the singer, named Emmylou Harris. "We told him about her—raving," Roberts recalled.

A raven-haired southern beauty with sultry eyes, Harris had done one album that went nowhere, but she still maintained a strong work ethic. At the time members of the Burritos saw her, she was a solo folk singer at a Georgetown bar called Clyde's. "I was the jaded, cynical, old 25-year-old. I'd had a baby and a broken marriage and I'd worked as a waitress and I'd been on food stamps," she recalled. She'd heard Parsons's name but wasn't impressed. When he phoned her to come get him in Baltimore, her response was abrupt: "I said 'Excuse me, I have to work tonight. You can take the train—I'll pick you up at the train station.' I can't believe I had the moxie to do that."

In her tiny Ford Pinto, Harris drove to the train station in Washington, D.C., to pick up someone she knew only as a voice on the phone. "The funny thing is," Harris said, "that night, somebody rear-ended me. I'm surprised I didn't go up in flames. That was the beginning of the relationship with Gram."

Parsons was out to see if Harris could cut it as a country singer. There in her kitchen, for the first time the two joined voices: "So I thought of one of the hardest country duets I could think of to do which was 'That's All It Took' and she just sang like a bird. And I said 'That's it.' The rest of the night she just kept getting better and better." Harris followed Gram's vocal lead by watching his eyebrows go up or down.

Harris told a different story: she said the duo first sang together at Clyde's. Nonetheless, their historic but short-lived collaboration was born. Gram Parsons hadn't just gotten lucky, he'd won the lottery. Parsons's counterpart had the kind of charisma and star power that had been lacking with his prior collaborators.

In 1971, one of the most successful country-pop chart artists of the decade, former folkie John Denver, had a hit with the anthemic "Take Me Home, Country Roads." The Nitty Gritty Dirt Band also enjoyed pop success with Jerry Jeff Walker's bluegrass ballad, "Mr. Bojangles." More important, for the first time the band brought together in Nashville a divergent group of country, bluegrass, and hybrid artists young and old for their acclaimed album *Will the Circle Be Unbroken* volume one. Just three years prior, when the Byrds got an icy reception at the Opry, such an album would have been unlikely—if not impossible.

In 1972, the Eagles came out of the gate quickly with Jackson Browne's "Take It Easy," and Linda Ronstadt covered Johnny Cash and Patsy Cline on her solo record. Many artists seemed to be capitalizing on Gram's vision except for Gram himself. In a letter to Frank David Murphy, he lamented what his vision was becoming: "I've some sort of 'rep' for starting what (I think) has turned out to be pretty much of a 'country rock' (ugh!), plastic dry—fuck. Excuse the strong language."

Mo Austin of Reprise Records gave Gram the chance to make his own solo statement. At the time, Gram was weaning himself off heroin but still drinking heavily and gaining weight. His first two choices to produce the album, Keith Richards and Merle Haggard, bowed out. His next pick was Ric Grech, but Grech had a kidney stone; he would end up doing some work on the album uncredited. It would be the better part of a year after Gram and Emmylou met before she finally got her phone call and plane ticket to come to LA.

Just like when he was sixteen and hired the best sideman he could find in Bobby Braddock, Gram went to Las Vegas and convinced members of Elvis's band to play on his first solo album. After years of creating fictional ties to Presley, this one Parsons didn't have to conjure. He was using Presley's musicians to make his first true solo record.

Glen Hardin from Wellington, Texas, assumed the role of musical director. Minden, Louisiana, native James Burton on guitar and Dobro had played with Ricky Nelson, wrote the song "Suzy Q," and provided the distinctive intros to Elvis classics like "Suspicious Minds." Fiddler Byron Berline hailed from a little Kansas border town and had played with the Rolling Stones at Gram's urging. Elvis's drummer, Ronnie Tutt, was from Dallas, Texas. Rounding out the roster of Cosmic American all-stars, Birmingham, Alabama, native Emmylou Harris would become nothing less than Parsons's vocal soul mate. An old friend from the pre–Sub Band days, Barry Tashian, provided important contributions on guitar and vocals.

In September 1972, along with multi-Grammy-Award-winning engineer Hugh Davies, the musicians gathered at Wally Heider Studio 4 in Hollywood to start laying down tracks. On her first trip to the West Coast, Harris walked around wide-eyed, having no idea what to expect. "We had a fantastic band, they were consummate musicians," Harris remembered. "Gram brought out a sense of camaraderie in people. He enjoyed what he was doing. He was such a nice guy." From a safe distance of decades, Harris was remembering her mentor at his best when, in truth, Parsons was a wreck.

Gram came into the studio a stoned-out, drunken mess, too wasted to play. It didn't help that the honeymoon with Gretchen was over and his life with her was becoming more volatile. Due to his drunkenness, Gram had been thrown out of Chris Hillman's birthday party by the guest of honor himself. At a party thrown by John Phillips, Gram passed out at the piano, recalled Phillips in his memoir.

Gram looked to be on his way to doing exactly what he told Jon Corneal he wouldn't: following his mother's alcoholic path to an early grave. It took a come-to-Jesus session with friends for Parsons to realize he was pissing away his first and perhaps only shot to make the kind of record he'd always wanted. He cut down on the substance abuse enough to function in the studio.

What ensued over the next month turned out to be a moody, beautiful array of songs. With a female counterpart, Parsons could touch on a deeper range of emotion than his previous work with the Burritos. Byron Berline's rousing fiddle on the opening track, "Still Feeling Blue," signaled the record's strong country direction. James Burton's comfy-as-a-featherbed Dobro underscores Emmylou's first lead vocal with Gram on the tale of forbidden love, "We'll Sweep out the Ashes."

Parsons's fragile voice reflects world-weariness in the next track, "A Song for You." Chris Ethridge has been quoted describing Gram's "soulful, help me" voice. Nowhere is that quality more evident than here:

Take me down, to your dance floor
I won't mind the people, when they stare

The next song, "Streets of Baltimore," was co-written by Harlan Howard and Tompall Glaser, the same guy who introduced the Byrds at the Opry and got so furious when Gram ad-libbed "Hickory Wind." There's Gram's bluesy side on "She." Emmylou's audition song, "That's All It Took," feels like her coming-out party on the record. Another classic, Gram's "The New Soft Shoe," has a spot-on, mood-setting instrumentation. The record ends with a final James Burton guitar-driven rave-up, another Gram original, "Big Mouth Blues."

For her work Emmylou made a cool five hundred bucks and bought a sweet new Martin guitar. In the ensuing weeks, she said she wondered if the record would ever come out. Gram wrote about his satisfaction with the record, which he planned to call "*GP.*" "There's plenty of boogie on GP—I keep my love for variations. I do love the album and all the guys (and 1 girl Emmylou Harris) I'm working with now."

Gone was the need to hide behind a rhinestone suit. Gram's vision of Cosmic American music had taken a big step forward. Harris told Holly George-Warren about the significance of that accomplishment: "Gram's writing brought his own personal generation's poetry and vision into the very traditional format of country music, and he came up with something completely different."

At the end of 1972, Gram turned his attention to putting together a touring band. Fortunately, he passed on the first name that came to mind, the Turkeys, settling on the Fallen Angels. They were booked on a circuitous six-week journey through Colorado, Texas, Chicago, up the East Coast, and into New York. Gretchen came along for the ride. Phil Kaufman, whom Gram had met through the Rolling Stones in 1969 and had fired as the Burritos' road manager, was now back in the fold.

Kaufman called an old-school Nashville steel-guitar player Neil Flanz in hopes of hiring him for the tour. Flanz had played the Opry many times with greats like Charlie Louvin, but he had no idea who Gram Parsons was. "When I played with our group that night and mentioned the offer to go on Gram's tour, our keyboard player said 'Grab it!'" Flanz chuckled. "I was on a plane to LAX the next day."

Jon Corneal drove out to Los Angeles to fill in during rehearsals until drummer N. D. Smart could get on board. At Phil Kaufman's place, Corneal took a shine to a jacket Kaufman was wearing: Gram's old Nudie coat worn in the Sub Band's fleeting cameo in Peter Fonda's film, *The Trip*. It's a Nudie Cohn classic, resplendent with submarines, torpedoes, and rhinestones.

"You really like that jacket, don't you?" Gram asked Corneal. "You can have it." Perhaps this was Gram's peacemaking gesture for all the times he'd dropped Corneal. Decades later, holding the coat at his Auburndale home Corneal said, "I'd let it go for seventy-five thousand."

As the debut of what was billed "Gram Parsons and the Fallen Angels Tour" grew closer, Emmylou Harris was concerned Parsons was doing more partying than rehearsing. Gram was hitting the bottle again. "The drinking did bother me," Harris remembered. "But when you're really young, you don't think that you or anyone you know that age is really in any trouble. I was naïve about it."

Hard reality was waiting in Boulder, Colorado, where the band was booked for the tour's opening three-night stand. Parsons was wrecked and the first show a disaster. "We just didn't learn the intros or any particular structure to the songs on the GP album," Flanz recalled. "I think the state of consciousness was such that we weren't at all worried. It was pretty grim." Out in the audience was one of Gram's first girlfriends from Winter Haven, Donna Class, whom he had not seen since New York in 1966. She joined him backstage.

"He was doing cocaine and drinking," Class said with some sadness in her voice. When he pulled a key out of a vial loaded with powder and offered it to Class, she declined. In response Gram told her, "You always were a lady." Backstage in Boulder was the last time the two childhood friends spoke.

Hearing how badly the tour started, executives at Warner Brothers, who were funding the tour, considered pulling the plug. By the third show, the group had discovered a guitarist named Jock Bartley, who would later team up with Rick Roberts to form Firefall. In hopes of adding a little more structure, Warner Brothers made drummer N. D. Smart bandleader and hired Bartley for the rest of the tour. The Fallen Angels were given the okay to go on to Texas, but if there were more reports of bad shows and erratic behavior, there's little doubt Gram's inconsistent performances could have meant an end to it all.

"As for Boulder, that was a disaster, but we got things straightened out by doing some serious rehearsing," remembered Flanz. February 21, 1973, the afternoon the Fallen Angels pulled into Austin, Texas, they had permission to rehearse at the evening's venue, the Armadillo World Headquarters. "We did some serious woodshedding"—practicing until they got it right—Flanz said.

The Fallen Angels could not have found a better venue for their first Texas gig. Located at 525 ½ Barton Springs Road in South Austin, the Armadillo World Headquarters was founded by a group of local artists and writers who liked to call themselves Mad Dog Inc. The old armory building had been transformed into a post-hippie haven with large murals on the walls and a sprawling space for more than 2,000 concert-goers. The venue had high, arched ceilings, a concrete floor, cinder block walls, and lousy acoustics. The Armadillo was the perfect place for disaffected college kids away from home for the first time to find a new sense of community. Crowds welcomed musicians like Willie Nelson and later, Waylon Jennings, artists who didn't fit into the Nashville mode, didn't care, and weren't about to compromise.

To promote the show, Gram was booked for an interview at Austin's KOKE radio station. Deejay Rusty Bell was a big promoter of "progressive" country artists, but Gram and Emmylou weren't about to accept that label. She quickly corrected Bell and said they were playing "regressive country." Neil Flanz agreed: "Most of the GP album was hard-core country with hip lyrics. Nashville was countrypolitan."

Gram seemed content to play what he called "card tricks on the radio," answering Bell's questions with silent head nods for yes or no. When the station's Emergency Broadcast System box kept squawking, Bell said he didn't know what to do. Parsons yanked the contraption out of the wall.

That night a large audience turned out at the Armadillo. For Parsons, this was finally validation of his vision. Backstage, photographer Burton Wilson snapped a series of photos of the band warming up; Jock Bartley sat to the far side tuning his guitar.

"It was just minutes before my first gig with them," Bartley recalled. "That was the gig and little tour that followed that propelled my entire career and life, frankly." Before a crowd of fifteen hundred or more screaming hippies, the Fallen Angels gave a tight, focused performance.

Bartley knew that first night something special was happening: "I had a realization on stage that night about life-changing opportunities and about jumping through the window of opportunity when, if you're lucky, it opens for you."

"It was an amazing feeling, it really was," Neil Flanz marveled. "I think everyone in the band was elated." To a steel player accustomed to appearing before staid crowds, the Armadillo was a revelation: "They were heading towards the stage trying to touch us. I'd never seen anything like it." Flanz credited Gram's charisma.

After the Armadillo World Headquarters triumph in Austin, the group was booked for a four-night stand at Houston's Liberty Hall. That's where Gram, Emmylou, and superstar-on-the-rise Linda Ronstadt met up with a group of kindred spirits who called themselves the Sin City Boys.

By the early 1970s, contemporary music was in a funk. Stars like Joplin, Hendrix, and Morrison died. The Beatle splintered and rock and roll was going through a kind of metamorphosis needed once in a while to rejuvenate fans and rekindle their passion for live shows. The country wave provided a new direction. Plenty of former folkies were getting on the bandwagon.

The infusion of young country-rock artists brought a new excitement to Liberty Hall, Houston's premier underground concert venue located at 1610 Chenevert Street. After it opened in 1971, Chris Hillman's final lineup of the Burritos had come through town. The following year, Hillman and Stills appeared there with Manassas. Soon after, country rock kings-in-waiting Bernie Leadon and the Eagles, played live at Liberty Hall. A small but boisterous group of Burrito Brothers devotees would bombard the offshoot bands with requests for "Sin City."

The so-called Sin City Boys were a group of college-aged guys who met up at one of the city's influential places for new music, Disc Records. "College wasn't working out," remembered one of the group's charter members, Bob Webb. "Girls, beer, smoking dope, and listening to music were about all I needed." Webb, along with store manager Larry Sepulvado and a few others, decided it would be cool to come up with a Sin City patch and fly it like biker gang-colors.

During the sound check this loose confederation of Houston hellraisers walked in wearing their Sin City-emblazoned jackets. Gram had on a loose-fitting shirt, blue jeans, and "hair tousled as if he had just woke up," recalled Sepulvado. He wore a pair of turquoise bracelets and looked a little too West Coast for this down-home group of shit kickers. "In one hand he held a bottle of bourbon, which was communally passed around as the conversation progressed," remembered one of the Sin City stalwarts named Nimrod Funk.

Gram seemed puzzled about what these guys were doing and who they were, but he was happy to get a Sin City patch and assured the boys he would have it put on his jacket. When the group hit him up to play his old Burritos standard, Gram confessed the Fallen Angels hadn't rehearsed it. "But stranger things have happened in the past," he hinted.

"He really appreciated our recognition and praise of his latest effort, GP. We didn't talk too long, maybe ten minutes," Funk wrote. "But in that short time a real bond of friendship was established." Gram was needed backstage and the Sin City crew moved into front-row seats, where they held court for the entire four-night stand.

A sixteen-year-old songwriter from San Antonio, Steve Earle was another country-rock devotee who ran away from home to attend the Liberty Hall gigs. Earle, like many of the young men in the audience, became smitten with the lady on stage singing alongside Gram. At times, Parsons and Harris performed very close together, their microphones practically touching. There was obvious sexual tension between the two, much to Gretchen's chagrin.

After the Friday night show, the Fallen Angels' tour-bus driver took off and left Gram and Gretchen behind. The band of Sin City brothers quickly offered the two a ride back to the Plaza Hotel in their old blue Chevy station wagon. "As we pulled away from Liberty Hall the muffler nearly scraped off," said Funk. Gram was tipsy and kept asking to go to the Old Quarter club to see Townes Van Zandt.

After finding out it was too late to see another show, the group dropped the young couple at their hotel. "The image of Gram and Gretchen standing on the steps of the Plaza is still with me, had a touch of romance to it," wrote Funk. "The lighting was just right, the Plaza was just right. It was another wonderful ending to a fantastic evening." But Gram had yet to sing "Sin City."

That all changed on Saturday night. With the front row Sin City contingent now twenty strong, after the first set Gram retreated backstage and wrote out the lyrics to "Sin City" on a sheet of paper. In front of the jam-packed, 400-capacity hall, Gram strode out onstage to begin the second set. Emmylou walked out accompanied by Linda Ronstadt, who was in town opening for Neil Young. It was the first time the two women had met.

With Gram leading the way sporting his new Sin City colors and Harris and Ronstadt singing the lyrics he'd scribbled out, they broke into an impromptu version of the long-awaited song. "The Sin City Gang rose in unison as if the national anthem was being played," remembered Funk. "When the notes faded away, there was an uproar that just wouldn't quit."

After the show, two of the boys from the front row took the jackets off their backs and presented them to Harris and Ronstadt. In later years, Ronstadt wore the jacket in an Annie Leibovitz photo shoot for *Rolling Stone*. One of the last pictures of Gram and Emmy together included her Sin City jacket.

The last night of the historic Houston appearances, with Gram's permission, the Sin City group presented Emmylou with yellow roses as a thank-you for honoring their long-awaited song request. Gram received a bottle of champagne. "Now this group of boys goin' around causin' trouble just decided tonight to start spreading a little love around Liberty Hall," Gram joked on stage. "They're wonderful."

Gram announced another special guest in the audience: "We have Mr. Neil Young with us tonight. Besides Neil Young we have Miss Linda Ronstadt. And they make a pretty fair couple." Young spent most of the night by the side of the stage. To have Neil Young in the audience was further validation of Gram's growing status as a solo artist. It all came together in Texas.

Also that Sunday night, a group from a place appropriately called "Space City Video" recorded the performance. For years, that videotape was lost to posterity. In the late 1980s, Sepulvado finally tracked it down. "A local record collector was keeping it in his refrigerator," he remembered. "When we took it out the tape was stuck together." Enough of it was usable for commercial release, however.

Neil Young sent a limo to take Gram and the band to his hotel. There a raucous, booze-and-drug-fueled impromptu jam session lasted until five in the morning. Gretchen—who often danced close to the stage, shouted, and competed with little luck for her husband's attention—was not invited.

At a stopover in Arkansas, the tension between Gram and Gretchen boiled over. Instead of spending time with his wife, Gram decided to play piano at the motel bar until closing time. Boiling mad, Gretchen made a scene trying to get him out. Police were later called to the couple's motel room to break up a loud argument. Drunk and angry, Gram tried to resist the cops and ended up getting hit with mace. Road manager Phil Kaufman had to bail him out of jail.

Gram and Emmylou made it their routine to hole up in the very back of the bus and work on material with acoustic guitars. In March, Gram reconnected with his Bolles School classmate and pen pal Frank David Murphy. Murphy had a chance to hang out with Gram and meet the young chanteuse with him. "I had this red, '71 Charger with Gram and Emmylou doing duets in the back seat," Murphy recalled. "That was Gram at his most gentlemanly, most gentle, just hanging out with friends, no raucousness, no wildness. I wish people could see that."

In Boston, an aspiring songwriter named Tom Brown showed up for the Fallen Angels' show at a club called Oliver's. Brown brought with him lyrics to a song he'd scribbled out in about twenty minutes: "It can't be explained, but from the moment I finished writing I knew with absolute certainty that he would write a melody and cut the song. The adventures in the song were mine, but the designations 'Grievous Angel' and the king with an amphetamine crown referred to Gram. The title came when I remembered how sad and forlorn I once saw him looking." In just a matter of months Gram fulfilled Brown's premonition and brought his lyrics to life.

The group capped its six-week tour March 9, 1973, with a well-received show at Max's Kansas City in New York City. In *Penthouse* magazine, Bud Scoppa talked about Gram and Emmylou's performance: "Together, their voices can summon the angels or the devils, and sometimes both at the same time. When they harmonize, Gram invariably stops playing his acoustic, grips the mike in both hands and he and the stand tilt over to Emmylou. He seems overjoyed at her presence."

Had this musical marriage been given time to blossom, it would have spilled over into a relationship. Emmylou admitted many years later she was on the verge of telling Gram she was falling in love with him. In Emmylou, Gram found a perfect partner—someone who knew instinctively the burning drive artists have to *create*. It's the kind of compulsion that can lead you to forsake a lot of life's important commitments, including spouses and children.

A Warner Brothers publicist told *Crawdaddy!* magazine, "Sitting in a bar after a gig were Gretchen and Gram. When Emmylou came in there was a whole change in his personality. . . . His eyes would light up."

Ginny Wynn, a Warner Brothers staff photographer, described meeting Emmylou and seeing her with Gram for the first time: "They looked like two little kids having a sleepover." More important, Gram "introduced and raved about her" to Wynn.

*   *   *

With the tour over, each artist was offered a one-way ticket anywhere in the United States. Neil Flanz went home to Nashville. His days as a Fallen Angel were over. "I've gotten more recognition for doing that six weeks of work than my entire career in Nashville," he said. Others in the band scattered for the time being, but another Parsons solo record was already in the planning stages.

Gram wanted to spend some down time with Gretchen and reconnect with family in New Orleans. In the summer of 1973, alongside the stellar group of studio musicians he hired for *GP*, Gram would reach a creative peak in his solo career and play a couple of memorable gigs. But there seemed to be nothing to keep his personal life from crashing down around him.

# ❧ 22 ❧

## Darkness and Light

In the summer of 2009, Gram Parsons's daughter, Polly Parsons, summoned the strength to break her family's cycle of addiction. In Austin, Texas, Polly opened Hickory Wind Ranch. It had taken years of pain getting past her own issues to reach the point where she could begin helping others: "By 16, I became horribly addicted to cocaine and alcohol. I never mentioned who my father was, so no one knew until I was about 25. I was terrified that my outcome would be written in stone if I acknowledged the fact that I came from people who couldn't manage to stay on the planet."

For years, Polly forbade anyone to mention her father's name or play his music in her presence. "What is it that made musicians like my father spin out of control?" she asked.

Polly was behind the wheel of her late-model Nissan, her close friend Shilah Morrow sitting in the passenger side. A reporter was with them to do a story on the place that represented Polly's new mission in life: a refuge for women in the throes of substance abuse, a new ray of hope in the corner of Cosmic America Gram's daughter was now calling home.

"You know what this place reminds me of?" Polly asked her friend.

Tipping her cowboy hat and nodding toward the house, she answered, "Joshua Tree Inn."

"Doesn't it?" Polly said. "I thought that too."

\* \* \*

In the spring of 1973, Gram and Gretchen accepted an invitation to go with Bob and Bonnie Parsons on a sailing trip to the West Indies. The weeklong voyage would give Gram's now twelve-year-old half-sister Diane a chance to spend time with the absentee brother she adored. Alcohol abuse and stress had taken a toll on Gram and his father. Bob Parsons no longer resembled the strapping bon vivant who tooled around Winter Haven in a Jag. Gram too looked haggard from the weight gain and weeks of hard work and partying on the road.

Bob and Gram clashed about the young couple bringing marijuana on the boat; Bob thought it a bad example to set in front of Diane. Like so many adults of his generation, Bob didn't consider his own boozing in the same light as pot smoking, even though his health was deteriorating.

One memorable photo from that trip shows Gram in the Grenadine Islands wearing a brimmed hat, playing acoustic guitar for a few people, and enjoying some moments of peace in a far-off tropical place.

One night on the boat, Bob finally confessed to his son that even as Big Avis lay dying, he'd brought her alcohol in the hospital. That stunning admission, and Gram and Gretchen smoking pot near young and impressionable Diane, ratcheted up the tension on board. Finally, Bob asked Gram and Gretchen to leave the boat. The confluence of events drove a wedge between Gram and his New Orleans family; they never saw each other again. "After his break with Bob, he was never the same," Gretchen told filmmaker Gandulf Hennig, "His joy was gone."

Bob Parsons's daughter Becky said that her father never meant to cut off Gram and Gretchen; it was merely Bob's attempt at "tough love."

\* \* \*

Not a moment too soon, Warner Brothers executives came up with the idea of sending their artists on a country rock world tour. For Gram it meant sharing the stage with a constellation of stars he'd worked with and musicians he admired: the man some called the greatest guitar picker on the planet, ex-Byrd Clarence White; two former Burrito Brothers, steel player extraordinaire "Sneaky" Pete Kleinow and bassist Chris Ethridge; and others who worked on *GP*, Emmylou Harris and fiddler Byron Berline.

The first weekend in June 1973, a two-show minitour to test the idea ended at the Tower Theater in Philadelphia's Upper Darby Township. With a couple of former Byrds, Burrito Brothers, and his new vocal soul mate in tow, Gram could cherry-pick from much of his catalogue. That night's set included "Hickory Wind," "Sin City," "We'll Sweep Out the Ashes," "Streets of Baltimore," and the arresting duet Parsons planned to put on his next solo album, a cover of the Everly Brothers' "Love Hurts." There were some tense moments with guitarist Clarence White, who accused Gram of hogging the spotlight. Yet Parsons was so impressed by White and drummer Gene Parsons (no relation), they made plans to record together.

Set to start recording his next record in July, Parsons and Phil Kaufman headed out to Joshua Tree to relax and find a spiritual center. "I spend a lot of time up at Joshua Tree in the desert just looking at the San Andreas Fault," Gram told an interviewer. "And I say to myself, 'I wish I was a bird drifting up above it.'"

\* \* \*

On July 15, Parsons received terrible news: While loading his gear from a club gig at 2 a.m., guitarist Clarence White, the man Gram had just shared a stage with the month before, had been struck and killed by a drunk driver. Besides being a world-class musician, twenty-nine-year-old White was also a husband and father. In a terrible show of judgment considering how White was killed, Parsons showed up drunk for the Catholic funeral mass.

Despite many notable musicians attending the final graveside rites, there was no music to provide an appropriate sendoff for such the revered guitarist. Finally, Parsons and Bernie Leadon broke into a traditional ballad recorded by the Burritos, "Farther Along." Parsons found the funeral sterile and depressing and said he would not want to be grieved in this way. "We were in the limo at Clarence's funeral," Roger McGuinn attested, "and Gram said he didn't want this to happen to him. It was sort of agreed, that wouldn't happen to him."

*   *   *

Parsons's desperately needed musical reprieve came just days later. In the same studio, the same group of all-star musicians who'd recorded *GP* gathered to begin making his next record, *Grievous Angel*—the title taken from Tom Brown's lyric. This time, Bernie Leadon was on board, N. D. Smart from the Fallen Angels tour was there, and Linda Ronstadt added some background vocals to a new ballad Parsons had written in the wake of White's death, "In My Hour of Darkness."

Ric Grech turned down Gram's offer to record and tour. "Ric had come to see that it wasn't safe for him to follow Gram any further," said Jenny Grech. "He loved him, but it was too dangerous."

Around the time Parsons was recording his new album, his Laurel Canyon home burned down—the cause was a mystery. Parsons managed to escape with a singed black bag containing his songbooks and a few personal items; many other valuables were lost. Gretchen moved back into her father's house and Gram took up residence in Phil Kaufman's party pad.

One of his friends said it took Parsons three tumblers of tequila before he could steady his hands enough to get the first cigarette of the day lit. His marriage was on the verge of collapse. Gram was hopelessly enamored with making music and was pursuing a lifestyle of debauchery to numb himself. In his notebook, the lyrics Parsons scrawled to one of his tunes, "Ooh, Las Vegas," are a nearly illegible scrawl.

The album's opening track, "Return of the Grievous Angel," came from Brown's inspired lyrics and Gram's melody. The title song evokes Jack Kerouac's oft-used literary themes of heading west by train: "switchman waved his lantern goodbye and good day, as we went rolling through." Gram calls out to Elvis's lead guitarist, "Pick it for me, James." After the song's description of the kickers, cowboys, and honky-tonks along a journey of twenty-thousand roads, Gram and Emmy harmonize, "They all lead me straight back home to you."

The studio players give Parsons's ode to Big Avis, "Brass Buttons," an appropriate but not overly sentimental feel. The overdubbed crowd noise makes it sound like Gram is performing the Louvins' "Cash on the Barrelhead" in a cowboy bar. Jesse Chambers, the man who first sang "Love Hurts" with Gram in the Legends, said the version with Emmylou left him stunned.

To Parsons, "Love Hurts" was a statement of fact. His friend Jim Stafford said it's his favorite Parsons recording: "It's all there. All the pain in his life is just laid out there. It's just astonishing to me."

In the album's final track, "In My Hour of Darkness," Parsons tells the story of three friends he'd lost. One was a "young man, went driving through the night"—actor Brandon De Wilde, who died in a 1972 car accident along a "deadly Denver bend." Another was "an old man" named Sid Kaiser, a father-figure whom *Crawdaddy!* magazine identified as Gram's "drug connection." And finally, of Clarence White, Gram wrote, "the music he had in him, so very few possess."

The completion of *Grievous Angel* marked the end of Gram and Emmylou's musical collaboration. From the beginning of the *GP* sessions in September 1972, and through these final recording sessions in the summer of 1973, the two had been together ten months.

*Rolling Stone* later gave five-star status to *Grievous Angel*. To know it came out of Gram's summer in hell is a testament to how pain and inner turmoil can be transformed into timeless art. In Emmylou's estimation, Gram had dried out and was looking and sounding far better than he had for the *GP* sessions. Perhaps it was just wishful thinking: "I felt he was on the upswing. He had stopped drinking. He seemed to me like he had more and more sober moments. He seemed healthier."

Others thought he was just doing a better job of hiding it.

Photographer Ginny Wynn was present during the *Grievous Angel* sessions. By her estimation Gram was serious and dedicated, often recording multiple songs in a single session. She took the memorable photo of a bloated Gram at the Burrito King in Los Angeles. During a car ride the same day, she photographed him looking world-weary, slumped in the back seat, a Corona six-pack by his side and cigarette in hand. After the old Cadillac overheated and the two were waiting for it to cool down, Wynn snapped the iconic images of Gram splayed out across the hood like a broken-down rock star king of the world.

Wynn captured some loving moments between Gram and Gretchen at a picnic. He's wearing a straw hat and a "Gram Parsons and the Fallen Angels Tour" T-shirt. She remembered Parsons taking forever to choose a single image "from about 200 photos I took" for the cover of his new album. It's a close-up and casual picture of Gram with a mustache; he's wearing a turquoise bracelet, staring intensely into the lens.

*　*　*

Soon after the recording sessions had ended, Gram went back to the Joshua Tree Inn to celebrate completion of the record with Margaret Fisher, his high school friend with whom he had recently reconnected. She'd been in California indulging in the same dangerous excesses as Gram. He'd been in a good mood, she said: "He just kept playing his new record over and over." Two other friends with them had left and; Gram had gone out and scored some morphine. The two former Florida boarding schoolers, the "throwaway kids" from wealthy families, were now mainlining drugs in a desolate desert motel.

For Gram, talking about deep-seated problems never came easily. "Gram had trouble having real close friends," Byron Berline told the *Cosmic American Music News*. "We all knew each other, and we cared for one another, but Gram hadn't any close friends he could talk to when he had any troubles."

Gram had been drinking all day even before he decided to take a second hit of morphine. It was against Fisher's better judgment, but what could she do to stop him? This time there was no singing doctor to pull him back from the precipice. Gram had ingested a lethal cocktail of drugs and alcohol.

As he lay on the bed in room number eight, Gram's breathing became labored, finally stopping altogether. In a panic, Fisher followed the junkie code: Do what you can yourself but don't bring the cops into it. By the time she summoned help, it was too late. Gram Parsons was declared dead at a hospital in Twentynine Palms. Joshua Tree, the place Gram considered a spiritual center, had become his portal to the other side. In the words of Bob Buchanan, Gram had "hurt himself" one too many times.

*  *  *

On September 19, 1973, Gram Parsons had become yet another rock-and-roll casualty in an era of excess, a time when young men wore their dangerous habits like a badge of honor. In his cause-of-death ruling, the coroner noted the victim's chronic abuse of drugs and alcohol. Gram's premonitions of an early death became a self-fulfilled prophecy.

After witnessing the light go out of her friend's eyes, Margaret Fisher says she will remain forever haunted by "the worst day of her life": a cross that is forever hers to bear. With his reckless habits and debilitating addictions, at twenty-six Gram Parsons wasn't far enough along the road to redemption. His death was all about timing.

Others close to Parsons flirted with the same fate. Jim Stafford said, "I'm lucky I didn't drink myself to death." Jon Corneal swore angels appeared to him in the shattered windshield of a car he'd wrapped around a pole trying to outrun the cops. He'd been drunk and out of his mind.

Elvis Presley's death four years later convinced Roger McGuinn to go straight: "I was seven years younger than him and I was doing prescription drugs and illegal drugs, everything I could get my hands on. Drinking like crazy, and then Elvis died. I said I'd better clean up."

Without mentioning Fisher, Gram had told Gretchen he was going out to Joshua Tree to clear his head and get away from the sycophants surrounding him. The next time she saw her husband was in the coroner's office, where she did have a chance to kiss him goodbye. In New Orleans, the Parsons's phone rang at 3 a.m. Bob was in the hospital being treated for cirrhosis; it was up to Bonnie to tell Diane her big brother was dead. Bob checked himself out of the hospital and flew to Los Angeles to claim the body.

"The tears would not end, the pain would not go away," Little Avis said of her late brother, the protector she once adored. "Once the pain got so bad, I knew my heart would burst. I got on my knees and asked Christ to take my pain away."

Ginny Wynn sat in a grocery store parking lot staring at the photo Gram had chosen to be on the cover of his upcoming album. "I remember how eerie it was looking at that photo of Gram looking into my camera lens," she recalled. "It was like having one foot in the here, and one in the hereafter."

*    *    *

Phil Kaufman felt guilty he hadn't been there to oversee what Gram was doing and keep him from going over the edge. He and a friend procured an old hearse and headed for Los Angeles International Airport to hijack Gram's body before Bob Parsons could claim it. Kaufman told airport employees alternate plans had been made to transport Gram's body for burial. Workers let him sign out the coffin containing his friend's remains.

To fulfill a pact he'd made with Parsons two months earlier, Kaufman and his buddy drove back up to Joshua Tree. Near a favorite place of Gram's called "Cap Rock," the men dragged the coffin out of the hearse and opened it. Kaufman put a Sin City jacket inside, poured five gallons of gasoline over his friend's remains, and lit it.

The two men abandoned Gram's burning coffin by the side of the road, leaving it to be discovered by park rangers. By then, the fire had gone out, leaving the remains only partially charred. Members of Gram's family considered it an act of cruel and selfish stupidity; others found it to be a fitting funeral pyre true to Gram's wishes and outlaw nature.

It was September 21, Diane Parsons's thirteenth birthday. Her family waited until after the party to break the news that her brother's body had been stolen. Despite his fragile health, Bob Parsons was able to claim what was left of Gram's remains. His daughter Becky said it was all about bringing Gram home and giving him a proper resting place. "A big thing in the South is going somewhere to pay respects," she said.

*    *    *

After having their grief drawn out and intensified, Gram's family got their turn to say goodbye to the son and older brother they loved.

Gram's old girlfriend Donna Class flew in from Colorado to be with the family. A rare photo shows Avis, Diane, and Becky standing alongside their brother's coffin. After the private funeral service, Gram Parsons's body was interred at the Garden of Memories in Metairie, Louisiana.

Gram was back home in Cosmic America to stay. Many years later Becky commissioned a bronze likeness of Gram strumming the guitar with the words, "God's Own Singer."

Bob Parsons succumbed to alcoholism in 1975 at the age of fifty. Little Avis appeared to have escaped her family's dark legacy of addiction, yet she too met a premature end in a 1993 boating accident. Bonnie died of alcohol-related causes in 2011.

Of the body-snatching incident, Gram's niece Avis Johnson Bartkus surmised, "It's kind of cool—If it's not your family." To this day, she has a hard time understanding why so many of Parsons's fans make the pilgrimage to Joshua Tree, the scene of his "horrible demise."

Polly Parsons recalled, "I was told a different story every month for about six months. He died in a fire, he had a heart attack." She was not yet seven years old when he died. She would forever carry the same giant hole in her heart Coon Dog's suicide had left for Gram. Polly added, "My mother's mother committed suicide in our backyard two weeks after my father died."

*   *   *

For years, Polly tried to fill the emptiness the same toxic way as her father—with booze and drugs: "Finally, I got to discover him by myself, on my own terms, and it wasn't pretty." She locked herself in a room, listened to his music, wrote things down, prayed, and cried. Finally, after about twelve days in a cathartic bubble, she emerged.

"Okay," she said. "I'm ready."

Polly Parsons reclaimed her father's legacy by wearing his name proudly and even playing his music. She organized memorial concerts that drew musicians influenced by his music: Elvis Costello, Dwight Yoakum, and Lucinda Williams. Norah Jones was joined onstage by none other than Gram's buddy in country music, Keith Richards, for a rendition of "Love Hurts."

It was after her move to Austin that Polly came to realize substance abuse was the family demon. "How was I going to come through it and not just recycle the history of my past?" she asked. The answer came through the establishment of Hickory Wind Ranch.

"The idea is there really is hope, that if you're in a sober-living situation in the language that you speak, you have a fighting chance."

She says the experience has brought her closer to her father: "I really feel that he's as close as I need him to be, emotionally and spiritually. I'm just his little girl, doing the best I can."

\*     \*     \*

After his long winter trek home in 1969, Bob Buchanan got a job in the auto industry and worked until retirement. "My life has been marvelous that it's lasted this long . . . I've met some wonderful people and traveled." After Gram's death, he knew he'd made the right decision to go home and let his ego suffer—if it meant his body and soul no longer had to: "Call it a guardian angel or common sense or a gut feeling. Those feelings can save your life."

Gram Parsons paid a terrible price to achieve the international fame he'd craved, and even that was overshadowed by singer Jim Croce's death in a plane crash the very next day. Through the years, however, Gram's early exit and the ensuing theft of his body have become one of the most talked-about legends in rock-and-roll history.

Those who appreciate Parsons for who he was and what he'd accomplished in his tragically short career couldn't care less how he died. What matters is the ever-growing stable of artists who point to Parsons's work as an important influence. His Cosmic American vision has done exactly as he'd hoped: it continues to bring people together in a shared love of the music.

His legacy has taken on a life of its own, especially in some of the places Gram called home. His influence has outgrown the tragic sadness of Joshua Tree; his story can be defined in its rightful domain— the places that helped give rise to the music Gram loved, that his fans still love—among them some of the most popular and influential musicians in the business.

From Harvard's halls to the streets of Greenwich Village; from Florida youth centers, southern family rooms, porches, garages, to the Ryman; and in long-forgotten concert halls and recording studios, we can celebrate Gram Parsons the artist—not the addict.

"Gram knew Jesus, he was brought up with it," said his Byrds compatriot Roger McGuinn. "I'm not worried. I know Gram is in heaven."

# ※ 23 ※

## Calling Me Home

Even if Gram Parsons had never achieved widespread postmortem fame thanks to the body-snatching incident, by now his legacy would be just as universal and deserved. That pioneering vision is forever tied to the music he wrote, the greats whose songs he recorded, and the legend he mentored, Emmylou Harris. In the decades after his death, tribute albums, concerts, and biographies have legitimized the role Parsons played in the evolution of modern music and freed him from that half-charred coffin abandoned in the desert.

"The Angels Rejoiced Last Night," one of the last songs recorded by Gram and Emmylou, shows that even outtakes from the *Grievous Angel* sessions were stellar. The musical marriage of their voices never sounded better than on Charlie and Ira Louvin's bluegrass ballad of old-fashioned sin and redemption. Framed within Gram and Emmylou's harmonies and Byron Berline's plaintive mandolin, the story about a brother and sister's hard-hearted daddy and the loss of their God-fearing mother never sounded so achingly beautiful.

Emmylou later remarked it was her favorite song from those 1973 sessions with Gram. In 1976, that song and another heart-rending ballad, a cover of the Everlys' "Sleepless Nights," were released on an album of the same name.

Gram once scribbled on the back of a phone message a list of records for his friend Frank David Murphy to "run right out and get." At the top of the list he advised, "Any Louvin Brothers record will do." But if it came right down to it, he told Murphy to own Charlie and Ira's landmark album, *Satan Is Real*. "The Angels Rejoiced Last Night" remains one of the most memorable songs from that record, along with the track covered by the Gram-era Byrds, "The Christian Life."

Emmylou kept the circle unbroken by putting at least one Louvin Brothers song on her solo albums. Her first top-ten country hit in 1975 was the Louvins' "If I Could Only Win Your Love." Harris's own composition, "From Boulder to Birmingham" was her way of working through her musical mentor's sudden and shattering departure:

> I would walk all the way from Boulder to Birmingham
> If I thought I could see, I could see your face

Harris also carried on Gram Parsons's vision, attributed her own considerable success to meeting him, and dutifully answered questions about whether love was beginning to blossom within their short-lived musical marriage. Harris's career, including Grammy awards in the country and folk genres, is right out of Gram Parsons's own playbook.

Respected musicians like James Burton agree that with or without Harris, Parsons would have gone on to an enormous career or at the very least gotten the wide critical acclaim he had been lacking. If only Parsons could have gotten a little Louvin Brothers–style redemption from the demons plaguing him. Before it all came to a sudden stop, Harris was helping him find the way down that musical road to a better place in life.

*   *   *

On a stage in Nashville, a crowd of Grand Ole Opry legends, country music's icons, heard these words spoken about Harris and Parsons: "In the early 1970s, she met Gram Parsons, who would become a collaborator and mentor. Parsons showed how meaningful, soulful and poetic country music could be, playing her songs by Merle Haggard, George Jones, the Louvin Brothers, and Buck Owens, among others.

She toured as a harmony singer in Parsons' band and joined him on his landmark recordings."

Those words were part of Emmylou Harris's induction into the Country Music Hall of Fame. And there to induct her was the great-grandfather of Cosmic American music himself, Charlie Louvin. Speaking of Gram and Charlie and the rest of her musical influences, Harris told the audience, "They're there, to the right of me, to the left of me, backward and forward. They've been there since the beginning, and they're with me still. And now they're going to be with me up in bronze on the wall."

Three years later, in her song "The Road," Harris again lamented Parsons's loss concluding, "no one was to blame." She confessed "probably" loving Parsons and wondering, "Can you see me from some place, up there among the stars?"

\*　\*　\*

"Landmark" is the same word used in the Rock and Roll Hall of Fame to describe the Byrds' *Sweetheart of the Rodeo* album, for which Parsons was primarily responsible. The Byrds were inducted in 1991, and "Hickory Wind" is noted as one of the group's essential songs.

Those who felt Parsons belonged in the Country Music Hall of Fame decided to try to help him get there. On a drive from Boston to Buffalo and "bored out of his gourd," Parsons fan Will Harnack turned on some of his music and had a revelation: "You've heard a song a zillion times, but you still can't believe how perfect it is." From that point, Harnack started to think about how Parsons wanted to build a bridge for a new audience to the music he loved.

It had been almost thirty-five years since Parsons died. Harnack felt it just wasn't right that what little people knew about Parsons revolved around the tragicomic episode surrounding the theft of his corpse and failed immolation of his body. "So around Rochester, I got really pissed. This just wasn't right," he remembered. "About ten miles later, I got the idea to start a petition. A petition to get him inducted into the Country Music Hall of Fame." Thousands of Parsons fans worldwide added their names to Harnack's petition.

\*　\*　\*

While his fans waited and lobbied for Parsons to be honored, a Country Music Hall of Famer made an unforgettable visit to Gram's boyhood home.

Waycross City Auditorium looms over Pendleton Street looking more like a church than a run-down basketball gymnasium. Age lines wander through her brick and mortar in a distinct stair-step pattern. Single strands of ivy creep up the outside walls. The old gray wooden ticket windows appear to have closed to their last customers long ago.

It was here that the king of Cosmic American music, Elvis Presley, along with the Louvins, Mother Maybelle, and the Carter family, passed the torch to nine-year-old Gram Connor. Here in Waycross, Gram caught the spark the day he bought his first Elvis single on that distinctive yellow Sun label. Faraway voices on the radio introduced him to Hank Williams, Little Richard, Ray Charles, and Jerry Lee Lewis.

There's not a more appropriate place to celebrate Gram Parsons's music and life than in Waycross, Georgia. On carefree days and warm play-out nights, Gram Connor enjoyed the only lasting sense of home he ever had. Those who grew up with Gram remember this musical son of the South who told tall tales—Coon Dog's boy.

Across the street from the auditorium stands the massive oak tree local musician and entrepreneur Billy Ray Herrin swears Gram was talking about climbing in the lyrics to "Hickory Wind." On this day, the man standing underneath is the song's co-author, Bob Buchanan, visiting Gram's old hometown for the first time. Buchanan too was showing signs of the battle he'd fought—the struggles to stay alive after hurting himself in the 1960s. Despite myriad health problems, his spirit was soothed for having come to this place. Puffing on a Dominican cigar, he appeared at peace.

Buchanan's eyes wandered to a branch twenty feet above him arching down to ground level where he could lean on it comfortably. "Gram might have even climbed this. I know I would have. . . . I'm tempted to right now but I know my doctor would tell me I shouldn't," Buchanan laughed.

He talked about feeling the spirit of the little town where Gram Connor lived: "I understand 'Hickory Wind' even better now," he said

"Just being down home, back home where you grew up. That's why we wrote it. I'd been back home in Saginaw. Gram had been down here. We had that good down-home feeling like when we were kids. You're eight years old, twelve years old, life is free and fun. Then you end up in Hollywood, California, with all the producers and money makers and money grabbers, you see life take a hell of a turn and it isn't pretty. Unfortunately Gram didn't get through all that."

Buchanan's somber tone turned thankful when talking about why he somehow managed to survive the exact same excesses that claimed the lives of more than a few friends.

"You look back and see what happened and realize that it's not for us to figure out, the human mind can't do that. It's a God job." Buchanan's voice trailed off and his eyes were gazing at the canopy of nature surrounding him. "It's incredible to see all this. The older I get the less I know, and it's wonderful. You know, with or without us, this thing will keep growing."

A maroon Suburban pulled up and an older man in a blue plaid shirt, blue jeans, and cowboy hat got out. Lighting a cigarette, he walked to the front steps of the building and greeted the small group waiting for him. More than a half-century after he'd appeared here with Ira and a kid from Memphis named Presley, Charlie Louvin was back at the City Auditorium in Waycross.

At eighty-two Charlie was still performing a hundred nights a year around the country. He'd come to Waycross to play a festival in Gram's honor. Parsons's hippie soul-man buddy Leon Russell was booked to headline Friday night of the weekend-long tribute. Charlie Louvin was to headline Saturday night.

Seated on the front steps, Louvin could have been the Marlboro man. The industry giants he has walked among and influenced in his storied career stretch far and wide. He told a tale of recording in the legendary Castle Studio at Eighth and Church Streets in Nashville's Tulane Hotel. It was December 18, 1947: "Lonzo and Oscar were trying to record 'Who Pulled the Plug from the Jug?' If you screwed up you had to start from the top again, they must have started that song fifty times," Louvin remembered. As the comedy duo ran long, other artists had to wait in the hall. Well past midnight, when it was finally Charlie and Ira's turn to record, already waiting outside was the next artist in line, Hank Williams.

At a show in Dyess, Arkansas, Louvin recalled meeting a twelve-year-old boy who looked to be right off the farm. Charlie needed to use the bathroom, and the dark-haired youngster showed him where to find it. To repay the boy's kindness, Charlie invited him to see the show. "I told him to come on in and set down and he said, 'I can't, I'm waiting on friends.' I knew that wasn't true, he had on a pair of overalls, no shirt, no hat, no shoes. I just said, set right down here and when your friends show up you can have them set down." This was Charlie Louvin's introduction to young Johnny Cash.

"As we pulled away from the school, under a light bulb outside the gym I happened to look back, saw him wave so I waved back," Louvin recounted. In his biography, Cash wrote about that defining moment: "Charlie waved back, and how much that meant to me. It was like it had been when I was three years old and standing by the railroad track and waving at the engineer as the train went by. It was awfully important that the engineer waved back. I'd shout, 'He saw and he waved.' That's the way I felt when Charlie Louvin waved at me."

*   *   *

If Gram Parsons were here on this day he'd have been every bit as star struck as his old buddy Bob Buchanan, who sat down on the front steps with Louvin and introduced himself. He spoke of meeting Gram and establishing a fast friendship through their mutual admiration for music of the Louvin Brothers.

"Gram was the one who introduced your music to that psychedelic sixties crowd in Los Angeles," Buchanan said. "Gram was a gentle man with a big heart. He liked people and he fought for them. He was on their side."

Louvin thought for a moment: "It's a shame he couldn't have been one of 'em."

"Well that's the problem, it got to his head so big he started hanging around with the Rolling Stones and all that Nudie crazy stuff and trying to be a star," Buchanan said. "He was having cocaine and whiskey for breakfast and that's what killed him. . . . nobody could talk any sense to him."

Replied Louvin, "Well, I was the designated driver before that title came along. My brother was a drinker. That's what broke us up."

*　*　*

With his cigarette smoked, Louvin climbed the stairs and was led into the auditorium. Above the entryway was an eye-catching sign: "No Tobacco Products Allowed." The place was set up as a gymnasium with basketball goals and bleachers, and the ceiling was beginning to fall down in places. Most of the stage where Gram Connor witnessed history had been boarded up, but there was still enough visible to imagine the King of Rock and Roll there in 1956.

Louvin talked about the tyrannical way Colonel Tom Parker ran that 1956 tour. According to Louvin, Parker had all the plates destroyed of posters that featured "the Louvin Brothers as the headliners and Elvis as an also." Night in and night out, Parker would think nothing of scheduling an extra show and not informing others on the bill. "Finally, we elected Ira to confront Colonel Tom and tell him we wouldn't play unless he came back here with something green in his hand." Parker simply canceled that night's extra concert, leaving hundreds of fans outside disappointed.

He remembered the confrontation between Ira and Elvis backstage at a show in the Carolinas. "I was standing six feet from it," said Louvin. After Ira called Elvis a "white n——," Elvis smiled and told Ira he was only giving the people what they wanted to hear. "That was the end of the conversation. Some people said it was a fight. But he never cut a Louvin Brothers song. That statement probably cost the catalogue ten million dollars."

About his influence on Gram Parsons, Louvin said something surprising: "If I'd a got to meet him, I would have apologized for that." Then he recounted how life as a working musician can be grueling and thankless, the kind of life that leaves certain people open to substance abuse to make it through the hard times. "It gets in your blood and it doesn't bother you to go hungry. You got that hope that things will get better. You have to have that or you'd commit suicide."

Louvin beamed when talking about being the one who slipped the Country Music Hall of Fame medal around Emmylou Harris's neck. Being back in Waycross was also important: "It means a whole lot to me. I don't do a show where I won't sing 'Cash on the Barrelhead' or 'The Christian Life.'" Louvin was glad to hear that Waycross city leaders had set aside a million dollars to renovate the auditorium. He thought it a good idea to commemorate Parsons here and all the history that's happened within these walls.

The shadows of Friday evening grew longer; Louvin was booked to play the next night, but still wanted to head to the fairgrounds and meet Leon Russell. He walked back outside the auditorium and paused on one of the top steps: "I wish I would have had the chance to convert Gram. Not to religion, but just get him out of where he didn't want to be." He paused for some pictures, stooped down and pulled one of many weeds protruding through the front walkway, and loaded back into the Suburban. At eighty-two, Charlie had finally relinquished the driving to his guitar player and oldest son, Sonny Louvin.

* * *

Down the memorial highway and across the railroad tracks, music could be heard blocks from the Okefenokee fairgrounds. Outside the sign read: "Annual Gram Parsons Guitar Pull and Tribute." Beyond the chain-link fence, a down-home crowd had gathered: older-looking hippies, young couples with babies, fans camped out next to an RV, others under the stars on lawn chairs and blankets. People set up booths to sell their wares.

Many of the musicians, with group names like the Crabgrass Cowboys, Deepwell, and Devils in Disguise, have been playing this festival for years. From places like Ottawa, Canada; Columbia, South Carolina; and Marietta, Georgia; most traveled unpaid to be part of it.

It was all a stone's throw down the highway from the house where Gram threw Saturday morning parties and did his front-porch stage shows. On this weekend, Billy Ray Herrin's twelve-year-old grandson, Ashton, belted out "Big Mouth Blues." At Waycross College, youngsters Tracie Mattox and Luke Johnson performed soulful versions of Gram standards like "A Song for You."

Later that night at the Cypress Creek Bar, a trio of Waycross teens, the Woodgrains, put a funk and reggae spin on their version of "She." Gram's college friend and International Submarine Band mate Ian

Dunlop performed barefoot with khaki shorts, pink T-shirt, and a black sequin-studded cowboy shirt. In the early morning, Bob Buchanan stood in the parking lot puffing on a cigar and telling backstage stories about the Monterrey Pop Festival in 1967.

On that Friday evening at the fairgrounds, to the east the crowd could see a shooting star's fleeting streak across the cloudless sky. Introduced as the "one and only Master of Space and Time," the old cosmic cowboy Leon Russell mounted the stage aided by a cane. Beneath his cowboy hat flowed the trademark mane of white hair and a long, whiter-than-white beard. Songs like "Jumpin' Jack Flash" and even "Wild Horses" took on that infectious Leon Russell boogie. He kept lyrics in front of him on a laptop.

Russell paused long enough to talk about a green silk top hat Gram had given him as a gift around 1970. "On tour it got laid around, thrown around, sat on and stepped on," Russell recounted. "And one day I noticed a little tag pokin' out from inside the headband that read 'MGM studios, 1932, Al Jolson.'"

If you go on YouTube and dial up "Joe Cocker's Mad Dogs and Englishmen tour" from 1970, you'll see Leon singing and playing in the top hat Gram gave him. Russell also played on the Byrds' first hit, "Mr. Tambourine Man," as a member of an elite group of Los Angeles studio musicians known as "the Wrecking Crew," the real band behind many of the biggest hits of the 1960s.

There was a sprinkling of grandpas and grandmas in attendance and no evidence of so-called Grampires, a derisive term used to describe those with a strong affinity for Parsons's music and tragic life story. And there was no bitter, cynical, revisionist talk about how Parsons's lasting appeal arose only from the unfortunate circumstances surrounding his death. People around here will tell you with conviction, that's just not true.

The next evening, rain chances diminished from 50 to 20 percent to partly cloudy and clearing. Moths flew in a frenzy inches from floodlights giving minimal illumination to the goings-on back at the Okefenokee fairgrounds. Dave Griffin, the tribute's founder and host, whom many people referred to as "Uncle Dave," seemed to be in perpetual motion. When he wasn't giving musicians a generous introduction, he was often playing right alongside them. His host band, appropriately named Hickory Wind, took the stage early that evening with an uplifting version of "Mr. Tambourine Man."

In came Charlie Louvin, festooned in dark pants and matching vest, chartreuse long-sleeved shirt, black boots, and cowboy hat. Though Louvin is a living, breathing face right off of Cosmic America's Mount Rushmore, he clearly wasn't concerned about star treatment. He stopped at the front gate and pulled out a twenty-dollar bill to pay the way in for a man with a cane.

Louvin's set list included old favorites and obscurities, a little gospel, a few covers, and a tip of the hat to the songwriters he's known and worked with: Johnny Cash, Kris Kristofferson, Glen Campbell, Mother Maybelle, and Merle Haggard. In between each number, Louvin sprinkled in some homespun country humor.

Then the Country Music Hall of Fame inductee had another surprise: "We also are doing a song tonight that we have never done on the stage before. There's a young man, his name is hangin' on this festival. He recorded some Louvin Brothers songs and we owe him a lot. He introduced our music to rock-and-roll people he was workin' with. He wrote this song . . . all over Waycross I see the name, 'Hickory Wind.'"

In a plaintive voice weathered and worn by more than sixty years of shows and a hundred-thousand roads, Charlie Louvin began to sing the lyrics scribbled on a piece of white notebook paper he was holding. Most could not see the man standing at the foot of the stage behind one of the large speakers, Bob Buchanan, the song's co-writer. As Louvin sang the second verse, he walked away. His eyes and face overcome with emotion, Buchanan retreated to a backstage area to gather himself.

Louvin's voice had a vintage, soulful tone as if poured from an aged, oak cask. When his first-ever rendition of "Hickory Wind" ended to the crowd's enthusiastic approval, Buchanan walked back toward the front of the stage. Not ready to talk about the impact of what he'd just seen and heard, it was all he could do to utter three words: "It was beautiful."

\*   \*   \*

At a stop on the Fallen Angels tour in 1973, Phil Kaufman wanted to surprise Parsons by inviting Buchanan to walk onstage unannounced for a duet of the song they'd co-written five years previous. It was the only time the two performed their signature song together live. Gram confessed after the show he was so loaded he didn't recognize Buchanan.

Like a soldier with post-traumatic stress disorder, Buchanan had come to associate music with his own addictions. For decades he'd put the musical side of himself into a deep hibernation. That weekend in Waycross, decades of winter started to thaw.

Later that night, Buchanan was invited onstage to do his own version of "Hickory Wind." With Charlie Louvin's help, the healing warmth of music and memories in the heart of Parsons's boyhood home had brought down the walls. Louvin succumbed to pancreatic cancer just fifteen months later. The indelible images of that night endure in a live recording Charlie released about six months prior to his passing.

At its best, the power of music brings about change, heals the soul, and binds generations of us together. In these swampy lowlands, where alligators' nighttime eyes glow fiery crimson, "Hickory Wind," one of Gram Parsons's most memorable compositions, has become more than a song. It evokes romantic glimpses of childhood. It conjures southern memories of banjo, dobro, fiddle, and steel—and a yearning to feel innocent, joyous, and safe at home.

# Acknowledgments

The best part of journalism is the journey. If I could write this book all over again, I would. It was a privilege to get to know so many people who've made up that broad mosaic of music history, especially in the South.

Special thanks to my enthusiastic photographer and road buddy on this project, Michael Robinson. I am most grateful to Jim Carlton who gave us the enduring gifts of friendship, memories, quick wit, and most of all, credibility. He opened many, many doors. So too did the Cosmic American den mother Peggy Hanson, a generous soul who seems to know everyone pivotal to Gram Parsons's legacy. Special thanks also to Becky Gottsegen, who trusted me enough to share the bitter and sweet aspects of growing up Bob Parsons's daughter and Gram Parsons's stepsister. Thanks also to Gram Parsons's niece Avis Johnson Bartkus who shared her memories, her mother's bittersweet memoirs, and family photos.

To the good people in Waycross, Georgia—thank you. Billy Ray Herrin made us feel welcome right away. Henry Clarke, Boo Clarke, Richard Smith, Clyde Goble, Arlene Dixon, and Nancy Gill were very kind to share their memories. So was Roger Williams. Dave Griffin's annual Gram Parsons Guitar Pull and Tribute is a reminder that Parsons's true legacy lies not in the overblown legend surrounding his death in the desert, but in the music and the emotion that music continues to evoke.

Thanks to Carl Chambers whose Dizzy Rambler online website (http://www.dizzyrambler.com), is the definitive, interactive primer for anyone interested in Polk County Florida's considerable music history.

Thanks to Jesse Chambers, Jon Corneal, and Bobby Braddock. I am most grateful to Jim Stafford for showing me the home where so much history happened, and for giving me a firsthand tour of his own remarkable rise to stardom and success. Thanks to former Journeyman Dick Weissman for giving me his perspective on the often-overlooked folk era in American music.

Thanks to Frank David Murphy for sharing his memories and memorabilia. Special thanks to the ageless Rufus McClure at the Bolles School in Jacksonville, Florida. Thanks to Margaret Fisher for meeting with me in Jacksonville. Thanks to Paul Broder, Larry Piro, and David W. Johnson. Thanks to Mick Marino, Ian Dunlop, and Barry Tashian.

Thanks to Bob Buchanan and the late Country Music Hall of Fame inductee Charlie Louvin. I will never forget the visit to City Auditorium and finding out the true meaning of "Hickory Wind." Thanks to Vince Martin and Bobby Ingram for the Coconut Grove memories. Thanks to David Amram, the creative force of nature. Thanks to all my friends at the Kerouac Project of Orlando.

Thanks to Donna Class. Special thanks to Marilyn Platt for sharing the letters Gram wrote to her. Thanks to former Shilos bandmates Paul Surratt and Joe Kelly. Thanks to Michael Buffalo Smith and Johnny Batson for the Carolina connections. Thanks to Les Dudek for sharing his youth center memories. Thanks to Susan Martin and Jeff Lemlich, scholars of Florida's garage band days.

Thanks to Karen Wyatt at the Newseum for helping uncover the historic Ted Polumbaum photos of Gram Parsons at Harvard. Thanks also to Nyna and Judy Polumbaum for their kindness.

Thanks to the Gram Parsons biographers: Sid Griffin, Ben Fong-Torres, Jason Walker, Jessica Hundley, and Polly Parsons and David Meyer, whose book is a research tour de force. I also found Gandulf

Hennig's 2006 documentary, "Fallen Angel" very informative as were Pamela Des Barres's memoirs.

Thanks to those who shared their Gram Parsons photos: Les Leverett, Larry Sepulvado, Ginny Wynn, and the estate of Burton Wilson. Thanks to Jock Bartley, Rick Roberts, and Neil Flanz.

Thanks to Will James, Gram National and International. Thanks to Little Avis's friend in Winter Park, Dan Jovi. Thanks to Ray, Fred, and Bill at Rock and Roll Heaven in Orlando for helping me track him down. Thanks to Jim Abbott, Johnny Rogan, and Holly George-Warren for encouragement. Thanks to Emma and Tom Smith, as well as Rick Norcross.

Thanks to Camilla and Roger McGuinn. Randy Brooks shared his memories of meeting and interviewing the Byrds at the Opry in 1968.

Thanks to my proofreader Bonny Fesmire. Thanks also to John Byram. Thanks to Amy Gorelick, Stephanie Williams, and everyone at University Press of Florida. Thanks to scholars William McKeen and Clay Motley. Thanks to Michael Ray Fitzgerald for honest feedback.

Thanks to Josh Rosenthal at Tomkins Square for giving me the honor of writing liner notes to Charlie Louvin's *Live in Waycross*, a Gram Parsons tribute CD.

My love to the home team: Karen, William, and Kristen and my family members and friends who've provided encouragement.

In Cosmic America, Gram Parsons's true legacy is alive and well.

# Notes

**Preamble, Gram Parsons at Nineteen**

*"Up Close, Parsons looked—to my own sophomore eyes—remarkably self-possessed"*: David W. Johnson, "Parsonage," *Folk Roots*, January/February 1995. Used with author's permission.

**Chapter 1. Cosmic Roots**

*"She never talked about any of it"*: Author's interview with Avis Johnson Bartkus, August 7, 2011.
*"His heart was back home"*: Ibid.
*"plastic"*: Gram Parsons letter to Frank David Murphy, December 27, 1972.
*"white man's blues"*: Jason Gross, "Sid Griffin Interview," *Perfect Sound Forever Online Magazine*, http://www.furious.com/perfect/, July 2001.
*"Cosmic American Music"*: Gram Parsons quoted by James Calemine, "Reflections on Gram Parsons: The Complete Reprise Sessions," http://www.swampland.com.
*"Radio did not obey the law"*: William McKeen, "What We Talk About When We Talk About Elvis," *American History*, August 2007.
*"The transistor radio was a big breakthrough"*: Author's interview with Roger McGuinn, June 3, 2010.
*"I don't know if I'm playing with fire"*: Gram Parsons to Chuck Casell, *Big Mouth Blues: A Conversation with Gram Parsons*, recorded interview, A&M Records, March 3, 1972.

## Chapter 2. Legacy versus Legend

*"Oh, he was a beautiful boy"*: Author's interview with Margaret Fisher, April 2, 2008.

*"I tried to be as far from him"*: Ibid.

*"Imagine"*: Ibid.

*"inconvenient kids"*: Ibid.

*"Not now"*: Ibid.

*"rock's greatest cult figure"*: Keith Richards, "The Immortals," *Rolling Stone,* April 2005.

*"pure musicians"*: Keith Richards, *Life* (New York: Little, Brown and Company, 2010), 248.

*"Gram wrote great songs"*: Ibid., 249.

*"They're underground classics"*: Author's interview with Jim Stafford, December 5, 2008.

*"could've been quite a driving force"*: Chris Hillman quoted in Bob Mehr, "Concert Preview: Living to tell the Tales," *Memphis Commercial Appeal,* April 25, 2008.

*"loose"*: Author's conversation with Bobby Braddock, May 2007.

*"A close examination of Parsons's lyrics reveals"*: Dr. Clay Motley, Western Kentucky University, "American Music: Gram Parsons and Southern Religious Folklife" (paper presented to International Country Music Conference: Nashville, Tenn., May 23, 2009).

## Chapter 3. Pilgrimage to Waycross

*"I would get country music mixed with some rockabilly"*: Gram Parsons to Casell, *Big Mouth Blues.*

*"You just knew"*: Author's interview with Henry Clarke at Hickory Wind music store, September 2008.

*"They'd say 'Gram, I want you to listen to this record'"*: Ibid.

*"I knew how to play the Boogie Woogie"*: Author's interview with Nancy Gill, December 8, 2008.

*"Couldn't read a lick of music"*: Author's interview with Dickey Smith at Hickory Wind music store, September 2008.

*"Mrs. Smith, I just wrote a song"*: Ibid.

*"He called it 'The Gram Boogie'"*: Ibid.

*"Shoot to shoot"*: Nancy Gill interview, December 8, 2008.

*"Play-out nights"*: Dickey Smith interview, September 2008.

*"There were some weeks"*: Author's interview with Claud Goble at Hickory Wind music store, September 2008.

*"He would take us out there"*: Henry Clarke interview, September 2008.

*"Boy, we thought"*: Dickey Smith interview, September 2008.

*"I was much more comfortable with him"*: Undated writings of Avis Parsons Johnson.

*"I'm sure there was a lot of stress"*: Avis Johnson Bartkus interview, August 7, 2011.

*"She was one of the prettiest women"*: Henry Clarke interview, September 2008.

*"It would have been embarrassing"*: Dickey Smith interview, September 2008.

*"Then I got down to Florida"*: Ibid.

*"The guy who taught me how to ski"*: Ibid.

*"He was not that arrogant"*: Henry Clarke interview, September 2008.

"*I got chastised*": Ibid.

"*The adults would eat later*": Nancy Gill interview, December 8, 2008.

"*There was a lot of wild stories*": Ibid.

"*Besides me and Henry*": Dickey Smith interview, September 2008.

"*If we ever had a concert*": Henry Clarke interview, September 2008.

"*C'mon*": Dickey Smith interview, September 2008.

"*Mr. Dynamite*": Elvis Presley "Souvenir Photo Album," 1956. Author and publisher unknown.

"*Just to try to get a peek*": Dickey Smith interview, September 2008.

"*Talked corn but wore a big diamond*": A. Musik Lover, *Waycross Journal-Herald*, December 23, 1956.

"*The rather tall, dark complexioned youth*": Ibid.

"*Heartburn motel*": Ibid.

"*That's all I'd hear*": Claud Goble interview, September 2008.

"*Someone's gonna pay for this*": Author's interview with Roger Williams, editor of the *Waycross Journal-Herald*, September 2008.

"*He came on*": Gram Parsons to Chuck Casell, *Big Mouth Blues*.

"*Now, this is the kind of music I like*": Author's interview with Charlie Louvin, April 19, 2009.

## Chapter 4. Like Elvis

"*I often wondered*": Author's interview with Haywood "Boo" Clarke, Waycross, Ga., September 2008.

"*They were not named*": Stanley Booth, *Rhythm Oil: A Journey through the Music of the American South*, 61.

"*daring*": Ibid.

"*busting out of jail*": Douglas Brinkley, "Bob Dylan's America," *Rolling Stone*, May 14, 2009.

"*If he saw something*": Author's interview with Richard Smith, Hickory Wind Music Store, Waycross, Ga., September 2008.

"*I remember he just came in*": Haywood "Boo" Clarke interview, September 2008.

"*everywhere he went*": Henry Clarke interview, September 2008.

"*He was a very stunning and dashing figure*": Ibid.

"*If I'd had any sense*": Dickey Smith interview, September 2008.

"*Gram Connor and his friends*": Ibid.

"*conceited and lying*": Ibid.

"*At one point*": Ibid.

"*My God, Gram*": Ibid.

"*Gram was intelligent*": Henry Clarke interview, September 2008.

## Chapter 5. Coon Dog's Secret

"*My husband Wendall was a house mover*": Author's interview with Arlene Dixon, Waycross, Ga., September 2009.

"*They cut the home into four pieces*": Ibid.

"*He had a lot of high praise*": Ibid.

"It doesn't bother me": Ibid.

"I knew Gram well enough to know": Author's interview with Rufus McClure, May 5, 2009.

"Gram's daddy was like the emcee": Dickey Smith interview, September 2008.

"Here's Dickey": Ibid.

"It was a prism": Undated writings of Avis Parsons Johnson.

"Take care of my Avie": Louise Cone quoted by David Meyer, *Twenty Thousand Roads*, 42.

"just like he always did": Claud Goble interview, September 2008.

"My mother was one of the first": Henry Clarke interview, September 2008.

"It's amazing": Claud Goble interview, September 2008.

"Oh man": Haywood "Boo" Clarke interview, September 2008.

"I love you Gram": Undated writings of Avis Parsons Johnson.

"She was recently divorced": Avis Johnson Bartkus interview, August 7, 2011.

"I suspect it may have added": Ibid.

"I hate to mention": Nancy Gill interview, December 8, 2008.

"He was a victim": Ibid.

"Right after the funeral": Claud Goble interview, September 2008.

"The Snivelys took Gram and my Mother": Avis Johnson Bartkus interview, September 7, 2011.

"I was left to find comfort": Undated writings of Avis Parsons Johnson.

"I'll never come back": Henry Clarke interview, September 2008.

"If I ever get in a wreck": Author's interview with Paul Broder, February 8, 2009.

"They disintegrated": Dickey Smith interview, September 2008.

"That's the last I saw of them": Haywood "Boo" Clarke interview, September 2008.

"The school made no effort": Rufus McClure interview, May 5, 2009.

"I think Gram's mother went to more drinking": Dickey Smith interview, September 2008.

"a male comforter": Undated writings of Avis Parsons Johnson.

"It's what saved him": Author's interview with Billy Ray Herrin, September 2008.

## Chapter 6. Gram's Domain

"It's just a flood": Author's interview with Jim Carlton, June 2007.

"Gram's domain": Ibid.

"This was a pretty cool pad": Ibid.

"about whatever girl": Ibid.

"I still remember": Author's conversation with Jim Carlton and Parsons's unnamed neighbor, June 2007.

"carpetbagger": Henry Clarke interview, September 2008.

"I met him": Undated writings of Avis Parsons Johnson.

"I'm not crazy about it": Gram Parsons letter to Connie O'Connell, January 1960.

"Everyone was calling": Jim Carlton interview, June 2007.

"Gram, like the measure,": Author's interview with Donna Class, a former girlfriend from Winter Haven High, February 4, 2009.

"It's all right": Ibid.

*"I thought that was the coolest thing"*: Jim Carlton interview, June 2007.

*"My God"*: Ibid.

*"I knew that wasn't true"*: Donna Class interview, February 4, 2009.

*"I still remember"*: Ibid.

*"Every song I sing"*: Ibid.

*"It must really seem absurd"*: Lyrics quoted during Donna Class interview, February 4, 2009.

*"I had to work"*: Jim Carlton interview, June 2007.

## Chapter 7. Red Coats, Pacers, and Legends

*"teen room"*: Donna Class interview, February 4, 2009.

*"buddied up"*: Undated writings of Avis Parsons Johnson.

*"She made a big speech"*: Ibid.

*"We told her about how much we liked Bob"*: Ibid.

*"I liked to pretend she was my mother"*: Ibid.

*"I was over there a lot"*: Donna Class interview, February 4, 2009.

*"other mother"*: Jim Carlton interview, June 2007.

*"The photographers knew"*: Avis Johnson Bartkus interview, August 7, 2011.

*"I remembered how big Flat Top was"*: Author's interview with Jim Stafford, December 2009.

*"I remember when Gram came back"*: Ibid.

*In my memory, the music was everywhere*: Bobby Braddock, *Down in Orbundale*, 85–86.

*"It was absolutely like a religious experience"*: Author's interview with Jim Stafford, November 2008.

*"FABULOUS guitarist"*: Bobby Braddock, *Down in Orbundale*, 85–86.

*"If you don't get an education"*: Jim Stafford interview, December 2009.

*"Jesus, a swimming pool!"*: Ibid.

*"The thing we didn't do"*: Ibid.

*"Our set list had to be just abysmal"*: Jim Carlton interview, June 2007.

*"He just steals the show"*: Ibid.

*"Tell you what"*: Ibid.

*"When I met him"*: Jim Stafford interview, December 2009.

*"My name is now Ingram Cecil Parsons"*: Jim Carlton interview, June 2007.

*"He had some distress"*: Ibid.

*"ceased to exist"*: Ibid.

*"I remember Gram"*: Author's interview with Gram Parsons's half-sister Becky Gottsegen, July 9, 2009.

*"My signature will be worth something"*: Ibid.

## Chapter 8. The Youth Center Circuit

*"You'd mash down on the accelerator"*: Jim Carlton interview, June 2007.

*"There were juke joints"*: Jim Stafford interview, December 2009.

*"We took pride"*: Jim Carlton interview, June 2007.

*"Garage bands were everywhere"*: Susan Martin, "Playin' the Peninsula," http://www.fl6osrock.bravehost.com.

"Funderful Forty": Taken from http://www.cflradio.net.

"As a kid of about 14": Susan Martin, "Playin' the Peninsula."

"You felt you were really legit": Jim Carlton interview, June 2007.

"We were laughing": Don Felder, Heaven and Hell, 25.

"I remember seeing Jerry Lee Lewis": Jim Stafford interview, December 2009.

"I always thought": Ibid.

"Gram was showing an interest": Author's interview with Gerald "Jesse" Chambers, September 26, 2008.

"I got this real good guitar player": Ibid.

"That's what appealed to us": Author's interview with Jon Corneal, October 28, 2008.

"I remember standing and crying": Gerald "Jesse" Chambers interview, September 26, 2008.

"wasn't terribly impressed": Ibid.

"gold-plated everything": Jon Corneal interview, October 28, 2008.

"they found out": Becky Gottsegen interview, July 9, 2009.

"freewheeling kid": Jim Stafford interview, December 2009.

## Chapter 9. High Times and Earliest Recordings

"I've been accused": Author's interview with Carl Chambers, July 11, 2008.

"Hi-Time was something": Ibid.

"You need to wash that stuff out": Gerald "Jesse" Chambers interview, September 26, 2008.

"The most wonderful Gibson guitar": Ibid.

"that was like manna from heaven": Ibid.

"I was recording Jesse": Carl Chambers interview, July 11, 2008.

"And now some young and upcoming musicians": Jack Stir recorded by Carl Chambers, http://www.dizzyrambler.com.

"Oh that's tiring": Ibid.

"Clark was there": Jon Corneal interview, October 28, 2008.

"There were some strong personalities": Gerald "Jesse" Chambers interview, September 26, 2008.

"The band argued": Author's correspondence with Sam Killebrew, May 29, 2009.

"My wife and I": Author's conversation with Pete Davis, Lakeland, June 2009.

"I thought I was at Columbia": Jim Carlton interview, June 2007.

"I remember him": Author's correspondence with Bobby Braddock, June 13, 2007.

"Bobby was really an incredible keyboard player": Jon Corneal interview, October 28, 2008.

## Chapter 10. Folk in the Other Room

"It always just seemed really natural": Donna Class interview, February 4, 2009.

"Avis and her first cousin": Ibid.

"sitting at the piano": Buddy Freeman quoted in a booklet by Mark Leviton, "Gram Parsons: The Early Years 1963–1965."

"Gram was kind of isolated": Donna Class interview, February 4, 2009.

"Gram had received some in the mail": Ibid.

*"Gram was around for tenth grade"*: Ibid.

*"restriction"*: Jim Carlton interview, June 2007.

*"I got custody"*: Ibid.

*"It was all his idea"*: Jim Stafford interview, December 2009.

*"He had a line"*: Jon Corneal interview, October 28, 2008.

*"He was into playing music"*: Ibid.

*"I pushed the Casswin guys"*: Author's correspondence with Rick Norcross, May 4, 2009.

*"full bore"*: Jim Carlton interview, June 2007.

*"Gram used to come over"*: Rick Norcross correspondence, May 4, 2009.

*"the kitty"*: Author's correspondence with Rick Norcross, April 1, 2009.

*"This provides the salary"*: *Lakeland Ledger,* November 29, 1964.

*"I thought Gram was adorable"*: Author's interview with Emma Smith, August 30, 2008.

*"He hit on my girlfriend"*: Author's correspondence with central Florida folk musician who asked not to be named, April 29, 2009.

*"reading them the riot act"*: Jim Carlton interview, June 2007.

*"I do think my father's inability to keep his pants on"*: Becky Gottsegen interview, July 9, 2009.

*"They raised the children"*: Ibid.

*"I wished very much that mother was poor"*: Undated writings of Avis Parsons Johnson.

*"She was getting too close"*: Avis Johnson Bartkus interview, August 7, 2011

*"I wasn't surprised"*: Donna Class interview, February 4, 2009.

*"There was no overriding shame"*: Jim Carlton interview, June 2007.

*"They didn't do it for his welfare"*: Rufus McClure interview, May 5, 2009.

## Chapter 11. Shilos and Bolles

*"the big brown box"*: WYFF online coverage of implosion, http://www.wyff4.com, September 20, 1997.

*"Are you guys going to do 'In the Hills of Shiloh'?"*: Author's interview with Joe Kelly, November 19, 2008.

*"That's how we happened to meet"*: Ibid.

*"We hit that harmony"*: Author's interview with Paul Surratt, December 6, 2009.

*"It was just really exhilarating"*: Joe Kelly interview, November 19, 2008.

*"I went home that night"*: Paul Surratt interview, December 6, 2009.

*"Here he is the judge"*: Ibid.

*"Buddy insisted we all go out"*: Joe Kelly interview, November 19, 2008.

*"The entire group was extremely confident"*: Paul Surratt interview, December 6, 2009.

*"Hoot Tour"*: John Phillips, *Papa John,* 118

*"dazzling musicianship"*: Ibid., 96.

*"Friday Coca-Cola Hi-Fi Hootenanny"*: Mark Leviton, "Gram Parsons."

*"Recording Artist Likes Greenville's Folk Music"*: Ibid.

*"Gram demonstrated"*: Rufus McClure interview, May 5, 2009.

*"Where are you from?"*: Roger Williams interview, September 2008.

*"He was on the fast track"*: Ibid.

*"good music"*: Paul Broder interview, February 8, 2009.

*"He'd be just as likely to play"*: Ibid.

*"I do remember"*: Ibid.

*"He hid that he was running"*: Rufus McClure interview, May 5, 2009.

*"Suicide by attrition"*: Ibid.

*"We got there"*: Gerald "Jesse" Chambers interview, September 26, 2008.

*"I don't know why we're here"*: Jim Stafford interview, December 5, 2008.

*"Bob Hubbard became"*: Rufus McClure interview, May 5, 2009.

*"smoking circle"*: Roger Williams interview, September 2008.

*"I would every now and then go by"*: Ibid.

*"PROFESSIONAL"*: Ibid.

*"There was no real gray area"*: Ibid.

*"I said to myself"*: Author's interview with Marilyn Garrett Platt, May 18, 2009.

*"couuuntry"*: Jon Corneal interview, October 28, 2008.

*"That twangy country thing"*: Marilyn Garrett Platt interview, May 18, 2009.

*"We were so young"*: Paul Surratt interview, December 6, 2009.

*"I can still in my mind's eye see him"*: Marilyn Garrett Platt interview, May 18, 2009.

*"The sun is setting"*: Gram Parsons letter to Marilyn Garrett, February 17, 1964.

*"You're the Shilos' type of girl"*: Ibid.

*"His voice just had a sadness"*: Marilyn Garrett Platt interview, May 18, 2009.

*"good," and "excellent"*: Mark Leviton, "Gram Parsons."

*"You Can't Beat Our Meat"*: Jim Carlton interview, June 2007.

*"I never had dreams"*: Marilyn Garrett Platt interview, May 18, 2009.

## Chapter 12. Chicago Surfinanny

*"George almost had a stroke"*: Gram Parsons undated letter to Marilyn Garrett.

*"Gram and George were always arguing"*: Paul Surratt interview, December 6, 2009.

*"I've been staying here on the weekends"*: Gram Parsons letter to Marilyn Garrett, April 15, 1964.

*"He went to that fancy Bolles school"*: Joe Kelly interview, November 19, 2008.

*"Here we are in a fancy hotel"*: Paul Surratt interview, December 6, 2009.

*"I wish we could have done that"*: Ibid.

*"I have a trust fund"*: Joe Kelly interview, November 19, 2008.

*"It was a premonition"*: Ibid.

*"The Shilos mean a lot to me"*: Gram Parsons undated letter to Marilyn Garrett.

*"After a 21-firecracker salute"*: Unknown author, *St. Petersburg Evening Independent*, April 20, 1964.

*"We're now beginning our last month of school"*: Gram Parsons letter to Marilyn Garrett, dated "Monday."

*"He would show up"*: Paul Broder interview, February 8, 2009.

*"We got really hammered"*: Ibid.

*"There was a falling out"*: Joe Kelly interview, November 19, 2008.

*"We were gonna sing"*: Ibid.

*"long talk"*: Paul Surratt interview, December 6, 2009.

*"We're the only two"*: Ibid.

*"Oh, you can't do that!"*: Ibid.

*"If you want to do it"*: Ibid.

"That was my first time to New York": Ibid.

"I had met Gram years earlier": John Phillips, *Papa John*, 269

"We played live": Paul Surratt interview, December 6, 2009.

"You're still in high school?": Ibid.

"We really enjoyed your set": Ibid.

"respected folk singer": Walker, confirmed in author's correspondence with Jason Walker, December 6, 2009.

"was messy": Jim Carlton interview, June 2007.

"His drug use": Jim Carlton liner notes, "Gram Parsons, Another Side of this Life."

"wooing song": Joe Kelly interview, November 19, 2008.

"Gram always had a notebook": Ibid.

"After the Journeymen": Author's correspondence with Dick Weissman, May 2011.

"There were two sets of demos": Ibid.

"Gram played and sang": Ibid.

"It had been recorded over!": Ibid.

"My mindset": Joe Kelly interview, November 19, 2008.

## Chapter 13. Senior Year and the Derry Down

"He'd see that little red glow": Roger Williams interview, September 2008.

"It wasn't that he got huffy": Author's interview with Frank David Murphy, June 30, 2009.

"Then we'd go to the Mayflower Hotel": Roger Williams interview, September 2008.

"We had a real hootenanny": Frank David Murphy interview, June 30, 2009.

"As you, no doubt, already know": Gram Parsons letter to Marilyn Garrett, January 10, 1965.

"All future plans may be postponed": Ibid.

"the Mighty 690" and "the Big Ape": Http://www.thebushmen.net.

"I don't know how he felt about the Beatles": Paul Surratt interview, December 6, 2009.

"September of '64": Frank David Murphy interview, June 30, 2009.

"DC Five": Ibid.

"They got in so much trouble": Ibid.

"Derry Down": Jack McClintock, "Youth is Full of Pleasance," *Tampa Tribune*, undated.

"We were really going to go Old English": Ibid.

"Hi, my name's Gram Parsons": Live recording of the Shilos at the Derry Down opening, December 20, 1964. Courtesy of Jim Carlton.

"a great big flop": Ibid.

"just for the hell of it": Jim Carlton interview, June 2007.

"It was pretty austere": Donna Class interview, February 4, 2009.

"It was a big success": Jim Carlton interview, June 2007.

"high cotton": Joe Kelly interview, November 19, 2008.

"There's a certain strength to the group": Paul Surratt interview, December 6, 2009.

"Avis was wonderful": Ibid.

"I'm glad you are rid of Keith": Gram Parsons letter to Marilyn Garrett, January 15, 1965.

"Honestly, some day I'm going to lose control": Ibid.

"She was eating ice cubes": Paul Broder interview, February 8, 2009.

*"You could tell Avis had a serious problem"*: Ibid.

*"Gram was not very kind"*: Ibid.

*"What seventeen - or eighteen-year-old understands"*: Ibid.

*"Could you love this?"*: Avis Johnson Bartkus interview, August 7, 2011.

*"The saddest part"*: Ibid.

*"I can still go back and listen to that tape"*: Joe Kelly interview, November 19, 2008.

*"Luckily, no one minded"*: Paul Surratt quoted in Mark Leviton, "Gram Parsons."

*"If I had any idea"*: Paul Surratt interview, December 6, 2009.

*"She wasn't good enough"*: Ibid.

*"I'd give a thousand dollars"*: Ibid.

*"We would greatly appreciate"*: Shilos letter reprinted in Mark Leviton, "Gram Parsons."

*"He submitted"*: Paul Broder interview, February 8, 2009.

*"I think Bob Hubbard really turned him around"*: Ibid.

*"Do you think?"*: Rufus McClure interview, May 5, 2009.

*"If you give me your commitment"*: Ibid.

*"Gram is a capable student"*: Ibid.

*"We're going to have to do"*: Gram Parsons letter to Paul Surratt, May 27, 1965.

*"cash in on this thing"*: Ibid.

*"Gram was really blown away"*: Paul Broder interview, February 8, 2009.

*"He got a letter"*: Jim Carlton interview, June 2007.

*"I want you to play around"*: Ibid.

*"Bolles noted singer/songwriter"*: The Bolles School yearbook, "Turris, 1965."

*"I suppose looking into the future"*: Inscription provided by Paul Broder.

*"being observed quite attentively"*: Karen Johann, "My Memories of Gram," *Cosmic American News*, Winter/Spring 1992.

*"He really seemed to be singing to me"*: Ibid.

*"His father also married the boss's daughter"*: Ibid.

*"I thought it was the most tragic thing"*: Ibid.

*"So I did"*: Ibid.

*"made a positive influence"*: Ibid.

*"We talked woman to woman"*: Undated writings of Avis Parsons Johnson.

*"I turned to somebody and asked"*: Frank David Murphy interview, June 30, 2009.

*"Prereminiscence"*: Paul Broder interview, February 8, 2009.

## Chapter 14. "A Country Beatle"

*"Now here I am flipping the bird"*: Jim Stafford interview, December 2009.

*"I kept running into people"*: Ibid.

*"The layout is still the same"*: Ibid.

*"I spent three months"*: Ibid.

*"made a little history"*: Ibid.

*"drinking Jack Black straight"*: Dickey Smith interview, September 2008.

*"Why should I cry?"*: Undated writings of Avis Parsons Johnson.

*"She had left twelve children"*: Ibid.

*"We went down and played"*: Joe Kelly interview, November 19, 2008.

"I'm headed north": Ibid.

"That's the first time I'd ever been really depressed": Paul Surratt interview, December 6, 2009.

"It was a really enlightening experience": Paul Broder interview, February 8, 2009.

"Fred was a natural linkup": John Sebastian quoted by Richie Unterberger, liner notes to *Tear Down the Walls,* by Martin and Neil, Electra Records, 1964

"healing instrument": Tony Ruiz and Henry Llach, "The Other Side of Greenwich Village 60s Folk Scene Part 2," *Perfect Sound Forever* online magazine, http://www.fredneil.com/the-other-side-of-greenwich-village-60s-folk-scene.

"Did you like that pot": Paul Broder interview, February 8, 2009.

"I had never even heard of LSD": Ibid.

"It appeared to me that Gram was cooking up heroin": Dick Weissman correspondence, May 2011.

"He was a little disenchanted": Jim Stafford interview, December 2009.

"I just blurted it out without thinking": Ibid.

"he kind of perked up": Ibid.

"He may have had a little more vision": Ibid.

## Chapter 15. The Polumbaum Photos

"Stringing for Life occupied most of my dad's working hours": Judy Polumbaum, "Abiding Moments," *Off Deadline: The Daily Iowan* 2008.

"I'd never been so scared": The Newseum, "Ted Polumbaum (1924–2001) Retrospective."

"There was all this talk": Author's conversation with Larry Piro, February 2010.

"He looked like a normal high school kid": David W. Johnson, "Parsonage."

"All of a sudden, he appeared": Ibid.

"Gram immediately wanted to find other musicians": Ibid.

"We got together": Author's interview with Ian Dunlop, November, 1, 2008.

"so surprised": Donna Class interview, February 4, 2009.

"He had an acoustic guitar": Sid Griffin, *Gram Parsons: A Musical Biography,* 47.

"I am now officially a Harvard Freshman": Gram Parsons letter to Avis Parsons, September 1965.

"He easily could have done well": Jet Thomas quoted in David W. Johnson, "Parsonage."

"The second-highest promotional contract": Writer unattributed, "Yardling to Rock, Signs RCA Contract," newspaper unattributed, October 21, 1965.

"Bobby asks questions": William Fripp, "Will Harvard Spoil Gram Parsons?," *Boston Globe,* October 31, 1965.

"It's not that Gram Parsons": Ibid.

"We barely look old enough": Author's conversation with Ian Dunlop in Waycross, Ga., September 2009.

"Suddenly the world turned 180 degrees": Rufus McClure interview, May 5, 2009.

"When I turned them on to these singers": Sid Griffin interview with John Nuese, *Gram Parsons,* 48.

"It was probably four or five months later": Conversation with Ian Dunlop, September 2009.

"*Mainly I was turned off*": Sid Griffin, *Gram Parsons*, 56.

## Chapter 16. Orlando, New York City

"*This looks nothing like a remember it*": Author's visit with Becky Gottsegen to Winter
 Park, Fla., December 2009.
"*Gram had just had his wisdom teeth pulled*": Ibid.
"*He was so proud of Gram*": Ibid.
"*There was a deep well*": Author's interview with Dan Jovi, June 10, 2009.
"*Bob kind of released the reins*": Avis Johnson Bartkus interview, August 7, 2011.
"*In this strange, amoral household*": Ibid.
"*The first time we were in the house*": Dan Jovi interview, June 10, 2009.
"*The Beatles were a big deal*": Ibid.
"*I never saw him without a drink in his hand*": Ibid.
"*bizarre*": Ibid.
"*parents*": Jim Carlton interview, June 2007.
"*the babysitter*": Ibid.
"*Avis hung a picture of Bonnie in the closet*": Becky Gottsegen interview, July 9, 2009.
"*They're not just your concern*": Gram Parsons letter to Avis Parsons, November 8, 1965.
"*Everybody had to get the most obscure information*": Frank David Murphy interview,
 June 30, 2009.
"*We went to New York*": Conversation with Ian Dunlop, September 2009.
"*I didn't like the lifestyle*": Donna Class interview, February 4, 2009.
"*This place was dreary, cold and dank*": Buddy Freeman quoted in David Meyer, *Twenty
 Thousand Roads*, 167.
"*I remember it was the first time*": Conversation with Ian Dunlop, September 2009.
"*I told him*": Gerald "Jesse" Chambers interview, September 26, 2008.
"*It was a very, very funny experience*": Conversation with Ian Dunlop, September 2009.
"*We drove back inland*": Ibid.
"*The South is rich in that heritage*": Ibid.
"*I think because of Nuese's little glasses*": Jim Carlton interview, June 2007.
"*I was really quite impressed*": Conversation with Ian Dunlop, September 2009.
"*You know he really shouldn't be doing that*": Ibid.
"*When they did The Russians Are Coming*": Becky Gottsegen interview, July 9, 2009.
"*No one paid unusual attention*": Jim Carlton interview, June 2007.
"*I remember Ian*": Author's interview with Barry Tashian, July 19, 2009.

## Chapter 17. Staying Behind, Safe at Home

"*I have strong opinions about Gram*": Gerald "Jesse" Chambers interview, September
 26, 2008.
"*I don't know if I'd have gone in that direction*": Ibid.
"*There were things I saw Gram do and promises he didn't do*": Ibid.
"*That's when I was aware*": Ibid.
"*It was a good decision*": Ibid.
"*I was secure*": Nancy Ross quoted in Pamela Des Barres and Paul Kempricos, *Rock
 Bottom: Dark Moments in Music Babylon*, 230.

*"I've been looking for you"*: Ibid.

*"I remember him doing 'Luxury Liner'"*: Barry Tashian interview, July 19, 2009.

*"I was actively fighting for this little soul"*: Pamela Des Barres and Paul Kempricos, *Rock Bottom*, 230.

*"He had to choose"*: Ibid.

*"Fred and I always hooked up"*: Author's interview with Bob Buchanan, January 27, 2009.

*"Fred wandered off"*: Ibid.

*"Fred would hurt himself too much"*: Ibid.

*"It was kind of her little toy"*: Ibid.

*"I've gotta play you this stuff"*: Jon Corneal interview, October 28, 2008.

*"Jon, as good as you are"*: Ibid.

*"I was writing songs"*: Ibid.

*"We'll get country people"*: Gerald "Jesse" Chambers interview, September 26, 2008.

*"Are you crazy?"*: Ibid.

*"I suspected"*: Bob Buchanan interview, January 27, 2009.

*"some heavyweights"*: Ibid.

*"Gram would play"*: Jim Carlton interview, June 2007.

*"I was sleeping on the couch"*: Jon Corneal interview, October 28, 2008.

*"I was eatin' like a pig"*: Ibid.

*"Now, Gram, he dropped acid"*: Ibid.

*"He and Nancy were up and down"*: Bob Buchanan interview, January 27, 2009.

*"It was tearing him up"*: John Nuese quoted in Sid Griffin, *Gram Parsons*, 52.

*"I was probably drinking large jugs of wine"*: Jon Corneal interview, October 28, 2008.

*"I'm not gonna drink myself to death"*: Ibid.

*"He never spoke about Coon Dog as his real Daddy"*: Ibid.

*"For me it was Gram and his happiness"*: Nancy Ross quoted in Pamela Des Barres and Paul Kempricos, *Rock Bottom*, 230.

*"Not knowing what she was doing"*: Bob Buchanan interview, January 27, 2009.

*"The main thing about Gram"*: Sid Griffin, *Gram Parsons*, 53.

*"It was all Gram's show"*: Bob Buchanan interview, January 27, 2009.

*"Gram led me to believe we could do some of my tunes"*: Jon Corneal interview, October 28, 2008.

*"You don't write very good songs"*: Ibid.

*"You lying son of a bitch"*: Ibid.

*"I just backed off"*: Ibid.

*"Pretty Polly"*: Nancy Ross quoted in Pamela Des Barres and Paul Kempricos, *Rock Bottom*, 231.

*"The band knew trouble was brewing"*: Sid Griffin, liner notes to *Safe at Home: International Submarine Band*, Shiloh Records reissue, 1985.

## Chapter 18. Vinny's Place

*"I saw Fred Neil in Greenwich Village"*: Roger McGuinn interview, June 3, 2010.

*"He would show up in his Borsalino hat and his leather cape"*: Author's interview with Vince Martin, April 28, 2008.

*"Crosby and Stephen Stills sat on my floor"*: Ibid.

*"We played all the time!"*: Ibid.

*"I think what Gram found in Fred"*: Bob Buchanan interview, January 27, 2009.

*"In pop music there's too much imitation"*: Author unknown, "Where is it All Going?: An Interview with Fred Neil," *Hit Parader*, 1966.

*"Go get yourself another battery"*: Jim Carlton interview, June 2007.

*"Hey Bob, can you help me with this?"*: Bob Buchanan interview, January 27, 2009.

*"We both had a lot of home in us"*: Ibid.

*"I was not a happy camper"*: Ibid.

*"So I came up with the second lyric"*: Ibid.

*"If you don't have a little sympathy in there"*: Gerald "Jesse" Chambers interview, September 26, 2008.

## Chapter 19. A Country Byrd

*"It was the first tune"*: Author's interview with Roger McGuinn, June 3, 2010.

*"a nest of vipers"*: David Meyer, *Twenty Thousand Roads*, 214.

*"Gene had a problem with success"*: Roger McGuinn interview, June 3, 2010.

*"I felt like I was in a movie"*: Ibid.

*"I was kind of indifferent"*: Bob Buchanan interview, January 27, 2009.

*"We would have made fifteen grand"*: Jon Corneal interview, October 28, 2008.

*"John's the guy"*: Ibid.

*"He was already starting to shop out"*: Ibid.

*"I picked up every single"*: Gram Parsons interview by Michael Bate, March 1973. Used with permission.

*"You don't know anything"*: Ibid.

*"I allowed the silver-tongued devil"*: Jon Corneal interview, October 28, 2008.

*"It was just not happening"*: Roger McGuinn interview, June 3, 2010.

*"I wanted to do an extension of 'Eight Miles High'"*: Ibid.

*"I'm a full-fledged Byrd now"*: Jim Carlton interview, June 2007.

*"We had a commitment"*: Roger McGuinn interview, June 3, 2010.

*"We could pull that off"*: Ibid.

*"I think we were just tired"*: Ibid.

*"I guess it was a simpler time"*: Author's interview with Randy Brooks, November 28, 2008.

*"That was the first time"*: Lloyd Green quoted in Christopher Hjort, *So You Want to be a Rock and Roll Star: The Byrds Day-by-Day 1965–1973*," 163.

*"Great, great, how do you want me to approach it on steel?"*: Ibid.

*"the devil"*: Roger McGuinn interview, June 3, 2010.

*"just another gig"*: Ibid.

*"dear old David"*: Randy Brooks, "Soft-Singing Byrds Make Opry Debut Smashing Success Here," *Vanderbilt Hustler*, March 1968.

*"The endearing memory I have"*: Interview with Randy Brooks, November 2008.

*"I picked up on a tension"*: Ibid.

*"tweet tweet"*: Ibid.

*"Tompall Glaser said"*: Gram Parsons interview by Michael Bate, March 1973. Used with permission.

*"We did that and the Glaser Brothers just flipped out"*: Ibid.

*"What's the big deal?"*: Roger McGuinn interview, June 3, 2010.

*"dirty commies"*: Randy Brooks, "Soft-Singing Byrds Make Opry Debut Smashing Success Here."

*"an exploitation of country music"*: Ibid.

*"It's almost like he was predicting"*: Author's interview with Randy Brooks, November 28, 2008.

*"Well it was nice meeting you"*: Author's correspondence with Jeff Hartzer, December 18, 2008.

*"His voice and pen seem meant for the medium"*: *Los Angeles Times* review quoted in Ben Fong-Torres, *Hickory Wind: The Life and Times of Gram Parsons*, 81.

*"The close harmony vocals"*: *Hitweek* review quoted in Christopher Hjort, *So You Want to be a Rock and Roll Star,* 171.

### Chapter 20. The Lost Burrito Brother

*"By the time I got out there"*: Jon Corneal interview, October 28, 2008.

*"Mick and Keith take us out to Stonehenge"*: Roger McGuinn interview, June 3, 2010.

*"I knew right off"*: Gram Parsons interview by Michael Bate, March 1973. Used with permission.

*"I was naive"*: Roger McGuinn interview, June 3, 2010.

*"I'm the first one to say"*: Ibid.

*"I'd say Sweetheart of the Rodeo is the most revered Byrds album ever"*: Ibid.

*"Keith had an affinity for country music"*: Gram Parsons interview by Michael Bate, March 1973. Used with permission.

*"He was beautiful"*: Andee Nathanson to Jessica Hundley, http://www.rhino.com podcast.

*"He was discovering his sound"*: Ibid.

*"Finally Chris Hillman came around"*: Gram Parsons interview by Michael Bate, March 1973. Used with permission.

*"I was blown away"*: Roger McGuinn interview, June 3, 2010.

*"I've got these two old melodies"*: Chris Etheridge, quoted in Holly George-Warren, liner notes to *Gram Parsons: The Complete Reprise Sessions,* Rhino Entertainment, 2006.

*"Gram took my roommate, Miss Andee, and me"*: Ibid.

*"It is a killer vocal, man"*: Chris Hillman quoted in Sid Griffin, *Gram Parsons*, 93.

*"One afternoon, Nancy gaily announced"*: Pamela Des Barres and Paul Kempricos, *Rock Bottom*, 233.

*"It was a big, awful, horrible joke"*: Nancy Gill quoted in ibid., 234.

*"Before you know it, I'm sleeping on the couch"*: Jon Corneal interview, October 28, 2008.

*"When you're going out to a cold city"*: Bob Buchanan interview, January 27, 2009.

*"Uh, okay, where you going?"*: Ibid.

*"The ego is not that strong"*: Ibid.

*"That's why Gram named the album that"*: Ibid.

*"They said, 'What are you doin' back here? I watched you on TV, you had it made'"*: Ibid.

*"She got pretty heavy into partying"*: Avis Johnson Bartkus interview, August 7, 2011.

*"Then one morning, I woke up in a different frame of mind"*: Ibid.

*"I was home"*: Ibid.

*"We started listening to the first Flying Burrito Brothers album"*: Tom Leadon quoted in Mike Greenhaus, "Turning Back the Clock: The Mudcrutch Interview," *Los Angeles Times,* July 18, 2008.

*"knocked me out"*: Bob Dylan quoted in Jann S. Wenner, "Bob Dylan Interview," *Rolling Stone,* November 29, 1969.

*"is about the temptation of urban life"*: Stanley Booth, "The Gilded Palace of Sin," *Rolling Stone,* May 17, 1969.

*"They're so uptight about our sequined suits"*: Author unknown, "Country Trip, A Talk With Gram Parsons," *Fusion,* March 26, 1969.

*"Frey was in awe of Gram"*: Chris Hillman quoted in Sid Griffin, *Gram Parsons,* 92.

*"Eyes closed, Gram seemed entranced"*: Jon Landau, "Records," *Rolling Stone,* April 5, 1969.

*"and play rock star games"*: Chris Hillman quoted in Sid Griffin, *Gram Parsons,* 90.

*"Gram was so excited"*: Nathanson podcast, http://www.rhino.com.

*"Gram was as knowledgeable about chemical substances as I was"*: Keith Richards quoted in Fong-Torres, *Hickory Wind,* 155.

*"We lost him then, you know?"*: Bob Buchanan interview, January 27, 2009.

*"She soon took up residence with Gram"*: Pamela Des Barres and Paul Kempricos, *Rock Bottom,* 233.

*"Gram's chopper was pure redneck"*: John Phillips, *Papa John,* 269.

*"I brought Gram flowers in the hospital"*: Pamela Des Barres and Paul Kempricos, *Rock Bottom,* 236.

*"It got to the point where we couldn't work with him"*: Chris Hillman quoted in Sid Griffin, *Gram Parsons,* 90.

*"It was peer pressure, a macho thing"*: Roger McGuinn interview, June 3, 2010.

*"Bob was one of those people who said 'If you need help, come home'"*: Bonnie Parsons quoted in Judson Klinger and Greg Mitchell, "Gram Finale," *Crawdaddy!,* October 1976.

*"ancient"*: Keith Richards, Life, 247.

*"I'd be called 'round the house in an emergency"*: Hank Wangford, the Gram Parsons Project online interview archive, http://www.gramparsonsproject.com.

*"genteel, polite, well-mannered, well-educated, sympathetic, spiritual—and totally mad as well"*: Jenny Grech quoted in author unknown, "Parsons/Grech," *Record Collector,* September 1994.

## Chapter 21. Like a Bird

*"Remember the Armadillo"*: Armadillo World Headquarters memorial plaque at South First Street and Barton Springs Road, Austin, Texas.

*"I started hanging out at the Armadillo"*: Willie Nelson quoted in author unknown, "Willie Nelson: All-American Classic," *Independent,* 4–5.

*"where we really wanted to make our home"*: Gretchen Parsons quoted in Fredda Joiner, "An Interview with Gretchen Parsons," *Cosmic American News*, 1985.

*"I remember it being fun"*: Becky Gottsegen interview, July 9, 2009.

*"She is a beautiful young blond girl"*: Gram Parsons letter to Frank David Murphy, December 1972.

*"I said sure, why not"*: Gram Parsons interview by Michael Bate, March 1973. Used with permission.

*"When I heard her, I called Chris Hillman"*: Author's correspondence with Rick Roberts, January 2011.

*"I was the jaded, cynical, old 25-year-old"*: Emmylou Harris online interview, the Gram Parsons Project, http://www.gramparsonsproject.com.

*"I said 'Excuse me, I have to work tonight. . . . '"*: Ibid.

*"The funny thing is"*: Ibid.

*"So I thought of one of the hardest country duets"*: Gram Parsons interview by Michael Bate, March 1973. Used with permission.

*"I've some sort of 'rep'"*: Gram Parsons letter to Frank David Murphy, December 1972.

*"We had a fantastic band"*: Emmylou Harris quoted in Holly George-Warren, liner notes to *Gram Parsons: The Complete Reprise Sessions*, Rhino Entertainment, 2006.

*"soulful, help me"*: Ibid.

*"There's plenty of boogie on GP"*: Gram Parson letter to Frank David Murphy, December 1972.

*"Gram's writing"*: Emmylou Harris quoted in Holly George-Warren liner notes to *Gram Parsons: The Complete Reprise Sessions*.

*"When I played with our group that night"*: Author's interview with Neil Flanz, August 17, 2009.

*"You really like that jacket"*: Jon Corneal interview, October 28, 2008.

*"I'd let it go"*: Ibid.

*"The drinking did bother me"*: Emmylou Harris online interview, the Gram Parsons Project, http://gramparsonsproject.com.

*"We just didn't learn the intros"*: Neil Flanz interview, August 17, 2009.

*"He was doing cocaine and drinking"*: Donna Class interview, February 4, 2009.

*"As for Boulder, that was a disaster"*: Neil Flanz interview, August 17, 2009.

*"We did some serious woodshedding"*: Ibid.

*"regressive country"*: Emmylou Harris quoted in Holly George-Warren liner notes to *Gram Parsons: The Complete Reprise Sessions*.

*"Most of the GP album was hard-core country"*: Neil Flanz interview, August 17, 2009.

*"card tricks on the radio"*: Ibid.

*"It was just minutes before my first gig with them"*: Author's correspondence with Jock Bartley, May 2010.

*"I had a realization on stage that night about life-changing opportunities"*: Ibid.

*"It was an amazing feeling"*: Neil Flanz interview, August 17, 2009.

*"They were heading towards the stage trying to touch us"*: Ibid.

*"College wasn't working out"*: Bob Webb quoted in Nimrod Funk, "A Sin City Primer," *Cosmic American News*, 1986.

"hair tousled as if he had just woke up": Author's interview with Larry Sepulvado, October 2009.

"In one hand he held a bottle of bourbon": Nimrod Funk, "A Sin City Primer."

"But stranger things have happened": Ibid.

"He really appreciated our recognition": Ibid.

"As we pulled away from Liberty Hall": Ibid.

"The image of Gram and Gretchen": Ibid.

"The Sin City gang rose in unison": Ibid.

"Now this group of boys": Ibid.

"We have Mr. Neil Young": Ibid.

"A local record collector was keeping it in his refrigerator": Larry Sepulvado interview, October 2009.

"I had this red, '71 Charger": Frank David Murphy interview, June 30, 2009.

"It can't be explained": Bob Chessey, "An Interview with Tom Brown," *Cosmic American News,* 1986.

"Together, their voices can summon the angels or the devils": Bud Scoppa, "Gram Parsons Does a Week in the Gilded Palace of Sin," *Penthouse,* September 1973.

"Sitting in a bar after a gig were Gretchen and Gram": *Crawdaddy!,* October 1976.

"They looked like two little kids": Author's correspondence with Ginny Wynn, December 7, 2009.

"I've gotten more recognition for doing that six weeks of work": Neil Flanz interview, August 17, 2009.

## Chapter 22. Darkness and Light

"By 16, I became horribly addicted": Polly Parsons quoted in Margaret Moser, "Do Right Woman," *Austin Chronicle,* July 31, 2009.

"What is it . . . ?": Ibid.

"You know what this place reminds me of?": Ibid.

"After his break with Bob": Gretchen Parsons quoted in Gandulf Hennig, "Fallen Angel" documentary, 2004.

"tough love": Becky Gottsegen interview, July 9, 2009.

"I spend a lot of time": Gram Parsons quoted in author unknown, *Crawdaddy!,* July 1973.

"We were in the limo": Roger McGuinn interview, June 3, 2010.

"Rick had come to see": Jenny Grech quoted in author unknown, "Parsons/Grech," *Record Collector,* September 1994.

"It's all there": Jim Stafford interview, December 5, 2008.

"I felt he was on the upswing": Emmylou Harris quoted in Holly George-Warren liner notes to *Gram Parsons: The Complete Reprise Sessions.*

"from about 200 photos I took": Author's correspondence with Ginny Wynn, December 7, 2009.

"He just kept playing his new record": Author's interview with Margaret Fisher, July 2009.

"throwaway kids": Author's interview with Rufus McClure, May 5, 2009.

*"Gram had trouble having real close friends"*: Byron Berline quoted in Hank Korsten, "Byron Berline Talks about Gram Parsons," *Cosmic American Music News,* Fall/Winter 1986.

*"hurt himself"*: Bob Buchanan interview, January 27, 2009.

*"the worst day of her life"*: Margaret Fisher interview, April 2, 2008.

*"I'm lucky"*: Jim Stafford interview, December 5, 2008.

*"I was seven years younger"*: Roger McGuinn interview, June 3, 2010.

*"The tears would not end"*: Undated writings of Avis Parsons Johnson.

*"I remember how eerie it was"*: Author's correspondence with Ginny Wynn, December 7, 2009.

*"A big thing in the South"*: Becky Gottsegen interview, July 9, 2009.

*"It's kind of cool"*: Avis Johnson Bartkus interview, August 7, 2011.

*"horrible demise"*: Becky Gottsegen interview, July 9, 2009.

*"I was told a different story"*: Polly Parsons quoted in Margaret Moser, "Do Right Woman."

*"Finally, I got to discover him by myself"*: Ibid.

*"How was I going to come through it . . . ?"*: Ibid.

*"The idea is there really is hope"*: Ibid.

*"I really feel that he's as close as I need him to be"*: Ibid.

*"My life has been marvelous that it's lasted this long"*: Bob Buchanan interview, January 27, 2009.

*"Call it a guardian angel"*: Ibid.

*"Gram knew Jesus"*: Roger McGuinn interview, June 3, 2010.

## Chapter 23. Calling Me Home

*"run right out and get"*: Gram Parsons letter to Frank David Murphy, December 1972.

*"In the early 1970s, she met Gram Parsons"*: Emmylou Harris's Country Music Hall of Fame induction, April 27, 2008.

*"They're there, to the right of me"*: Emmylou Harris's induction speech, April 27, 2008.

*"Landmark"*: Http://www.rockhall.com/inductees/thebyrds.

*"bored out of his gourd"*: Author's correspondence with Will James Harnack, January 31, 2010.

*"So around Rochester, I got really pissed"*: Ibid.

*"Gram might have even climbed this"*: Author's conversation with Bob Buchanan, September 18, 2009.

*"I understand 'Hickory Wind' even better now"*: Ibid.

*"You look back and see what happened"*: Ibid.

*"Lonzo and Oscar were trying to record"*: Author's conversation with Charlie Louvin, September 18, 2009.

*"I told him to come on in"*: Ibid.

*"As we pulled away"*: Ibid.

*"Charlie waved back"*: Johnny Cash, *The Man in Black* (Grand Rapids, Mich.: Zondervan, 1975), 51–52.

*"Gram was the one who introduced your music"*: Bob Buchanan to Charlie Louvin, September 18, 2009.

*"the Louvin Brothers as the headliners"*: Author's interview with Charlie Louvin, September 18, 2009.

*"Finally we elected Ira"*: Ibid.

*"I was standing six feet from it"*: Ibid.

*"If I'd a got to meet him"*: Ibid.

*"It means a whole lot to me"*: Ibid.

*"I wish I would have had the chance"*: Ibid.

*"On tour it got laid around"*: Leon Russell, concert in Waycross, Ga., September 18, 2009.

*"We also are doing a song tonight"*: Charlie Louvin, concert in Waycross, Ga., September 19, 2009.

*"It was beautiful"*: Author's conversation with Bob Buchanan, September 19, 2009.

# Discography

## The Shilos

*Gram Parsons: The Early Years, Volume I (1963–1965)*
Sierra
February 1979
Contains tracks recorded with the Shilos, one in 1964, the others in early 1965.

*Fallen Angels: Legendary Country Rock Recordings*
Camden International
2000
Contains "November Nights" and "Just Can't Take It Anymore" with the Like

## The International Submarine Band

"The Russians Are Coming"/"Truck Driving Man"
Ascot 2218
1966

"Sum Up Broke"/"One Day Week"
Columbia 4–43935
1966

Rereleased by Sundazed 2005

"Blue Eyes"/"Luxury Liner"
LHI
1968

"Miller's Cave"/"I Must Be Somebody Else You've Known"
LHI
1968

The above two were combined on a Sundazed/Shiloh release 2008

*Safe at Home*
LHI–S–12001
April 1968
Rereleased as *Gram Parsons*
Shiloh RI 4088
May 1979

## The Byrds

*Sweetheart of the Rodeo*
1968

*Sweetheart of the Rodeo* Expanded Edition CD
Columbia Legacy
1997

*Sweetheart of the Rodeo* Legacy Edition
Sony
2003

*The Gilded Palace of Sin*
A&M SP 4175
March 1969
US #164

"The Train Song"/"Hot Burrito #1"
A&M 1067
1969

*Burrito Deluxe*
A&M SP–4258
April 1970
US—

*Close Up the Honky Tonks*
A&M SP–3631
July 1974
US #158
Contains songs from the first three Burritos albums, plus several
    unreleased tracks.

*Honky Tonk Heaven*
Ariola 87–585 XDT (Dutch)
1974
Contains several previously unreleased tracks.

*Sleepless Nights*
A&M SP–4578
May 1976
US #185
Contains unreleased tracks from 1970 Burritos and three duets with
    Emmylou Harris.

*Dim Lights, Thick Smoke*
Edsel
March 1987
Contains some hard-to-find Burritos tracks, including "Bony Maronie" and
    "The Train Song."

*Farther Along*
A&M CD 5216
1988
Contains best of Gram Parsons–era Burritos, with some previously
 unreleased tracks.

*Out of the Blue* (UK)
A&M 540408–22
April 1996
Contains songs from the first three Burritos albums, plus several
 unreleased tracks.

*Gram Parsons with the Flying Burrito Bros: Live at the Avalon Ballroom*
Amoeba Records
2007

## Gram Parsons

"She"/"That's All It Took" (US)
Reprise
January 1973

*GP*
Reprise MS 2123
March 1973
US—

Rereleased on *GP/Grievous Angel*
Reprise 9 26108–2
February 1990

"The New Soft Shoe"/"She" (UK)
Reprise
March 1973
UK–

*Cosmic American Music: The Rehearsal Tapes 1972*
Magnum America
1995
Demos for *GP* with a number of covers and liner notes by Sid Griffin.

"Love Hurts"/"In My Hour of Darkness" (US)
Reprise
January 1974
US


## Gram Parsons and the Fallen Angels

*Live 1973*
Sierra GP 1973
February 1982

*More Gram Parsons and the Fallen Angels Live 1973*
Sierra GP/EP 104
September 1982

*Live 1973*
Sierra SXCD 6003
December 1994
Contains the entire unedited broadcast that made up the earlier LP and EP.

"Love Hurts"/"New Soft Shoe"
Sierra
1983


## Gram Parsons and Emmylou Harris

*Grievous Angel*
Reprise MS 2171
January 1974
US #195

Rereleased on *GP/Grievous Angel*
Reprise 9 26108–2
February 1990

*Complete Reprise Sessions*
Rhino
2007
*GP* and *Grievous Angel* albums remastered with interviews outtakes.

*Gram Parsons: Another Side of This Life—Lost Recordings, 1965–66*
Sundazed Music
2001

*Warm Evenings, Pale Mornings 1963–1973*
Raven
August 1992
Australian compilation that covers each phase of Parsons's career.

*Hillbilly Fever—Vol.5: Legends of Country Rock*
Rhino Records R2 71904
1995
Various artists, contains "Luxury Liner" with ISB, and "Sin City" with FBB.

*Sacred Hearts and Fallen Angels: Anthology*
Rhino
2001
Retrospective covering ISB through GP/ELH, contains "Knee Deep in the
    Blues" with ISB.

*Big Mouth Blues: A Conversation with Gram Parsons*
Sierra
2002
Interview by Chuck Casell in 1972.

*Gram Parsons: The Early Years Box Set*
With the Shilos, the Like, unreleased solo recordings, interview, DVD of
    Fallen Angels in Houston.
Sierra
2009

# Selected Bibliography

Booth, Stanley. *Rhythm Oil: A Journey through the Music of the American South*. New York: Vintage, 1999.

Braddock, Bobby. *Down in Orburndale: A Songwriter's Youth in Old Florida*. Baton Rouge: Louisiana State University Press, 2007.

Crosby, David Gottlieb, Carl. *Long Time Gone: The Autobiography of David Crosby*. New York: Dell, 1988.

Curtis, Kurt. *Florida's Famous and Forgotten: An Illustrated Encyclopedia*. Altamonte Springs: Florida Media Inc., 2005.

Des Barres, Pamela, and Paul Kempricos. *Rock Bottom: Dark Moments in Music Babylon*. New York: St. Martin's Press, 1996.

Doggett, Peter. *Are You Ready for the Country?* New York: Penguin, 2000.

Einarson, John. *Mr. Tambourine Man: The Life and Legacy of the Byrds' Gene Clark*. San Francisco: Backbeat Books, 2005.

Felder, Don. *Heaven and Hell: My Life in the Eagles 1974–2001*. Hoboken, N.J.: John Wiley and Sons, 2008.

Fong-Torres, Ben. *Hickory Wind: The Life and Times of Gram Parsons*. New York: Pocket Books, 1991.

Griffin, Sid. *Gram Parsons: A Music Biography*. Pasadena: Sierra Records and Books, 1985.

Guralnick, Peter. *Last Train to Memphis: The Rise of Elvis Presley*. Boston: Little, Brown and Company, 1994.

Hjort, Christopher. *So You Want to be a Rock and Roll Star: The Byrds Day-by-Day 1965–1973*. London: Jawbone Press, 2008.

Hundley, Jessica, and Polly Parsons. *Grievous Angel: An Intimate Biography of Gram Parsons*. New York: Thunder's Mouth, 2005.

Lemlich, Jeff. *Savage Lost, Florida Garage Bands: The 60s and Beyond*. London: Limestone Records, 1991.

Meyer, David. *Twenty Thousand Roads: The Ballad of Gram Parsons and His Cosmic American Music*. New York: Villard, 2007.

Phillips, John, with Jim Jerome. *Papa John: A Music Legend's Shattering Journey through Sex, Drugs, and Rock and Roll*. New York: Doubleday, 1986.

Pierce, Patricia Jobe. *The Ultimate Elvis: Elvis Presley Day-by-Day*. New York: Simon and Schuster, 1994.

Poe, Randy. *Skydog: The Duane Allman Story*. San Francisco: Backbeat, 2006.

Richards, Keith. *Life*. New York: Little, Brown and Company, 2010.

Rogan, Johnny. *Timeless Flight: The Definitive Biography of the Byrds*. San Carlos, Calif.: Maiden Voyage Publishers, 1991.

Rosenberg, Neil. *Bluegrass: A History*. Champaign: University of Illinois Press, 1993.

Sullivan, Denise. *Rip it Up! Rock and Roll Rulebreakers*. San Francisco: Backbeat, 2001.

Walker, Jason. *Gram Parsons: God's Own Singer*. London: Helter Skelter Publishing, 2002.

Zimmerman, Keith, and Kent Zimmerman. *Sing My Way Home: Voices of the New American Roots Rock*. San Francisco: Backbeat, 2004.

Zollo, Paul. *Conversations with Tom Petty*. New York: Omnibus Press, 2005.

# Index

Hall, Nora Mayo, 77

"The Hand within the Glove" (Parsons, Gram), 88, 101

Hardin, Glen, 210

Harnack, Will, 233

Harris, Emmylou, 4, 5, 106, 207, 210, 212, 216, 237–38; Parsons, Gram, and, *51*, 209, 218–19, 224, 232–33; "The Road," 233; "That's All It Took," 211

Harrison, George, 192

Hartford, John, 157

Harvard, 101, 107–8, 116–17, 120–22, 124, 125, *143*, 171; Parsons, Gram, at, *145, 146, 147*

*Harvard Lampoon*, 129

Hash, 133

Hazelwood, Lee, 169, 182–83, 195

"Heartbreak Hotel" (Presley), 18

Hendra, Tony, 129

Hendrix, Jimi, 204, 215

Henley, Don, 208

Hennig, Gandulf, 221

"Here Tonight" (Clark, G.), 208

Heroin, 97, 116, 204; addiction to, 168–69, 205; Neil's use of, 97

Herrin, Billy Ray, 20, 29, 234, 238

"He Stopped Lovin' Her Today" (Braddock), 72

"Hey Baby" (Channel), 45

Hickory Wind (band), 240

"Hickory Wind" (Parsons, Gram), 10, 20, 184, 187, 189, 192, 195, 211, 233, 240; Buchanan on, 234–35; Buchanan performing, 241; Louvin, Charlie, performing, 240; lyrics of, 234; performance of, 201; writing of, 178–79

Hickory Wind Ranch, 220

High lonesome harmony, 154

"Highway 61 Revisited" (Dylan), 108

Hillman, Chris, 2, 4, *157*, 166, 174, 181, 183, 186, 188, 194, 215; in Flying Burrito Brothers, 196; in Manassas, 208; Parsons, Gram, and, 202–4, 211

Hi-Time (TV), 63, *64*, 68, 70

*Hitweek*, 191

Hokum, Suzi Jane, 169, 171

Holly, Buddy, 37, 115

Hootenannies, 77–78, 81

Hoot Tour, 83

Hoskins, Rob, 76

"Hot Burrito #1" (Parsons, Gram), 10, 197

House Un-American Activities Committee, 77

Howard, Harlan: "I Fall to Pieces," 204; "Streets of Baltimore," 211

Hubbard, Robert, 86, 87, 107

Hurricane Dora, 101

Hutt, Sam, 205

"I'd Love you to Want Me" (Lobo), 49

"I Fall to Pieces" (Cochran and Howard), 204

"If I Can Only Win Your Love" (Louvin Brothers), 232

"I Just Can't Take It Any More" (Parsons, Gram), 120–21

"I May Be Right" (Weissman), 103

"I Must Be Somebody Else You've Known" (Haggard), 172

Ingram, Bobby, 75

"In My Hour of Darkness" (Parsons, Gram), 223, 224

International Fruit Corporation, 40

International Submarine Band, 131–33, 166–68, 182, 212; Corneal in, 169–73; end of, 182–83; recording sessions, 171–72; *Safe at Home*, 173, 183, 191

"In the Hills of Shiloh" (Silverstein), 82

Iron Butterfly, 167

Jackson, Michael, 45

Jagger, Mick, 192, 194, 202; Parsons, Gram, and, 205

"Jailhouse Rock" (Presley), 40

Jazzmaster, 47

Parsons, Bob, 45, 50, 126; affairs of, 79; business of, 76; death of, 228; Derry Down establishment, 102–4; in hospital, 226; Little Avis on, 31, 38, 128, 199–200; marital problems with Big Avis, 79; Orlando home of, *154*; Parsons, Becky, on, 127; Parsons, Bonnie, and, 127, *136*; Parsons, Gram, and, 133, 171, 221; personality of, 31–32

Parsons, Bonnie, 79, 199–200, 221, 226; Little Avis and, 129; Parsons, Bob, and, 127, *136*; on Parsons, Gram, 204

Parsons, Diane, 39, 79, 127, *135*, 227

Parsons, Gram: "Big Country," 71, 72, 106; "Big Mouth Blues," 212, 238; "Blue Eyes," 171; "Brass Buttons," 111, 115–16, 120–21, 130, 224; Buchanan and, 178–79; Carlton, Jim, friendship with, 89, 114, 117, 132–33; Chambers on, 165; at Chateau Marmont hotel, 159; childhood of, 12–19; "City of God," 9; Corneal and, 172–73, 182; on country, 169, 172; on country rock, 210; cremation of, 227; death of, 8–9, 225–26, 229; drinking habits of, 94; drugs and, 5, 76, 116, 202; "Drug Store Truck Drivin' Man," 190; early acetate of, *64*, 71; early reel-to-reel, *64*; at Elvis concert, 17–18; Fisher and, 8–9; in Florida, 3–4; folk music and, 74–80; generosity of, 177–78; *GP*, 212–14, 216, 219, 222, 224; in grade school, 54; *Gram Parsons, Another Side of This Life*, 133; *Gram Parsons: The Early Years, 1963–65*, 72; gravesite of, *163*; *Grievous Angel*, 218, 223, 231; guitar and, 22; "The Hand within the Glove," 88, 101; Harris and, *51*, 209, 218–19, 224, 232–33; at Harvard, *145*, *147*; heroin addiction, 168–69, 205; "Hickory Wind," 10, 20, 178–79, 184, 187, 189, 192, 195, 201, 211, 233, 234–35, 240, 241; Hillman and, 202–4, 211; "Hot Burrito #1," 10, 197; "I Just Can't Take It Any More," 120–21; "In My Hour of Darkness," 223, 224; Jagger and, 205; jamming, *144*; "Joan," 72; "Just Can't Take It Anymore," 123; legacy of, 10, 231; in the Like, *143*; Little Avis and, 12–13; Louvin, Charlie, on, 237–38; "Luxury Liner," 167, 171; marijuana use of, 76–77; McGuinn on, 182, 184, 195; motorcycle accident, 203; Murphy and, *160*; Neil and, 97, 168; "The New Soft Shoe," 211; in New York City, 130–31; "November Night," 121, 123, 167; "One Hundred Years from Now," 184; "Ooh, Las Vegas," 223; "Pam," 42, 72; Parsons, Bob, and, 133, 171, 221; Parsons, Bonnie, on, 204; performing "Hickory Wind," 201; at piano lessons, 13; "Prereminiscence," 111; "Racing Myself with the Wind," 71; "Return of the Grievous Angel," 223; Richards and, 202, 204–5; Rolling Stones and, 194–95, 201–3; in school, 7–8, 91; "She," 211, 238; in Shilos, 81–84; "Sin City," 9, 198–99, 215, 216–17; "A Song for You," 211, 238; song list, *148*; Stafford and, 39–40, 113, 116–17, 132; "Still Feeling Blue," 211; "Surfinanny," 92; theft of body of, 227; "The Twelve Days of Khruschev," 88; urban folkie period, *65*; wedding to Burrell, 207–8; "Wheel of Fortune," 121, *152*; writing, *150*; as young teen, 59; "Zah's Blues," 97, 106

Parsons, Gretchen, *161*, 203, 204, 211, 217, 218, 221, 223; wedding of, 207–8

Parsons, Jan, 42

Parsons, "Little" Avis, 22, 26, 27, 29, 54, 59, 127, *135*, 207, 226; on Big Avis, 105, 110; delinquency of, 199; on family servants, 80, 114; Parsons, Bob, and, 31, 38, 128, 199–200; Parsons, Bonnie, and, 129; Parsons, Gram, and, 12–13

Parsons, Polly, 173, 198, 220; addiction of, 228–29; birth of, 171

Parsons, Robert Ellis, 38

Parton, Dolly, 4

Bob Kealing's previous books, the investigative chronicle, *Tupperware, Unsealed* and his literary journey, *Kerouac in Florida: Where the Road Ends*, have drawn critical praise in the *Wall Street Journal*, the *Journal of Popular Culture*, and many other publications nationwide. A three-time Emmy award–winning reporter and eight-time nominee with WESH-TV in Orlando, Kealing has covered and broken major stories nationally and internationally. Since 2004, Kealing has also been a part-time correspondent for NBC. He is co-founder of the nonprofit Jack Kerouac Writer-in-Residence Project of Orlando and has appeared on C-SPAN as an expert on the life of Jack Kerouac. Kealing lives north of Orlando with his wife and two children. Follow him on Facebook and Twitter @bobkealing.

The University Press of Florida is the scholarly publishing agency for the State University System of Florida, comprising Florida A&M University, Florida Atlantic University, Florida Gulf Coast University, Florida International University, Florida State University, New College of Florida, University of Central Florida, University of Florida, University of North Florida, University of South Florida, and University of West Florida.